ERASING AMERICA

ERASING AMERICA

LOSING OUR FUTURE BY DESTROYING OUR PAST

JAMES S. ROBBINS

REGNERY
PUBLISHING
A Division of Salem Media Group

Regnery® is a registered trademark of Salem Communications Holding Corporation

Cataloging-in-Publication data on file with the Library of Congress

ISBN 978-1-62157-816-1
ebook ISBN 978-1-62157-839-0

Published in the United States by
Regnery Publishing
A Division of Salem Media Group
300 New Jersey Ave NW
Washington, DC 20001
www.Regnery.com

Manufactured in the United States of America

10 9 8 7 6 5 4 3 2 1

Books are available in quantity for promotional or premium use. For information on discounts and terms, please visit our website: www.Regnery.com.

To E.L.R.

CONTENTS

ONE

ERASING
AMERICA

Imagine a time when people ask, "Do you remember America?"
Maybe they won't. Maybe it will be a place they read about in
a history book, a nightmare land of oppression, slavery, racism,
police shootings, sexism, bigotry, inequality, capitalism, imperialism, environmental pollution, and other deplorable sins. There
will be no monuments to anything good about America, no
stories that praise it. It will have become a dark chapter in human
history best left unremembered.

To others, America will have become, as the beat poet Richard Brautigan lamented in the 1970s, "a dream, a word people
would repeat like a fantasy, as if it all had been an idealized
moment in the past."[1]

It may sound impossible, but we are headed that way. The
United States is divided between factions of people who may as
well be living in different countries. In some respects they already
do. They have separate histories, cultures, and visions for the

1

future. They are two distinct nationalities, divided by mutual distrust and joined by mammoth public debt.[2] Politics has become a chaotic mud pit where old norms of compromise and respect for the law have been discarded in the unrestrained pursuit of power. And the time-honored tradition of American exceptionalism is being replaced with a dreary story of a misbegotten country founded on slavery and oppression by deeply flawed men who have been falsely elevated as heroes.

It hasn't always been this way. As recently as twenty years ago, liberals and conservatives shared a benign view of the origins of the United States and its mission. There were variations in style, but the song was the same. This was the country of the Pilgrims and Jamestown, of the self-evident truths of the Declaration of Independence, of the rights won through revolution and secured by the Founders in the Constitution. This was the country of the frontier spirit, of expansion, of unlimited possibilities. It was the country that atoned for slavery with the blood of the fratricidal Civil War. It was the country of economic dynamism, invention, and technology's cutting edge. It was a nation of immigrants welcomed by Lady Liberty lifting her lamp beside the golden door, the country in which dreams come true. This fabric of national unity was woven over the centuries as a narrative of optimism and inspiration born of freedom.

Yet recently this harmony has broken down. The old-school liberals who still had a tinge of national pride have left the building. The new and extreme progressive viewpoint has challenged the historical American consensus with a counter-narrative of victimization, shame, and guilt. While yesterday's liberals found it hard to say anything favorable about the United States without adding "but," today's progressives have nothing good to say at all. In the words of the filmmaker Michael Moore, America is "a nation founded on genocide, built on the backs of slaves and maintained through the subjugation of women to second class citizenship and economic disempowerment."[3]

This radical mindset has taken over the education bureaucracy, the mainstream media, and the Democratic Party. Its operative belief is that Americans should feel embarrassment instead of pride for their country's history and must do penance before the gods of political correctness for their national sins.

This assault on the past is based not so much on the facts of history as on its supposed meaning. Those who take pride in America emphasize stories that reflect the best about our country and inspire hope for the future. Progressives seek to demean and demolish, elevating the victims of the past as an indictment of the present. They wield history as a weapon on behalf of the aggrieved, never gratified by the progress made. Indeed, as one supposed injustice after another is rectified, their attacks become fiercer, their complaints more numerous, and the retrograde American patriot is intimidated into silence.

All our classic national touchstones are in question. The Founders, the Constitution, and traditional American heroes are scrutinized through an unforgiving moral lens which grotesquely magnifies every flaw. The attack extends to the national anthem, the American flag, and other symbols of nationhood. Tearing down reminders of the old Confederacy, progressives reopen the wound of slavery, the original sin of the Republic on which their self-proclaimed moral authority rests. The progressives stigmatize religious traditions and holidays. They seek to erase the U.S.

border and foment open conflict between Americans. The progressives have declared themselves a separate people who care nothing for the traditions and history that made America great.

WHY HISTORY MATTERS

History is the source of all life's lessons, the good and the bad. We turn to history to see what to embrace and what to avoid. As Thomas Jefferson wrote, "history by apprising [the people] of the past will enable them to judge of the future," to evaluate the "actions and designs of men," and to recognize "ambition under every disguise it may assume" and thus defeat it.[4] But we do not always succeed. George Santayana's dictum, "Those who cannot remember the past are condemned to repeat it," has become an enduring cautionary statement because so many mistakes must be remade before they are learned.

History is also the storehouse of meaning and the wellspring of inspiration. The past is where we find our heroes and heroines, our stories of struggle and triumph. We look back to see forward, to trace our national destiny, to reinforce the idea that America has a purpose. We catch a glimpse of the Puritan leader John Winthrop's shining city on a hill, a vision Ronald Reagan would invoke three and a half centuries later as "a tall, proud city built on rocks stronger than oceans, windswept, God-blessed, and teeming with people of all kinds living in harmony and peace; a city with free ports that hummed with commerce and creativity."[5]

Preserving this vision is especially important because America was founded on an idea, freedom. Since our nation is not based on blood or race or land, the idea of freedom must be continually nurtured or the enterprise falls apart. Those who attack that notion of American destiny and the fundamental legitimacy of freedom's experiment compromise the entire system. But an appreciation of this history promotes national unity. From our past we derive a common historical language and shared beliefs about what being an American means. These unite our people and integrate newcomers.

Freedom defined America long before our Republic was established. In 1535 John Calvin described the New World as a place people wanted to go to so no one would bother them. From Jamestown and Plymouth forward, freedom was the defining concept of the nation. Americans fought Great Britain to affirm their self-rule and adopted a Constitution to protect their God-given rights.

People came here for religious or economic freedom or simply to escape inherited social and political restraints. Here they could start new communities in which they would govern themselves. From this freedom, based on what Jefferson called the self-evident truths of human equality and individual liberty, the rest followed. The Soviet émigré Ayn Rand wrote that "everything that America achieved, everything she became, everything 'noble and just,' and heroic, and great, and unprecedented in human history—was the logical consequence of fidelity to that one principle" of individual rights.[6] And because of this, "the United States of America is the greatest, the noblest and, in its original founding principles, the only moral country in the history of the world."[7]

Knowledge and understanding of the past enables this vision to persist into the future. We cannot nurture the ideal, cannot hold fast to the tree of liberty, without the inspiration that history provides. A common civic myth—not a "fairy tale" but a heroic account of a people's origins—contributes to our national strength. And if you lose the ideal, you lose the country. America dies when freedom dies.

The breakdown of our unifying civic myth is both cause and symptom of our national distress. Progressives understand the importance of history to American identity, which is why they want to replace it with a wholly different narrative. So they are tearing down the sacred monuments of the civic religion with the iconoclastic zeal of Islamic State terrorists.

"He who controls the past controls the future. He who controls the present controls the past," wrote George Orwell in his masterwork *1984*. But while Orwell intended his dystopian novel to be a warning against twentieth-century totalitarianism, the Left took it as an instruction manual. Their language echoes Orwellian doublethink: exclusion is inclusion. Diversity is unity. Speech is violence. Ideas are aggression. Freedom is slavery. And the week President Trump was inaugurated, *1984* shot up to number one on the Amazon bestseller list.[8]

BREAKING NATIONAL UNITY

The United States has always been an exceptional nation, but it faces severe challenges in today's racial, economic, and cultural divisions, which are troublingly reminiscent of the period before the outbreak of the country's greatest conflict. The United States is in danger of becoming a failed state.

Divisions over American history were not always so stark. Even in recent decades there were limits to political and social disagreements. We all venerated George Washington and the Founders, acknowledged Lincoln's leadership in the great national crisis, revered the Constitution and the freedoms it enshrined, and saw the United States as a light among the nations. There were variations in emphasis between parties and historical eras, but the core was consistent. Today, however, vocal political and social activists have accepted and internalized the radical critique of America. The Left is trying to normalize this radical critique and recast the old civic pieties as foolish and oppressive.

Standards and frameworks based on the common understanding of history no longer exist. Ideas that were perfectly acceptable even a few years ago are now met with unhinged vitriol. Commonplace facts meet withering criticism and charges of political incorrectness. Traditional American reverence for the Founders and American symbols are recast as racist nationalism. The progressives want to eradicate the premises that formed the basis of American civic life for decades, even centuries. In so doing they have declared war on those who value American history and its unifying purpose.

But having destroyed the old consensus, the Left has not supplied a replacement that speaks for everyone. "That is not who we are!" bellowed Barack Obama about anything he did not like. But as Ross Douthat points out, since half the country supports Donald Trump and the Republican Party, "then clearly something besides the pieties of cosmopolitan liberalism *is* very much a part of who we are." Given the Left's increasingly judgmental attitude about the past, Douthat speculates that "maybe no unifying story is really possible."[9]

Indeed, those who talk about rebuilding the traditional vision of the country are dismissed as hopelessly backward. "Church . . . family . . . police . . . military . . . the national anthem . . . Trump trying to call on all the tropes of 1950s-era nationalism," MSNBC's national correspondent Joy Reid tweeted out during the 2018 State of the Union speech. "The goal of this speech appears to be to force the normalization of Trump on the terms of the bygone era his supporters are nostalgic for."[10]

But it is the progressives who are exclusionary. Their identity politics and ideology of victimization reinforce division and conflict. Perhaps the most important reason progressives cannot provide a new unifying narrative is that they have no interest in unity.

It's not just that radical ideas have entered the debate, but that politics has been overwhelmed by an entirely radical way of thinking—no compromise, no limits, no prisoners. Extreme ideas have fostered extreme behavior. In the politics of massive resistance, the end justifies the means. This kind of ideological, party-line thinking is inimical to the political traditions of this most non-ideological country.

The progressives tolerate no dissent, taking their position as a given and the long-established truths about America as nearly fascism. Viewpoints that a few years ago would have been commonplace are now called "shocking." Everything they don't like is a "trigger," justifying an emotional outburst. Even ordinary language can be vilified as a "dog whistle," a bullying tactic meant to shut down debate, which they don't believe in anyway.

Supposed victim classes are excused from personal responsibility, and guilt is universal for their presumed oppressors.
People are trained to be offended and to believe that their offense
matters because society rewards it. The British actor and comedian Stephen Fry observes that "it's now very common to hear
people say, 'I'm rather offended by that.' As if that gives them
certain rights." Fry said that whining about being offended "has
no meaning; it has no purpose; it has no reason to be respected
as a phrase. 'I am offended by that.' Well, so f-cking what?"[11]

Compromise has become a dirty word in these uncompromising times. But our political system, built on checks and balances, cannot function without it. The genius of the Founders
was their insistence that many interests be balanced in the course
of governing. They had little faith in universal theories of public
good and even less in the power of flawed human beings to
construct flawless societies. The more the utopian spirit domi-
nates politics, the less will get done and the more problems will
accumulate.[12]

James Madison famously observed that government is necessary because "men are not angels." But progressives see themselves as avenging angels sent to root out iniquity. Indeed, the
original theorist of progressive activism, Saul Alinsky, dedicated
his handbook for revolution, *Rules for Radicals*, to an angel—a
fallen angel—"Lucifer, the original radical who gained his own
kingdom."[13]

This uncompromising posture widens the cleavages in American society, leaving a small group of radicals with outsized power
and influence. These are the people Donald Trump referred to in
his acceptance speech at the 2016 Republican National Convention

when he said "America is a nation of believers, dreamers, and strivers that is being led by a group of censors, critics, and cynics."[14]

MAKING AMERICA GREAT AGAIN

President Trump's pledge to "Make America Great Again" was met with predictable howls. Most on the Left said the country was never great to begin with. Since the progressives had already distorted our history, it seemed like Trump was promising to resurrect a corrupt and horrible past. Progressives targeted July 4 to make #AmericaWasNeverGreat trend on Twitter.

"Trump's 'Make America great again' language is just like the rhetoric of the Klan," *The Atlantic* asserted.[15] Representative Cedric Richmond of the Congressional Black Caucus charged that the "slogan Make America Great Again is really code for Make America White Again."[16] Another critic said Make America Great Again seeks to "recover some idealized picture of what America supposedly used to be." It is a "longing for Mayberry."[17] Some more literal-minded folk even tried to pin down exactly which previous era Trump was referring to.

It is no surprise that those who think America was never great would take offense at Trump's slogan.[18] But this was not how mainstream Americans heard it. People want to feel good about their country and their history. They have a right to an uplifting story that engages their spirit and sense of possibilities. History should be about more than apportioning blame. To the Trump voters, MAGA was an appeal to this time-honored idea; not just restoring economic growth and international clout, but reviving the greatness of the American spirit. Part of making

America great again is restoring the American story, and with it our sense of destiny, dynamism, and optimism.

Ronald Reagan, another political outsider who came to Washington to shake up the system, made "Let's Make America Great Again" the theme of his 1980 nominating convention. Reagan sought to rebuild the country following the economic and political shocks of the 1970s that had mired the country in malaise. Reagan succeeded—his policies revitalized the economy, won the Cold War against Communism, and, most importantly, revived the optimistic, freedom-loving spirit of the country.

But the Gipper also knew it was up to each generation to sustain this vision. He repeatedly warned that "freedom is never more than one generation away from extinction." It is not passed to our children naturally, but must be "fought for, protected, and handed on for them to do the same." Reagan said that if we fail to transmit the American story and spirit, then "we will spend our sunset years telling our children and our children's children what it was once like in the United States where men were free."[19] Or as George Orwell wrote, it will be a time when "the past was dead, the future was unimaginable."

TWO

DRIVING DOWN OLD DIXIE

Statues, inscriptions, memorial stones, the names of streets—anything that might throw light upon the past had been systematically altered.
—George Orwell, *1984*

A clash on August 12, 2017, between left-wing demonstrators and right-wing counter-demonstrators in Emancipation Park, formerly Lee Park, in Charlottesville, Virginia, over the planned removal of a statue of Confederate General Robert E. Lee left one protestor and two policemen dead. Thirty-eight others were injured.

The Charlottesville incident spurred a nationwide purge of memorials to the Confederacy. Towns across the country began pulling down statues, removing plaques, renaming streets and schools, and otherwise erasing the memory of the former heroes of the South. "Liberals poured into the streets," wrote the satirist C. J. Hopkins, "tearing down Confederate monuments, and otherwise signaling their total intolerance of the racism they had tolerated until a few days earlier."[1]

The Lee statue in Charlottesville was covered with a tarp pending its removal. Baltimore removed four Confederate monuments under cover of night days after the incident. Over the next two weeks, memorials were removed from St. Petersburg to San Diego, from Brooklyn to Montana.[2] Democratic congressmen introduced the No Federal Funding for Confederate Symbols bill to rename ten military installations named for Confederate generals, including Forts Benning, Bragg, Polk, and Hood.[3] House Minority Leader Nancy Pelosi called for eight "reprehensible" rebel statues in the U.S. Capitol to be removed, insisting that Republicans must join in the cleansing if they "are serious about rejecting white supremacy."[4]

The mayor of Birmingham, Alabama, ordered his town's Confederate Soldiers and Sailors monument boarded up.[5] In Memphis, the city council had already voted in 2015 to remove from city parks statues of Confederate President Jefferson Davis and the rebel general and later Ku Klux Klan leader Nathan Bedford Forrest. The Tennessee Historical Commission had blocked their removal under the Tennessee Heritage Protection Act, which covers historical monuments on public property. But after the Charlottesville incident, Memphis sold the parks, valued at $4 million, for two thousand dollars to the nonprofit Memphis Greenspace, Inc., and the statues quickly came down.[6]

Some activists took the matter into their own hands. In Durham, North Carolina, members of far-left groups, including the Workers World Party and Democratic Socialists of America, tore down a statue of a Confederate soldier in front of the county courthouse.[7] Despite ample video evidence of the crime, a local judge insured that the vandals would not be prosecuted. A few days after the Durham incident a statue of Robert E. Lee in front of the Duke University chapel was removed after vandals broke off parts of its face.[8] A Confederate memorial in a Georgia cemetery was also heavily damaged.[9]

The vandalism has spread beyond tributes to the Confederacy. A statue of Philadelphia's controversial mayor Frank Rizzo was defaced with spray paint, and the Vietnam Veteran's Memorial in Washington, D.C., was marked with lipstick.[10] In Austin, a statue of the legendary blues performer Stevie Ray Vaughan was spray painted for unknown reasons. The musician's signature broad-brimmed hat may have been a source of confusion, though the electric guitar in his hand might have suggested to a more historically literate vandal that the figure depicted was not a soldier.[11]

Anti-Confederate iconoclasm is driven primarily by the shifting internal politics of the Democratic Party. The Democrats who erected these statues—often Confederate veterans or their families—have over time been replaced by new Democrats who abhor them. The new Democrats control many of the cities in which the monuments stand, so down they come. As Memphis Mayor Jim Strickland explained, "these statues no longer represent who we are as a modern diverse city with momentum."[12]

NBC's *Saturday Night Live* satirized Democratic leaders touting among other things a jobs program "converting *Confederate* monuments into statues of prominent *lesbian poets*."[13] This was meant as a joke about fossilized Democratic leaders trying to project a more "woke" image, but responses on Twitter suggested younger activists thought this was a good idea, and there is a precedent of sorts; in 2016 students at the University of Pennsylvania took down a prominent portrait of "dead white male" William Shakespeare and replaced it with a photo of "black, lesbian, mother, warrior, poet," Audre Lorde.[14]

President Trump said it was "sad to see the history and culture of our great country being ripped apart with the removal of our beautiful statues and monuments."[15] But he also noted that the decision whether to keep such statues is "up to a local town, community, or the Federal Government, depending on where it is located."[16] Nevertheless, Mr. Trump was castigated for his insufficiently swift and sweeping denunciation of the right-wing protestors in Charlottesville and his suggestion that there were good people on both sides of the statue controversy. The president's blanket condemnation of violent extremism on the Right and the Left reflected a time-honored and centrist American intellectual tradition.[17] The media, however, have adopted the line that the statues are nothing more than symbols of hate, condemning their defenders to odium.

Congressman Keith Ellison, the chairman of the Democratic National Committee, charged that President Trump had "greenlit" Charlottesville-style protests by the extreme Right, and that the left-wing protestors more accurately reflected American values than the president.[18] Ellison later posed smiling with a copy of *The Anti-Fascist Handbook* published by the violent ultra-left Antifa group, which even Nancy Pelosi has denounced.[19] CNN cast the net of blame even wider, running a story asserting that the Charlottesville tragedy "could not have occurred without the tacit acceptance of millions of ordinary, law-abiding Americans who helped create such a racially explosive climate," and that all Trump voters were "white supremacists by default."[20]

But opinion polls showed that Americans agreed with President Trump by wide margins. In an NPR/PBS News-Hour/Marist poll taken soon after the Charlottesville incident, 62 percent of the respondents said Confederate statues "should remain as a historical symbol," while only 27 percent said they should be removed. Eighty-six percent of the Republicans questioned, 61 percent of independents, and a surprising 44 percent of Democrats said the statues should stay. Only 47 percent of Democrats opted for removal. Even more surprising was that a 44 percent plurality of African Americans favored keeping the statues, against 40 percent seeking removal. Two-thirds of whites and Latinos wanted the monuments to stay.[21]

Polls also called into question the idea that, as one commentator wrote, "Confederate statues were erected as the loudest dog whistle to non-white subjugation in American history."[22] An *Economist*/YouGov survey found that 54 percent felt that statues of Confederate war heroes evoked Southern pride, while only 26 percent saw them as symbols of racism.[23] Statues honoring rank-and-file soldiers in particular tend to be tributes to those who died in the fight, put up by their fellow troops, families, and communities. Similar monuments—in some cases nearly identical—were being erected in Northern towns at the same time for the same purpose. Commemorating conflict and its human cost is part of the human condition. Monuments have always followed wars, in every country, since history began. And there have always been those, like the ancient Vandals or ISIS, who want to tear them down.

THE SPIRIT OF APPOMATTOX

People objected to removing statues not only out of respect for their history but also in the spirit of reconciliation that prevailed after the Civil War. To be sure, there were debates over the causes and consequences of the conflict,[24] but it was clear that two controversies that had dominated American politics since the Revolution—slavery and the question of unilateral state secession—were settled. The country sought to move on, and the symbol of national rebirth was Appomattox.

The name Appomattox—derived from Apamatic, an Algonquian tribe that was part of the Powhatan Confederacy—conjures one of the great dramatic stories in American history. It was the end of a race between Robert E. Lee's Army of Northern Virginia, withdrawing from the broken Confederate lines around Richmond and Petersburg, and General Ulysses S. Grant's Union forces, seeking to block Lee from linking up with General Joseph E. Johnston's Western Army, itself pushed north through the Carolinas by General William Tecumseh Sherman. Time ran out for the rebels when Major General George A. Custer's horsemen beat the Confederates to the supply trains waiting for them at Appomattox Station. After a final desperate attempt to break out, General Lee called for a truce. "There is nothing left me but to go and see General Grant," he said, "and I would rather die a thousand deaths."[25]

On April 9, 1865, Palm Sunday, the two generals met in the home of Wilmer McLean, a farmer who had seen the first major engagement of the war sweep across his fields in Manassas and had moved to where he believed the war could not find him. Lee arrived in his best dress uniform, Grant in muddy boots and a private's jacket. The mood was cordial but businesslike. After a brief discussion the surrender document was signed. The generals saluted, and Lee departed. A short time later officers from North and South, many of them West Point graduates and old friends, gathered in McLean's front yard to share their stories—and, being Americans, to gather souvenirs, as McLean's furniture disappeared piece by piece.

This was one of the pivotal moments in American history. Yet one hundred and fifty years after these men made peace, the *New York Times* inveighed against the "dangerous myth" of Appomattox, which supposedly glosses over the difficulties of Reconstruction and the resurgence of white Democratic rule, segregation, and Jim Crow in the South. From this revisionist perspective, Appomattox separates the war from what followed far too cleanly, as "white Americans fashioned a story of prodigal sons returning for a happy family portrait."[26]

This exercise in hindsight ignores the fervent desire of people in the North and the South in 1865 to repair the house divided. A "happy family portrait" may have seemed unattainable, and there was no guarantee that a lasting peace was possible.[27] After four years of war and hundreds of thousands of deaths, the meeting at Appomattox was the act of reconciliation so desperately needed. Invested therefore with great symbolic value, it became the accepted framework for the entire country, North and South, and was almost universally revered as an American rebirth. In a speech on Grant's eighty-seventh birthday, President William Howard Taft paid tribute to "the spirit of the peace at Appomattox represented on the one hand by the magnanimity and far-sightedness of Grant, and by the self-restraint and courage and farsighted patriotism—for that it was—on the part of Lee in bringing the struggle to a close."[28]

Grant reflected in his memoir that he "felt like anything rather than rejoicing at the downfall of a foe who had fought so long and valiantly, and had suffered so much," even though he believed their cause was "one of the worst for which a people ever fought, and one for which there was the least excuse." He drafted practical peace terms because he understood that "the people who had been in rebellion must necessarily come back into the Union," and "they surely would not make good citizens if they felt that they had a yoke around their necks." Grant let the Confederate troops keep their mounts because "it was doubtful whether they would be able to put in a crop to carry themselves and their families through the next winter without the aid of the horses they were then riding." He provided Lee's starving army with the rations he had captured from their own trains. And he prevented his men from gloating or celebrating over the Confederate defeat. "The war is over," he told his staff. "The rebels are our countrymen again."[29]

Many attributed the tone set by Grant and Lee to the shared values inculcated in their days as cadets at West Point. The Union veteran Morris Schaff, an Ohio Democrat and 1862 graduate of the U.S. Military Academy, wrote that "two West Point men met, with more at stake than has ever fallen to the lot of two Americans to decide." The choice before them was "between magnanimity to a gallant foe and a spirit of revenge; there was the choice between official murders for treason, and leaving the page of our country's history aglow with mercy." Since "these two West Point men knew the ideals of their old Alma Mater," they "met on the plane of that common knowledge" and chose an honorable peace. "I cannot avoid expressing the belief," Schaff wrote, "that the greatest hour that has ever come in the march of our country's years was on that April day, when Grant and Lee shaped the terms at Appomattox."[30]

The reunion of the opposing officers at Wilmer McLean's house was a spontaneous expression of that same spirit. "The officers of both armies came in great numbers," Grant wrote, "and seemed to enjoy the meeting as much as though they had been friends separated for a long time while fighting battles under the same flag." Imagine the scene of men in blue and grey coming together, comrades who had served together in the Old Army, in Mexico or on the frontier, West Point classmates, friends and relatives, congregating in good fellowship outside McLean's house, exchanging stories and keepsakes, after concluding their part in the bloodiest conflict in American history. As Schaff wrote forty years later, they "met as brothers and planted then and there the tree that has grown, blooming for the Confederate and blooming for the Federal, and under whose shade we now gather in peace."[31]

WITH MALICE TOWARD NONE

President Lincoln set the tone of reconciliation in his second inaugural address. "With malice toward none, with charity for all," he issued a call to "bind up the nation's wounds" and "to do all which may achieve and cherish a just and lasting peace among ourselves and with all nations."[32] Lincoln did not anticipate a punitive peace. Grant recalled that when the president met with Confederate peace commissioners in February 1865, he told them that he had only two demands: preserve the Union and abolish slavery. If they would agree to these points, he was "almost willing to hand them a blank sheet of paper with his signature attached for them to fill in the terms upon which they were willing to live with us in the Union and be one people."[33]

Politicians across the political spectrum have since acknowledged and admired Lincoln's leadership and generous spirit. "With victory at hand, Lincoln could have sought revenge," President Obama said in 2009 for the Lincoln bicentennial. But "what Lincoln never forgot, not even in the midst of civil war, was that despite all that divides us—North and South, black and white—we were, at heart, one nation and one people, sharing a bond as Americans that could bend but would not break." And this example should inspire Americans to remember they are "servants of the same flag, as representatives of the same people, and as stakeholders in a common future."[34]

Americans were tired of war. They were weary of the struggle that had disrupted innumerable families and taken so many lives. While many in the North resented having to fight a conflict they saw as the South's fault, there was also a sense among the Yankees that the rebels had been rightly punished. Testifying to the severity of that punishment were the scorched earth in the wake of Sherman's march, the smoldering ruins of Richmond, the devastated Shenandoah Valley, and innumerable rebel graves. "Mourning in every household," Sherman said of the South, "cities in ashes, and fields laid waste, their commerce gone, their system of labor annihilated and destroyed. Ruin, poverty, and distress everywhere...her proud men begging for pardon, and appealing for permission to raise food for their children; her five millions of slaves *free*, and their value lost to their former masters forever."[35] Sherman also reflected on the cost of the war to the North, not just the fearful casualties but also running up unprecedented federal debt that has never been repaid.[36]

Lincoln's assassination within a week of Lee's surrender did much to undermine the spirit of conciliation, at least temporarily. In other countries, particularly in the developing world, such an event would be the pretext for widespread rioting, vengeance, bloodshed, show trials, and mass executions. But the only persons tried for crimes by high-level military tribunals were the conspirators in the assassination of Lincoln and Henry Wirz, the commandant of the notorious Confederate prisoner of war camp at Andersonville, Georgia. All were found guilty. Wirz and four of the Lincoln conspirators were hanged.

Former Confederate President Jefferson Davis might have expected a similar fate. From early in the war Union troops sang they would "hang Jeff Davis from a sour apple tree." Soldiers visiting the Capitol attacked his former Senate desk with bayonets.[37] But Davis was not hanged or even tried, even after leading a rebellion that resulted in the deaths of around 750,000 Americans on both sides—more than the American dead in all other U.S. wars combined.[38]

Indicted for treason and detained at Fortress Monroe in Hampton, Virginia, Davis wanted to stand trial to argue his case, but federal prosecutors hesitated. Though most people would have considered secession alone to be treason, the law was ambiguous, and the exact charges were unclear. An unexpected acquittal would delegitimize the entire war effort. After Davis

had been confined for two years, a judge finally set his bail at
$100,000, which was promptly paid by an unlikely group that
included the pro-Union shipping and railroad magnate Cornelius
Vanderbilt, the abolitionist Gerrit Smith, who had given financial
backing to John Brown, and the *New York Tribune* editor and
ardent abolitionist Horace Greeley.[39] The case of *United States
v. Jefferson Davis* languished until the ratification of the Fourteenth Amendment in 1868, when Chief Justice Salmon P. Chase
reasoned that trying Davis would amount to double jeopardy. In
February 1869, the U.S. attorney entered a *nolle prosequi*, for-
mally ending the case. Mississippi even offered Davis his old
Senate seat back in 1875, but he was barred from serving by the
Fourteenth Amendment.[40]

In 1978, when the Democratic-controlled ninety-fifth Congress passed a bipartisan joint resolution restoring citizenship to
Jefferson Davis, who had been specifically excluded from a general amnesty in 1876, President Jimmy Carter remarked, "It is
fitting that Jefferson Davis should no longer be singled out for
punishment. Our Nation needs to clear away the guilts and enmi-
ties and recriminations of the past, to finally set at rest the divisions that threatened to destroy our Nation and to discredit the
principles on which it was founded."[41] The rehabilitation inspired
the three-time Pulitzer Prize-winning writer, poet, and civil rights
proponent Robert Penn Warren to write a thoughtful and sympathetic exploration of Southern myth and memory titled *Jefferson Davis Gets His Citizenship Back*, first published in the
New Yorker.[42]

Davis did not serve in Congress after the war, but many
former rebels did. The Confederate vice president, Alexander

Stephens, served for nine years in the postwar House before being elected governor of Georgia. Today he represents his state in the Capitol's Statuary Hall in an image carved by Gutzon Borglum, the sculptor of Mount Rushmore. Reconciliation was the spirit of the times. In 1876 a former Speaker of the House, Republican James G. Blaine of Maine, said he would have been surprised when he entered Congress at the height of the war to have been told he would one day serve there with sixty-one members who had taken up arms against the United States. The former rebels' presence, he said, was a testament to "a liberality and large-mindedness and magnanimity and mercy such as has not been shown in the world's history by the conqueror to the conquered."[43]

The Republican Party dominated the government after the war, capturing 77 percent of the House seats in the 1866 midterm election. "Did we inaugurate any measure of bloodshed and vengeance?" Blaine asked. "Did we take property? Did we prohibit any man all his civil rights? Did we take from him the right which he enjoys to-day to vote? Not at all."[44] The Fourteenth Amendment's restrictions on almost every rebel elected to Congress were lifted by the required two-thirds vote. And even though the legislature was composed of men who had been shooting at each other a few years before, the Congress was less polarized then than it is today.[45]

The fact that people who engaged in armed rebellion against the United States could later be welcomed back into the halls of government says something about those times as well as ours. For the generation that had fought the war, unity was more important than revenge. They made a deliberate choice to bind the nation's wounds and move on. As even Barack Obama recognized, they reached "for a more perfect Union together as Americans, bound by the collective threads of history and our common hopes for the future."[46] Today's progressives, caught up in a spirit of retribution for offenses they did not personally experience, are slashing those collective threads. They would execute a modern-day Jefferson Davis after a show-trial and pack his senior commanders and members of his government off to a supermax prison for life. So overheated and unserious is the political climate that progressives cry "treason" over a Donald Trump tweet.[47]

"GOD BLESS ROBERT E. LEE"

In the decades after the Civil War, Robert E. Lee emerged as the best known and nearly universally respected Confederate leader. Indeed, he had been known as a man of utmost integrity since compiling a perfect disciplinary record at West Point. Lee was offered—and declined—command of the Union armies in 1861, and during the war he was respected by his foes, many of whom had known him and served with him. Walker Percy, the twentieth-century Southern novelist and a foe of segregation, said that the widespread affection for Lee in the North and South was a reflection of "the American preference for good guys and under-dogs, and especially underdog good guys."[48] And Johnny Cash, a pacifist, humanitarian, and firm believer in racial harmony and inclusion, could still sing "God Bless Robert E. Lee."

General John Kelly, the White House chief of staff, never imagined he was making an inflammatory statement when he called Lee "an honorable man,"[49] but he walked into a buzz saw of frantic denunciation. Martin Luther King Jr.'s daughter Bernice King tweeted it was "irresponsible & dangerous, especially when white supremacists feel emboldened, to make fighting to maintain slavery sound courageous."[50] In *Vanity Fair*, Kelly was accused of pushing President Trump's "twisted logic."[51] This radical worldview is unable to appreciate, as Grant did, the tragedy of the honorable Lee's defending a dishonorable cause

General Kelly's explosive remark was occasioned by the decision by Christ Church in Lee's hometown of Alexandria, Virginia, to remove a marble plaque honoring its former parishioner, whose wife helped start the church endowment. The church also decided to remove a matching plaque in honor of its founding member and vestryman George Washington. Church leaders explained that the plaques, placed in 1870, "create a distraction in our worship space" and "an obstacle to our identity as a welcoming church and an impediment to our growth and to full community with our neighbors."[52] The plaques were said to make some in the ultra-liberal congregation "feel unsafe." The church whose motto is "All are welcome—no exceptions" decided to make an exception for the unwelcome Washington and Lee. This kind of historical revisionism, warned General Kelly, is "very, very dangerous" and shows "a lack of appreciation of history and what history is."[53]

The parish church in Lexington, Virginia, that Lee attended after the war was later named for him, but he is no longer welcome there either. The church, which is steps away from Lee's home, has reverted to its previous name in an effort to "move on."[54] Some have suggested renaming Lexington's Washington and Lee University. The first of its namesakes personally saved the institution from financial ruin. The second served as its president from the end of the war until his death in 1870 at age sixty-three and is buried in its chapel.[55] If the school follows the example of Christ Church and obliterates both names, it could simply be called "University." Lee Barracks at West Point, where Lee graduated second in the class of 1829 and served as superintendent from 1852 to 1855, is also taking fire.

The National Cathedral in Washington, D.C., removed two stained glass windows that honored Lee and Thomas J. "Stonewall" Jackson. The windows depicted Jackson in camp reading the Bible and the "last meeting" between Jackson and Lee during the Battle of Chancellorsville in 1863, after which Jackson was mortally wounded by friendly fire. A church official said removing the windows was "a Christian imperative."[56] The windows were installed in 1953 to "foster reconciliation," according to the Very Reverend Gary Hall, dean of the cathedral, and were being removed to foster even more reconciliation.[57] "It's not just about the windows or the inscriptions," the cathedral spokesman Kevin Eckstrom explained. "It's about what kind of history we're going to tell"[58]—or erase.

Spreading far beyond the old South, the anti-Lee tide has reached as far as the University of Southern California, whose Trojan mascot rode a white horse named Traveler. After the Charlottesville riot, someone in the USC Black Student Assembly, realizing that Lee's famous mount was named Traveller, commented that "white supremacy hits close to home." Pat Saukko DeBernardi, the widow of the man who introduced the first USC Traveler, a former 1950s movie horse, commented that "three weeks ago it was fine. So now the flavor of the day is, we all have to be in hysteria. It's more of a political issue. The horse isn't political and neither am I."[59]

Not to be outdone, the sports network ESPN removed an Asian-American named Robert Lee from the team of announcers for its broadcast of the University of Virginia's home opening football game. The network explained that it was trying to protect Lee's appearance from becoming a punchline but in fact drew national attention to a fluke that probably would not have been noticed. *Commentary* editor John Podhoretz tweeted, "ESPN did this out of fear of the yowling mob. And is part of it now."[60] The flap reinforced the idea that the channel some call the "Entertainment, Sports, and Propaganda Network" was more concerned with advancing the cause of liberal politics than with simply covering sports.

Even battlefield monuments are under attack. In September 2017, the "Robert E. Lee Statue Removal Act" was introduced by Congressional Democrats to develop a plan and timeline to take down the Lee statue at Antietam.[61] But battlefield monuments serve an important educational purpose. Representing both sides in a battle lends essential context. Note for example the addition of markers and an outdoor monument honoring Native Americans who fell at Little Bighorn (including the Indian scouts who served in Custer's command), alongside the white stones marking where Custer's cavalrymen fell. It is a useful model for building up history rather than tearing it down.

The same thing happened at Gettysburg. Veterans of Union regiments early on erected statues and monuments along their battlefield lines, while Confederates had been allowed only to place flat stone markers to indicate their unit frontages. Forty years after the battle, during a debate over a plan to erect a monument to Lee and his men, a Union veteran noted that it would be useful for the rebel side to be better represented. "The battlefield of Gettysburg, as it now stands, is a beautiful, one-sided picture," he wrote. "There is not a monument or inscription to show that an army equal in numbers and valor to our own struggled fiercely for three days to destroy it." In his view the absence of Confederate monuments diminished the magnitude of the Union victory.[62]

Lee himself had not been as interested in commemorating the war. In the summer of 1869, he was asked to participate in a gathering at Gettysburg hosted by the Battlefield Memorial Association to mark the positions of different units during the battle. Lee said he was too busy to attend, and added that he thought it wisest "not to keep open the sores of war, but to follow the example of those nations who endeavored to obliterate the marks of civil strife, and to commit to oblivion the feelings it engendered." His nephew Fitzhugh Lee, who also fought there, gave a similar response. "If the nation is to continue as a whole," he said, "it is better to forget and forgive rather than perpetuate in granite proofs of its civil wars."[63] The wounds were too fresh in 1869; only one Confederate officer attended the gathering, George Pickett's adjutant general, Colonel Walter Harrison.

The first Confederate memorial at Gettysburg, the Virginia Monument, was unveiled in 1917 before an audience of Northern and Southern veterans of the battle. Frederick William Sievers crafted a forty-one-foot-high monument with seven life-sized bronze soldiers posed dramatically at the base, topped with a fourteen-foot bronze statue of Lee on his horse, looking across the field at the "copse of trees" where Pickett's Charge, having reached the high-water mark of the Confederacy, broke. Many other rebel monuments followed along the battle lines, facing their Yankee counterparts.

The National Park Service has declared that the battlefield monuments at Gettysburg will not be "altered, relocated, obscured, or removed" and that "a hallmark of American progress is our ability to learn from our history."[64] But in Charlottesville and elsewhere General Lee has lost the battle. The Lee statue in Charlottesville that was at the center of controversy was covered in a black tarp pending removal, along with one of Stonewall Jackson. Statues of Lee and three others in New Orleans had already come down in May 2017. And in September 2017 the Lee statue in Dallas's Lee Park was removed after the city council denounced it as a "symbol of injustice."[65]

The work of Alexander Phimister Proctor, a Canadian-born sculptor famous for his Old West and animal subjects, the Dallas statue featured mounted figures of Lee and a young soldier. It was unveiled in June 1936 during the Texas centennial celebrations by President Franklin Roosevelt, a New Yorker, who declared that "all over the United States we recognize [Lee] as a great leader of men, as a great general. But, also, all over the United States I believe that we recognize him as something much more important than that. We recognize Robert E. Lee as one of our greatest American Christians and one of our greatest American gentlemen."[66]

Roosevelt's respect for Lee was very much the bipartisan norm. President Dwight D. Eisenhower, a Kansan, hung Lee's portrait in the Oval Office, along with Washington's, Lincoln's, and Ben Franklin's. Having studied Lee's campaigns as a cadet at West Point, he could relate to him as a commanding general. Under Lee's gaze atop the Virginia Monument, Ike had trained American armored troops during World War I on the ground over which Pickett had charged at Gettysburg. Speaking to the United Daughters of the Confederacy in 1953, Eisenhower had praised Lee as "one man who early showed to all of us that a man could be a soldier who could fight with all that was in him—and fight brilliantly—for ideals in which he firmly and honestly believed, but still, at the same time, could be a great and noble character."[67]

Campaigning in the South in 1964, President Lyndon Johnson invoked Lee in defense of the Civil Rights Act: "If we are to heal our history and make this Nation whole," he said, "prosperity must know no Mason-Dixon line and opportunity must know no color line. Robert E. Lee, a great son of the South, a great leader of the South—and I assume no modern-day leader would question him or challenge him—Robert E. Lee counseled us well when he told us to cast off our animosities, and raise our sons to be Americans."[68]

Robert E. Lee's citizenship was restored by Congress in 1975. The Democrat-controlled House voted 407-10 for restoration, the only opponents being some members of the Congressional Black Caucus and ultraliberals with an axe to grind. Elizabeth Holtzman of New York voted no because the bill did not include amnesty for Vietnam War draft-dodgers. John Conyers of Michigan, who would resign in disgrace forty years later, dismissed the measure as "Bicentennial fluff," speculating that "Lee may not have even wanted his citizenship restored."[69] The Senate passed the bill unanimously. "General Lee's character has been an example to succeeding generations," President Gerald Ford remarked at the signing ceremony, "making the restoration of his citizenship an event in which every American can take pride."[70]

ON HALLOWED GROUND

Montgomery Meigs served with Lee in the U.S. Army before the war with Mexico, describing him then as "kind and generous to his subordinates, admired by all women and respected by all men. He was the model of a soldier and the *beau ideal* of a Christian man."[71] But when Lee sided with Virginia after its secession, he earned Meigs's enmity. Now Quartermaster General of the Union Army, Meigs came up with a plan to make Lee's estate in Arlington uninhabitable.

In 1864 the Soldiers' Cemetery in neighboring Alexandria was almost full, and Meigs was directed to identify another appropriate spot to bury the Union dead. He chose the Lee estate, recently acquired by the federal government at a tax auction, ordering that the interments begin as close to Arlington House as possible, "rendering it undesirable as a future residence or homestead."[72] The first twenty-six bodies were buried along the border of Mrs. Lee's rose garden, which itself became the final resting place for 2,111 unknown soldiers. Meigs buried his own son, Lieutenant John Rodgers Meigs, killed by Confederate guerillas, at Arlington. Today father and son rest side by side.

After the war, the Lee family sued for the return of the estate. In 1882, in a remarkable testament to the rule of law, the Supreme

Court ruled 5-4 in the case of *United States v. Lee* that the seizure by tax sale was illegal. Arlington was returned to Lee's oldest son and heir, the former Confederate general George Washington Custis Lee. Three months later, Custis sold the estate back to the U.S. government in a ceremony with Abraham Lincoln's oldest son and then-Secretary of War Robert Todd Lincoln. So a piece of land that had been a tool of Montgomery Meigs's spite became a symbol of national reconciliation and ultimately America's most hallowed ground.

President John F. Kennedy visited Arlington House in March 1963. Looking out across the Potomac from the front porch, he said, "This is a heavenly scene. I can see why Lee loved this place so much. I could stay here for ever."[73] A few months later he would be laid to rest less than three hundred feet away beneath an eternal flame.[74] The Kennedy gravesite is not far from the site of a freedman's village where former slaves lived during and after the war. Some four thousand freed slaves are buried in Arlington in Section 27, and in Section 15 rests "Uncle Jim" Parks, a former Lee family slave who later became a groundskeeper at the cemetery, the only person buried there who was also born there.

From the beginning, rebel prisoners of war who had died of wounds or disease were buried at Arlington. In 1900 Congress authorized a Confederate section (Section 16) to bring together Southern soldiers previously buried elsewhere in Washington. Initially the United Daughters of the Confederacy opposed the idea, arguing that if the bodies were to be moved they should be returned to their native states.[75] Southerners were not always comfortable having their honored dead lying next to Yankees for eternity. In 1879, the Southern Memorial Association of Alexandria had thirty-four Confederate soldiers disinterred from the federal cemetery in the town and reburied in a mass grave in the Christ Church yard. The vestrymen have not announced whether they will expel these dead rebels along with the plaques honoring Lee and Washington.

The UDF soon accepted the idea of a Confederate section at Arlington, however, and commissioned an imposing memorial, unveiled by Democratic President Woodrow Wilson on June 4, 1914, Jefferson Davis's birthday, and sculpted by Moses Ezekiel, a Jewish artist who, as a Virginia Military Institute cadet, was wounded in the battle of New Market. After the war, Ezekiel became a world-famous artist, based in Rome, and was knighted by the king of Italy. His works include monuments to Jefferson (vandalized on his birthday in 2018) and Homer at the University of Virginia, statues of Stonewall Jackson at Charleston, West Virginia, and Edgar Allan Poe at Baltimore, and a memorial at VMI to his comrades who fell at New Market (*Virginia Mourning Her Dead*). Yet he considered the work at Arlington the crowning achievement of his career. Ezekiel is buried at the foot of the monument, identified, as he requested, simply as "Moses J. Ezekiel, Sergeant of Company C, Battalion of Cadets of the Virginia Military Institute."

But during the 2017 iconoclasm spasm, a group of Ezekiel's descendants called for his Arlington monument to be consigned to a museum or melted down.[76] The journalist Dan K. Thomasson wondered whether Section 16 might one day be emptied of Confederate graves. "Would that finally heal the wounds of slavery?" he asked. Or do we "acknowledge that history is unchangeable," and we should retain our reminders of those who "had to die on both sides to begin the drawn-out process of keeping the promise of our founders?"[77]

The people who had the most sympathy for the vanquished were those who had fought them. Colonel Oliver Wendell Holmes Jr. of the Twentieth Massachusetts regiment saw action in most of the major battles in the East and was thrice wounded. The future justice of the Supreme Court believed that the "soldiers who were doing their best to kill one another" were not as angry about the war as some back home. He likened the feeling of brotherhood between Yankee and rebel to magnetic poles, "each working in an opposite sense to the other, but each unable to get along without the other." And when it came to honoring the dead, "the soldiers of the war need no explanations; they can join in commemorating a soldier's death with feelings not different in kind, whether he fell toward them or by their side."[78]

First Lieutenant Ambrose Bierce of the Ninth Indiana fought in most of the large battles in the Western theater and was seriously wounded at the battle of Kennesaw Mountain in 1864. After the war he became one of America's foremost writers, often reliving sanguine battle scenes in his fiction. In "A Bivouac of the Dead" (1903), an essay composed after revisiting a West Virginia battlefield where he fought, Bierce concluded that the denial of marked graves for the Confederate dead in the nearby Grafton National Cemetery reflected a meanness of spirit. "Is there a man, North or South, who would begrudge the expense of giving to these fallen brothers the tribute of green graves?" he asked. Bierce, whose first job was working as a printer's devil for an abolitionist newspaper, harbored no sympathy for the Southern cause, but he wrote, "They were honest and courageous foemen,

having little in common with the political madmen who persuaded them to their doom and the literary bearers of false witness in the aftertime."[79] Bierce's only agenda was a soldier's
respect for another soldier.

The last great gathering of Civil War veterans took place in
1938 on the seventy-fifth anniversary of the Battle of Gettysburg.
Around 1,800 veterans were in attendance, many brought at
government expense. "In America the Blue and the Gray are
meeting at Gettysburg," the *Oakland Tribune* noted. "The
'Yanks' and the 'Confeds' are shaking hands, knowing this is
one country, and supporting its common purpose."[80] President
Franklin Roosevelt dedicated the Eternal Light Peace Memorial
on Oak Hill, on which is inscribed "peace eternal in a nation
united." Constructed of Maine granite and Alabama limestone,
it evokes the clash between Joshua Chamberlain's Twentieth
Maine and William C. Oates's Fifteenth Alabama on Little
Round Top. The elderly veterans gathered that day were "a frag-
ment spared by time," said Roosevelt. "They are brought here
by the memories of old divided loyalties, but they meet here in
united loyalty to a united cause which the unfolding years have
made it easier to see. All of them we honor, not asking under
which Flag they fought then—thankful that they stand together
under one Flag now."[81] Two ninety-one-year-old veterans, one
Union and one Confederate, used the sun's rays to light the
monument's eternal flame.

Previous presidents, including Barack Obama, have invoked
this reciprocal sense of honor. In a 2010 Memorial Day address,
he told the story of a group of women visiting a cemetery in
Columbus, Mississippi, to place flowers on the graves of rebels

fallen at Shiloh. They "noticed other graves nearby belonging to Union dead" that had no flowers. "So they decided to lay a few stems for those men too," he said, "in recognition not of a fallen Confederate or a fallen Union soldier, but a fallen American."[82]

The ease with which some today reject the spirit of reconciliation that generations nurtured after the Civil War is a symptom of the shallowness of our times. It does not change what happened or what the generations who fought the war experienced. Morris Schaff wrote that the "true measure" of the war for the United States was the same as that which the nineteenth-century British historian George Grote ascribed to the *Iliad* for the ancient Greeks: "a grand and inexhaustible object of common sympathy, common faith, and common admiration."[83]

Holmes believed that "the generation that carried on the war has been set apart by its experience," and he considered it their "great good fortune" that "in our youth our hearts were touched with fire."[84] But Holmes did not wish for future generations to face the same inferno, and the preservation of memory was necessary to prevent repeating that national nightmare. "I believe from the bottom of my heart," he said, "that our memorial halls and statues and tablets, the tattered flags of our regiments gathered in the Statehouses, are worth more to our young men by way of chastening and inspiration than the monuments of another hundred years of peaceful life could be."[85]

Americans should heed the lessons of those times. Those who have never fought in a fratricidal conflict, never suffered slavery, never faced the other challenges our forefathers faced lack the perspective, let alone the moral standing, to judge harshly those who did.

WHEN REBELS WERE COOL

Confederates have been an enduring fixture in popular culture, and the rebel cause has been portrayed in many ways. There is of course the notorious heroic depiction of the Ku Klux Klan in D. W. Griffith's 1915 silent epic *The Birth of a Nation*, based on the controversial book *The Clansman* by Thomas F. Dixon Jr. The film was wildly popular and encouraged the revival of the Klan in the twentieth century. It was also the first American film screened at the White House. Thomas Dixon and Woodrow Wilson were roommates at Johns Hopkins, and Wilson was even quoted in the movie praising the Klan.

Rebels were also played for laughs, as in Buster Keaton's 1926 silent masterpiece *The General*, based on a real-life Union railroad raid in April 1862. When asked why his character was a Southern train engineer instead of a Union soldier, Keaton (who was not a Southerner) joked, "It's awful hard to make heroes out of the Yankees."[86] Curiously enough, the actual 1862 raid was the occasion for the first awards in the North of the Medal of Honor. The event was revisited from the Union perspective in the 1956 Disney feature *The Great Locomotive Chase*, starring Fess Parker, in which making the Yankees the heroes was not hard at all.

Shirley Temple provided a heartwarming portrayal of a six-year-old Southern belle-to-be named Virgie in *The Littlest Rebel* (1935), dancing with Bill "Bojangles" Robinson, who played the family slave Uncle Billy. Virgie saves her Confederate captain father from execution for espionage with a spirited appeal ("My daddy isn't a spy!") to kindly Abraham Lincoln, played by the perennial Lincoln actor Frank McGlynn Sr.

All manner of "Deep South" tropes emerged in popular culture, such as malevolent "fat redneck sheriffs, hillbillies, moonshiners, The Klan, tobacco-chawin' Good Ol' Boys missing half their teeth," as well as "fire-and-brimstone preachers, iron-bound matriarchs, white-suited plantation owners, Southern Belles in flouncy gowns or short-shorts with crop tops, and possums."[87] You go from shotgun totin' Beverly Hillbilly Granny Moses (Irene Ryan) talking about "the war betwixt the Yankees and the Americans," to the inbred, banjo-picking Lonnie (Billy Redden) in John Boorman's 1972 thriller *Deliverance*. There is the bumbling Louisiana sheriff J. W. Pepper (Clifton James) in the James Bond film franchise and the emotionally complex Kentucky-born deputy U.S. marshal Raylan Givens (Timothy Olyphant) in the recent FX dramatic series *Justified*.

The Givens character is a contemporary reflection of the enduring and traditionally accepted view of the Confederate veteran as the anti-hero. He is a loner who lives by his own rules, a man with a dark past and a deeply held code of honor. The rebel spirit had an undertone of disrespectability, but that was what made it attractive dramatically. The rebel could not be the "good guy" hero because he had something to overcome. Instead, he was haunted by a guilty past or personal tragedy or simply being on the losing side of the war.

In *Gone with the Wind*, Clark Gable played Rhett Butler, a Confederate blockade-runner who had a questionable life story even before the war broke out. The 1939 movie, adapted from Margaret Mitchell's Pulitzer Prize-winning 1936 novel, won eight Oscars, including Best Picture and Best Supporting Actress (Hattie McDaniel, the first black winner of an Academy

Award). *Gone with the Wind* knocked *The Birth of a Nation* from its perch as the all-time top box office attraction. Though criticized later for promoting the Lost Cause view of the South, the film's producer, David O. Selznick, had expressly not wanted the film to be "an advertisement for intolerant societies in these fascist ridden times."[88] In 1977 the American Film Institute voted it the most popular film of all time and ranked it sixth in its "100 Greatest Movies" list in 2007. Yet in August 2017, the Orpheum Theater in Memphis, which had run the movie annually for thirty-four years, pulled *Gone with the Wind* from its schedule because the management determined the theater "cannot show a film that is insensitive to a large segment of its local population."[89]

In the 1953 Western *Shane*, Alan Ladd plays a wandering rebel gunfighter with a complicated past who champions the cause of Wyoming homesteaders in a range war with the unscrupulous cattle baron Ryker. Oscar-nominated Jack Palance portrays Jack Wilson, a menacing Yankee gunman working for Ryker who coolly kills Frank "Stonewall" Torrey, a sympathetic ex-Confederate farmer. Shane later guns down both Wilson and Ryker before riding off, wounded, to an unknown fate.

In John Ford's *The Searchers* (1956), another former rebel, Ethan Edwards (played by John Wayne), spends years on the trail of the Comanche Indians who had abducted his young niece. Ethan is a tough, uncompromising ex-Confederate cavalryman who still has not accepted Union authority. Victor Davis Hanson noted that in this and other films with rebel anti-heroes, Edwards's skill-set and attitude come to the fore "when frontier law fails and such assets are necessary, even if acquired in nihilist service to the losing side."[90] In 2008 the American Film Institute named *The Searchers* the greatest American Western.

John Wayne returned as a former rebel in 1969 in *True Grit*—this time as the one-eyed marshal Rooster Cogburn, who rode during the war with the Confederate raider William Quantrill. The Texas Ranger La Boeuf (Glen Campbell), a former Confederate who served with General Kirby Smith, says he heard Quantrill's band killed women and children. Cogburn retorts, "I heard that, too, and it's a damn lie." Wayne's Cogburn earned him the Academy Award for Best Actor.

In *The Outlaw Josey Wales* (1976), another Confederate raider (Clint Eastwood) rides with "Bloody Bill" Anderson, seeking vengeance after Union-leaning Jayhawker militiamen kill his family. Wales in some respects mirrors the romanticized highwayman Jesse James, who rode with Bloody Bill in real life. In this movie, the Jayhawkers are the ones killing women and children, and Union troops gun down disarmed Confederate POWs. The vengeance-minded rebel had appeared earlier in *Dallas* (1950), with Gary Cooper as Blayde "Reb" Hollister, a wanted ex-Confederate guerilla who is hunting down a gang of former Union troops who murdered his family in Georgia.

More recently, in AMC's *Hell on Wheels* series, a former rebel colonel and Mississippi slave owner, Cullen Bohannon (Anson Mount), improbably forms "an uneasy alliance" with the former slave Elam Ferguson.[91] Bohannon, like Josey Wales and "Reb" Hollister, is seeking revenge against Union soldiers who murdered his family during the war. His nemesis in the series, Thor Gundersen—the "Swede"—is an amoral and ruthless former Union soldier and POW who, it is implied, survived the notorious Confederate prison camp at Andersonville by resorting to cannibalism. These and many other examples show the dramatic value of Confederate characters, especially when Hollywood thought rebels were cool.

Like the rebel soldier, the Confederate flag has been used for a variety of purposes, from being the emblem of "massive resistance" to integration in the South in the 1950s to topping the orange 1969 Dodge Charger the *General Lee* in the 1980s television series the *The Dukes of Hazzard*.[92] It also shows up in the revered 1991 outlaw feminist road movie *Thelma and Louise*. Thelma "exchanges her housedress for a black T-shirt emblazoned with a skull and a Confederate flag cap" to "cast off symbols of conventional femininity" and "take up symbols stereotypically associated with lower-class, white masculinity." The t-shirt's slogan foreshadows the pair's fate: "Driving my life away."[93]

Controversy over the rebel flag surged in 2015 after the white supremacist Dylan Roof gunned down nine black churchgoers in Charleston, South Carolina, in the hope of starting a race war. Photos emerged of Roof posing with the Confederate flag as well as burning an American flag. Days after the shooting, Governor Nikki Haley called for the flag to be removed from the South Carolina statehouse grounds, where it had first been flown in 1962 to protest desegregation. Retailers pulled rebel flags from their shelves, flag-makers ended production, and Warner Bros. stopped making toy versions of the *General Lee*.

"Some unnamed genius at the company feels that the flag is 'offensive to some' and therefore it has no business on a classic TV comedy about a bunch of good ol' boys and girls in the

Southern mountains," wrote Ben Jones, a former Democratic congressman from Georgia who played Cooter in *The Dukes of Hazzard*. "This is a new level of 'P.C.' idiocy. I don't know about you, but I am tired of being insulted by morons."[94] A CNN poll taken in the wake of the Charleston shooting showed that 57 percent of respondents viewed the Confederate flag as "a symbol of Southern pride," while only 33 percent saw it as a symbol of racism. But there was a wide racial gulf on the issue: 66 percent of whites see the flag as a mark of pride, and 72 percent of blacks see it as racist.[95]

The latter narrative won out among pundits and the press, and across the country the Confederate flag was furled. Virginia and other states removed the symbol from license plates. The Department of Veterans Affairs banned displaying the flag at any cemeteries it administers, though it allows small flags at individual graves on Memorial Day. And the Six Flags Over Texas amusement park dropped its display of the national flags that have flown over Texas in favor of six American flags, so as not to fly the flag of the Confederate States. "We always choose to focus on celebrating the things that unite us versus those that divide us," the park explained.[96] The outspoken Texas agriculture commissioner Sid Miller called the move "another act of appeasement to the intolerant, liberal, and oftentimes violent left" that is "destroying and attempting to sanitize our nation's history."[97]

NASCAR asked fans not to fly rebel flags at races to "create an all-inclusive, even more welcoming atmosphere for all who attend our events."[98] The association even offered to exchange fans' rebel flags for American flags on race day. But the move backfired, and the next week at Daytona International Speedway "spotting a Confederate flag was easier than finding a souvenir shop, restroom or beer stand."[99] NASCAR fan Paul Stevens complained the organization was "jumping on the bandwagon" and was "too quick to try to be politically correct like everybody else" when they should just "let it pass, let everything die down."[100] And of course since NASCAR was telling fans not to fly a flag that symbolized rebellion, the response was obvious.

Confederate flag sensitivity combined with anti-Trump mania when Ivanka Trump tweeted out a vacation picture of her husband, Jared Kushner, and their son on a fishing trip. A boat sporting American and Confederate flags happened to pass by as the photo was shot and is visible in the background. Ivanka's inadvertent photobomb caused a liberal Twitter explosion. "Confederate flag over Jared's shoulder," noted the Obama administration's director of the Office of Government Ethics, Walter Shaub. "Is this a dogwhistle?"[101] Penn State's Michael E. Mann of Climategate fame, whom the *Yale Alumni Magazine* called "the most hated climate scientist in the US," chimed in with his opinion that "to any neo-nazi, this confederate flag [in the background] is a dog-whistle."[102] Another, less hysterical Twitter user observed, "someone posts pics of an excited kid happy he caught a fish and people go to politics.... [I]f anyone wants evidence of what's wrong with this country look no further."[103]

Confederate symbols large and small continue to disappear. J. E. B. Stuart High School in Fairfax County, Virginia, was renamed Justice High School.[104] King's Dominion amusement park in Virginia changed the name of its "Rebel Yell!" rollercoaster to "Racer 75."[105] (No word yet on whether British rocker

Billy Idol is dropping that tune from his set.) Dolly Parton erased the word "Dixie" from her "Dixie Stampede" shows to "remove any confusion or concerns," as if there were any.[106] This was after a *Slate* reviewer panned the show as "a lily-white kitsch extravaganza that play-acts the Civil War but never once mentions slavery."[107] And the University of Mississippi has banned the traditional playing of "Dixie" at sporting events.[108]

This is not the first time the song has been banned. In the late 1960s and early 1970s, many schools dropped "Dixie" as a spirit song because of racial sensitivities. This inspired the recording artist Mickey Newbury to write "An American Trilogy," later made famous by Elvis Presley. The song is a medley of "The Battle Hymn of the Republic," the civil rights era folk song "All My Trials," and a dirge-like rendition of "Dixie." Newbury premiered the tune to a celebrity-sprinkled audience at the L.A. folk club the Bitter End West on Thanksgiving weekend in 1970. When he finished, the crowd was silent for a moment, then Mama Cass Elliot jumped up applauding, and the rest of the audience, which included Kris Kristofferson, Barbra Streisand, and the feminist-folk icon Joan Baez, "screamed and hollered like you would not believe."[109]

A year after hearing Mickey Newbury perform, Baez recorded "The Night They Drove Old Dixie Down," which became a number-one Billboard adult contemporary hit. The sing-along anthem, originally recorded by the roots rock group The Band, was written by the Canadian musician Robbie Robertson and featured in Martin Scorsese's 1978 rockumentary *The Last Waltz*. It is one of the best-known cultural references to the old South and offers an important key to understanding contemporary politics.

The song's storyteller is Virgil Caine, a Southern dirt farmer whose name evokes the biblical Cain, who emerged from the first conflict of brother against brother as the original marked man. He speaks for the downtrodden, the little guy, broken but unbowed. The Band's Levon Helm said, "It was the kind-of heartbreaking, complicated story and performance that had even Northerners rooting for the proud and desperate Virgil."[110]

The song is about the end of the Civil War and after, but the message transcends "the winter of '65." Virgil Caine is an everyman, the hardworking guy beset by problems but holding on to his values and his inspiration. He stoically deals with what comes. His family is hungry, just barely alive. He doesn't mind chopping wood, doesn't care if the money's no good. He has inherited a difficult lot in life, like his father before him, and standing up to his troubles is the root of his dignity. This was his way of life. His brother died to defend it. And in defeat Virgil is a victim of an unfair system that took the very best.

Virgil is not the kind of guy at whom an Ivy League-educated social justice warrior should bark, "Check your privilege!" He is the prototypical everyman. He is the working-class voter the progressives have abandoned and can't get back. They secretly—sometimes openly—despise him. President Obama belittled those who "get bitter" and "cling to their guns and religion." Bill and Hillary Clinton both ridiculed "the coal people" they were going to put out of business with a free-energy pipe dream. Liberal politicians and progressive pundits promoted the idea that the denizens of "flyover country" didn't matter, that their time had passed, that their concerns were unimportant, and they had no place in the American future. The liberal bells were ringing, and all the progressives were singing. The metaphorical "Dixie" being driven down was a decent way of life that seemed to be slipping away. And that message resonates most strongly with those who believe the country being overrun is not the Confederate States, but the United States.

THREE

KILLING THE DEAD WHITE MEN

Already we know almost literally nothing about the Revolution and the years before the Revolution. Every record has been destroyed or falsified, every book has been rewritten, every picture has been repainted, every statue and street and building has been renamed, every date has been altered.
—George Orwell, *1984*

In the wake of the Charlottesville incident, President Trump got into a sharp exchange with journalists over the implications of taking down the Lee statue. "This week, it's Robert E. Lee," he said. "I noticed that Stonewall Jackson is coming down. I wonder, is it George Washington next week? And is it Thomas Jefferson the week after? You know, you really do have to ask yourself, where does it stop?"

Journalists pushed back hard, insisting that the issues were totally different. But the president held his ground, arguing that since Washington and Jefferson were slave owners, they would eventually be treated the same way. "You're changing history," Trump said. "You're changing culture."[1]

Historians mocked the president for his slippery-slope argument. "It's a ridiculous conflation," sniffed Professor Alice Fahs of the University of California, Irvine. Lee is "not a founding father, and it's as though Trump thinks he is. It's really astonishing. It's amazing."[2] But Professor Fahs and others who scoffed at the president had it backwards. He was not raising Robert E. Lee to the level of the Founding Fathers; he was predicting that critics would conflate the slave-owning Founders with Lee.

Trump was quickly proved right. Virginia's Democratic governor, Terry McAuliffe, a close Clinton family associate with sterling liberal credentials, blundered into a minefield when he innocently praised the legacies of the Virginia "patriots…Thomas Jefferson and George Washington, who brought our country together." McAuliffe received a swift, stinging rebuke from CNN Vice President Johnita P. Due, who wrote that "invoking Jefferson to condemn the white supremacists and neo-Nazis who were demonstrating Friday and Saturday is antithetical to Jefferson's beliefs—and certainly to the life he led." Due asserted that "our national healing cannot move forward if even well-meaning leaders don't recognize the role our Founding Fathers played in seeding white supremacy."[3]

Jeffrey Blount also slammed McAuliffe in the *Huffington Post*: "As he stood asking us to come together across the racial divide, he holds up before black people two men who enslaved their ancestors as the perfect ideal."[4] In other words, one person's Founding Father is another's founding slaver.

Calls for statues of Washington and Jefferson to be removed followed almost immediately. The former director of the Congressional Black Caucus Angela Rye said on CNN that teaching reverence for the Founders is a "problem" and that statues and tributes to Washington and Jefferson "all need to come down."[5] Al Sharpton told Charlie Rose that the Jefferson Memorial should be defunded.[6] A statue of Jefferson at the University of Virginia, which he founded, was splashed with red paint, and later Black Lives Matter protestors enshrouded Jefferson with a black tarp and erected a sign saying, "This is a racist rapist," no doubt referring to speculation that Jefferson fathered children with his slave Sally Hemings.[7]

Bishop James Dukes, pastor of the Liberation Christian Center of Chicago, called on Mayor Rahm Emanuel to remove a statue of George Washington from Washington Park on the city's South Side. "I think we should be able to identify and decide who we declare heroes in our communities," he said, "because we have to tell the stories to our children of who these persons are." The bishop suggested the park be renamed for the former mayor Harold Washington.[8] White House Chief of Staff John Kelly sarcastically suggested that in place of statues of George Washington "we can find some cult hero that we can put up there and say he really was the great one. Andy Warhol or someone like that."[9]

President Trump's prediction was on solid ground because he recognized what already existed. Liberals have long deplored the "dead white males" who founded the country. It is surprising that New York-born Terry McAuliffe thought it would be acceptable to invoke Washington and Jefferson as symbols of unity, given the progressive political milieu in which he operates. His views, however, are evolving rapidly as the 2020 presidential race approaches. When the issue of Confederate memory arose in

2015, McAuliffe said, "Robert E. Lee, Jefferson Davis, these are all parts of our heritage," and it would be best to "leave the statues and those things alone" on Richmond's Monument Avenue.[10] Two years later he called the statues "flashpoints for hatred, division, and violence" and said they should all come down.[11]

Liberals have come a long way since the 1960 presidential campaign, when John F. Kennedy told a North Carolina audience, "as a New Englander, I recognize that the South is still the land of Washington, who made our Nation—of Jefferson, who shaped its direction—and of Robert E. Lee who, after gallant failure, urged those who had followed him in bravery to reunite America in purpose and courage."[12]

THE FOUNDERS: AMERICA'S ORIGINAL SINNERS

The Founders were extraordinary men, and their influence is difficult to overestimate. They led a successful revolt against the most powerful country in the world and established an enduring system of government that has been a model and inspiration for freedom worldwide. It is perhaps the longest continuing such system under a written constitution, a fitting offspring of the British Mother of Parliaments. Washington, Jefferson, Adams, Madison, Hamilton, Franklin, George Mason, Patrick Henry, and others are the giants of our early history. The cities, parks, schools, and innumerable other institutions that bear their names are monuments to their greatness and wisdom. Try to assemble a list of comparably gifted politicians today. Who even gets close?

The United States has maintained a sense of unity by upholding a civic myth of the Founding and the richness of American history in general. Even during the crisis of the Civil War, both sides revered the founding generation of revolutionaries. It was not just because many Confederates were the sons and grandsons of that heroic generation—Robert E. Lee's father, "Light Horse Harry" Lee, was a cavalry commander in the Revolution, and two other Lees signed the Declaration of Independence. It was chiefly because even the Southern rebels accepted the fundamental legitimacy of what the Founders had wrought. And through later periods of change, and in particular the immigration surge of the late nineteenth and early twentieth centuries, American traditions, symbols, and heroes were respected. When in 1901 the authors of a historical dictionary wrote that George Washington was "universally deemed the greatest of Americans, and one of the noblest public characters of all time," even after discounting the "doubtful authority" of his early hagiographer Parson Weems, no one would have contested that description.[13]

The revisionist march against the Founders took hold in the twentieth century. Charles Beard made one of the most important early critiques in his 1913 treatise *An Economic Interpretation of the Constitution of the United States*, in which he propounded the idea that the Constitution was the product of a plot by the mercantile class against the agrarian Anti-Federalists. This work was highly influential, especially among the conspiracy-minded, and tied into the socialistic and Marxist influences of the Progressive Era. The Beard thesis was discredited by the work of later scholars, including John P. Roche, who used the records of the state ratification debates to demonstrate that the new Constitution was thoroughly discussed and had broad-based support. Furthermore, the very existence of the Bill of Rights, which the Federalists opposed, illustrates that it was a document that enshrined compromise at its core.[14]

Today the economic critique of the Founders has given way to one based on identity politics, according to which slavery is the original sin. So, for example, onetime Federalist villains like John Adams and the Broadway sensation Alexander Hamilton are enjoying a rehabilitation of their reputations because they were on the right side of the slavery issue. Jefferson, who was in Paris during the Constitutional Convention, is definitely on the outs, along with father of his country, George Washington, and the slave-owning architect of the Constitution, James Madison.

A black student at James Madison Memorial High School in Madison (double whammy), Wisconsin, petitioned to change the school's name. In the school's contentious racial climate, she feels "more than unsafe," and apparently it is President Madison's fault.[15] Inspired by the Wisconsin protest, a student newspaper at James Madison University in Harrisonburg, Virginia, asked if JMU should change its name. Ninety-one percent of the almost 2,700 respondents said no, with 5 percent saying change it and 4 percent unsure. Many comments in the survey suggested that the debate over slavery and the Founders needed more historical context. "Owning slaves was an economic reality of farming in James Madison's times," one student wrote. "We cannot nor should we try to erase history that we are uncomfortable learning about." Another student suggested that the Founders "saw owning slaves like millennials treat owning a smart phone," and while it was not "correct and moral" it is "part of our history and part of the society of the time."[16]

Patrick Henry High School in Minneapolis is also debating its name. One member of the predominantly black student body, Semaj Rankin, helped raise awareness about Patrick Henry's slave ownership. "The school should be renamed after someone of color or a civil rights activist," Semaj said, "someone that has helped build something in this country."[17] Unlike, apparently, Patrick Henry.

Appreciating what the Founders and their successors built—their achievements and legacy—is critical in evaluating how they should be remembered. This idea came to the fore in 2016, when Yale University considered renaming Calhoun College, named for the South Carolina Senator John C. Calhoun, an advocate for both states' rights and slavery and a member of Yale's class of 1804. To evaluate Calhoun, the university's Committee to Establish Principles on Renaming adopted the standard of "principal legacy," defined as "the lasting effects that cause a namesake to be remembered."[18] The committee wrote that "we ask about a namesake's principal legacies because human lives, as Walt Whitman wrote, are large; they contain multitudes." So, for example, the report's authors say we rightly remember Frederick Douglass as "an abolitionist and an advocate for civil rights," not for saying that Native Americans "were easily 'contented' with small things such as blankets, and who would 'die out' in any event."[19]

Noting in passing that the university's namesake, Elihu Yale, "served as the governor of an East India Company colony that engaged in the slave trade," the committee chose not to delve into a historical question that threatened the three-hundred-year-old Yale brand. The *New Criterion*'s Roger Kimball noted that Elihu Yale was in fact deeply and personally involved in the slave trade, and profits from it accounted for part of the fortune that was later donated to the university. Any reasonable examination of comparative guilt, then, would drop the Calhoun inquiry and "concentrate on the far more flagrant name 'Yale.'"[20] But that was beyond the committee's mandate. It determined that Calhoun's principal legacy was at odds with the mission of the university, and the college was renamed. The slave trader Elihu Yale escaped, at least this time.

The principal-legacy standard recognizes and allows for the complexities of the human condition. Someone may be worthy of admiration for great accomplishments even though his other deeds fell short. For example, principal legacy allows people to focus on Mahatma Gandhi's leadership as a nonviolent opponent of British colonial rule in spite of his racially-tinged views on black Africans.[21] It means liberals can overlook Robert F. Kennedy's authorization of FBI wiretaps on Martin Luther King Jr. and investigations of his "sexual endeavors"[22] and can drive past Chappaquiddick while hailing Ted Kennedy as the "Lion of the Senate." It allows fans of Bill Clinton to focus on what they see as the achievements of his presidency and not his unprincipled legacy of workplace sexual harassment. Hillary Clinton's close mentor Democrat Robert C. Byrd can be remembered for being a constitutional scholar and the longest serving senator in U.S. history rather than for being a former Ku Klux Klan "Exalted Cyclops." And the city of Washington can erect an eight-foot-high statue of its scandal-plagued "Mayor for Life," Marion

Barry, because, as the *Washington Post* reminds us, "all heroes have feet of clay. Some just get theirs bronzed over and bolted to a stand."[23]

The principal-legacy approach is surprisingly reasonable in these unreasoning times. It gives leave to *Vox*'s Matthew Yglesias to write that "the storybook hero version of [George] Washington makes sense because Washington really did participate in great acts worth celebrating, even if he also did terrible things like own human beings as personal property."[24]

But principal legacy is in the eye of the beholder. For the "woke" progressive, if a historical figure was a slave owner, it is not only his defining, damning characteristic, it is the only thing worth talking about. "George Washington was a slaveowner," Angela Rye said. "Whether we think they were protecting American freedom or not, he wasn't protecting my freedom." Rye contended that America was "built on a very violent past that resulted in the death and the raping and the killing of my ancestors. I'm not going to allow us to say it's okay [to criticize] Robert E. Lee but not a George Washington. We need to call it what it is."[25]

The podcaster Jimmy Williams spoke for many progressives when he said on MSNBC that "racism is not just in the South. It is in every state in this country. This country was founded on the backbone of racism and will continue to, sadly, for a long time to come."[26] It is completely uncontroversial in these circles to charge that the U.S. Constitution remains a racist document because of the concessions the Founders made to slavery, none of which are still in effect. A prominent progressive website doesn't think twice about publishing an article entitled "America's Economy Was

Built on Slavery, Not White Ingenuity."[27] The activists at "Black-tivist" can post a *Salon* article proclaiming, "American economy and power were built of forced migration and torture" and get a big progressive "Amen." It later emerged that Blacktivist was a Russian troll outfit seeking to sow division in American politics. But progressives and revisionists have echoed Moscow's propaganda lines since the 1930s, so the Kremlin was just returning the favor.[28]

There is a certain unintentional irony in progressive talk about the importance of slavery to the early American economy, since many slave owners made the same argument in their own defense. For example, the 1861 Mississippi secession declaration noted that slavery "supplies the product which constitutes by far the largest and most important portions of commerce of the earth," and "these products have become necessities of the world."[29] Those on the Left who believe that slavery was the engine of the American economy need to explain why, if this was true, the South lost the Civil War.

It is becoming impossible to have a reasonable discussion about the positive aspects of American history. Every topic has been subjected to withering revisionism. The very notion of patriotism has become divisive, splitting the country between those who honor and respect America's history and a vocal minority who despise it. Polls show that those who are proud to be an American far outnumber those who are not, but the views of those who are ashamed of the country seem to dominate the debate.[30] And it is difficult for those who have patriotic feelings to take seriously or even understand the views of those who so completely and shamelessly denounce the Founders and the

Constitution. Their lack of reverence is wholly foreign to those who take pride in the United States. It is fundamentally anti-American. And while it is certainly true that the Founders are not above criticism, today's progressives treat them as beneath contempt.

"YOU CAN'T CHANGE HISTORY, BUT YOU DON'T HAVE TO HONOR IT"

In many respects the war on history is an effort by Democrats to purge their own past. The Democratic Party was the bulwark of slavery. Ten of the fifteen presidents who preceded Lincoln owned slaves at one time or another; six of them were Democrats, three were Whigs, and Washington had no party. Democratic revisionism has wrecked the traditional Jefferson-Jackson Day fundraising dinner, since neither of these party founders is politically correct any more. Both have connections to slavery, and Jackson has the additional historical blemish of having driven the Cherokees, Choctaws, and other tribes from their homes in the East to Oklahoma along the Trail of Tears. Historians regularly rank both of them among the top ten presidents, but party activists do not see their principal legacies as presidents, statesmen, or founders of the Democratic Party. To them, a "Jefferson-Jackson" dinner may as well be a "slavery-genocide" celebration. This has led to a nationwide scouring of their names. "I see it as the right thing to do," said the Connecticut party chairman, Nick Balletto. "You can't change history, but you don't have to honor it."[31]

Colorado Democrats took an online poll for alternative names for their fundraiser, and were cautioned that "expecting our heroes to be perfect creates a standard that cannot be attained by anyone" and that choosing others would "simply open their past to investigation that they too will fail."[32] One observer noted that if Democrats refused to recognize all their slave-owning presidents and those who had sex scandals or abused women, they would be left with Franklin Pierce, Grover Cleveland, Harry Truman, Jimmy Carter, and Barack Obama.[33] In the end they chose "the Obama Dinner."[34]

The Obama Treasury Department had planned to expunge Jackson's portrait from the twenty-dollar bill, replacing him with the former slave and abolitionist Harriet Tubman, in what the *New York Times* called "the most sweeping and historically symbolic makeover of American currency in a century."[35] They also planned to feature feminists and other activists on the backs of the five- and ten-dollar bills. But this plan fell by the wayside with the accession of President Trump. Now Old Hickory's portrait not only remains on the twenty-dollar bill but also hangs in the Oval Office. Meanwhile in New Orleans, the site of Jackson's famous 1815 battlefield victory, a group called "Take 'em Down NOLA" threatened to pull down the statue of the general in Jackson Square.[36] Elsewhere in the Big Easy, a confused vandal spray painted "Take it down" on the base of the equestrian statue of fifteenth century French military leader and "Maid of Orleans" St. Joan of Arc. Apparently, anybody on a horse is fair game.[37]

The Democrat John C. Calhoun has been spurned not only by his alma mater but by the party of which he was a pillar. But

Calhoun was highly regarded for years as a statesman, a leader of the Senate in its "silver age," and an intellectual. An admiring John F. Kennedy included him in his Pulitzer Prize-winning *Profiles in Courage*. As chairman of a Senate committee to choose five illustrious senators to be honored with portraits in the Senate Reception Room, Kennedy picked Calhoun along with Henry Clay, Daniel Webster, Robert M. LaFollette Sr., and Robert A. Taft. "Sincerely devoted to the public good as he saw it," Kennedy said, "the ultimate tragedy of [Calhoun's] final cause neither detracts from the greatness of his leadership nor tarnishes his efforts to avert bloodshed."[38]

Erasing history goes beyond Democrats' embarrassment about their erstwhile heroes. There is a national mania to revisit, re-contextualize, or simply eliminate reminders of history that have suddenly become uncomfortable for the liberal elite.

Pittsburgh opted to remove a statue of its native son Stephen Foster, which had been erected in 1900 and funded by contributions from local citizens. Sculpted by Giuseppe Marchetti, the statue was unveiled as a chorus of three thousand school children sang Foster's songs.[39] The sculpture, which shows Foster seated and making notes, features a smiling, elderly, banjo-playing African American man just below him. The work was intended to convey how Foster—who wrote "Oh! Susannah," "My Old Kentucky Home," and "Camptown Races," among other songs—was inspired by African American musicians. But it is a short step from "inspiration" to the latest leftist taboo, "cultural appropriation." So the tribute to Stephen Foster, "the father of American music" and the country's first pop star, was deemed racist and had to go.[40]

The elaborate Pioneer Monument in San Francisco, which features the goddess Minerva on a pedestal surrounded by scenes from California's history, has come under fire for its allegedly "fetishized or romanticized, historically and culturally inaccurate images" of "colonial conquest."[41] Most controversial is a statue, called "Early Days," of a Spanish *vaquero* and a missionary priest with an Indian sitting at their feet. The missionary is stooped over, pointing skyward with his left hand while reaching out to the Indian with the other, symbolizing the Spanish effort to Christianize the local tribes. The San Francisco Arts Commission voted unanimously to take the statue down. These days there is nothing about "Early Days" that passes muster with progressive critics, except perhaps that the *vaquero* was a Spanish speaker.

Another symbol of "forced assimilation" is Junípero Serra, a Franciscan friar who founded the mission system in California. After Serra was canonized by Pope Francis in 2015, vandals struck his burial site at the Carmel Mission, "toppling statues and damaging grave sites," splashing paint in the cemetery and basilica, and scrawling on a headstone, "Saint of Genocide."[42] In 2017 another group attacked a Serra statue near the San Fernando Mission, painting its hands red and writing "murderer" on it.[43]

A cartoonish statue of Hiawatha in La Crosse, Wisconsin, was criticized at a public meeting in 2017 for not representing real Indians, even though when it was erected in the 1950s it was intended as a sincere, if aesthetically misguided, tribute. Yet a more realistic statue showing three Ho-Chunk Indians playing the traditional sport of lacrosse was called "just as insulting" by

Shaundel Spivey of La Crosse's Human Rights Commission. The problem is that the statue makes it look like "lacrosse is just this game that people play" (isn't it?), ignoring its original spiritual or ritualistic purposes. And just for good measure, someone at the same meeting questioned the elaborate 2016 monument to the Olympic hurdler and local hero George Poage, the first African American to medal at the games, with two bronzes in 1904. The concern was that "it might promote a stereotype of black men being good at sports," by which logic there could be no statues to any black athletes anywhere.[44]

The Joe Louis "fist" statue in Detroit was criticized for looking like a sideways black power salute and also for its suggestion of violence, though Louis was, after all, a boxer. And after the Cleveland Indians dropped their controversial "Chief Wahoo" logo, ESPN's Max Kellerman made an impassioned plea that Notre Dame should dump its "Fighting Irish" moniker and leprechaun mascot because "pernicious, negative stereotypes of marginalized people that offend even some among them should be changed."[45] Of course you can always find "even some" people who are upset about anything, so setting the bar that low would require wholesale changes in just about every walk of life. The former ESPN and current MLB Network host Brian Kenny, who is of Irish extraction, tweeted out his support for Kellerman: "Leprechaun cartoons are subhuman and offensive, and are used to keep us 'in our place,'" a charge that seems antiquated at best, or more likely a desperate plea for special victimhood status. The sportswriter Clay Travis observed, "no one with a brain actually believes this," and another sports fan wondered, "What, the ESPN ratings aren't low enough?"[46]

Even remembering the Alamo is getting to be problematic. Texas General Land Office Commissioner George P. Bush, oldest child of former Florida Governor Jeb Bush, has undertaken an effort to "reimagine" the historic battle site and shrine of Texas liberty. But Alamo Society board member Glenn Effler said the master plan for the reimagining is an example to "the nation and the world why you should never entrust a historic site to politicians and bureaucrats."[47]

The thirteen-day siege of the Alamo in 1836 and the climactic battle that followed is central to the Texas foundation narrative. Its defenders died in the name of "Liberty, of patriotism & everything dear to the American character."[48] The selfless sacrifice of William Barrett Travis, Jim Bowie, Davy Crockett, and their heavily outnumbered comrades is an example of pure heroism that has been likened to the Spartan stand at Thermopylae. In fact, the first Alamo monument bore the inscription, "Thermopylae had her messenger of defeat—the Alamo had none."[49]

The legend of the Alamo has not escaped the revisionist blender.[50] In the new version, Travis is reborn as a syphilitic womanizer, slave trader, and alleged murderer. Bowie becomes the Indian-slaughtering thief. Crockett is the coward who tried to surrender rather than fight to the death. The gaggle of defenders is made up of land-hungry mercenaries and outlaws. And Sam Houston, who avenged them at the Battle of San Jacinto, is an overweight drug addict. This revisionist version is what Santa Anna would have written if he had issued press releases. It was a predictable drift from the heroic version of the story presented by John Wayne in his epic 1960 feature film *The Alamo* to the darker 2004 offering starring Dennis Quaid and Billy Bob Thornton. Note also the satirical commentary on the issue that same year in the animated series *King of the Hill*, in which iconic cartoon Texan Hank Hill groused, "Damn revisionists. Why don't they ever make history better?"[51]

The current Alamo "reimagining" sterilizes the story. Rather than fighting over the meaning of the battle and the character of the participants, the project minimizes the importance of the event altogether. In the new thinking, the siege of the Alamo has to be viewed as only one aspect of the long history of the Misión de San Antonio de Valero. George P. Bush's proposed reimagined Alamo would have a Plexiglas-enclosed park with an artificial stream, overlooked by a restaurant atop a new "multicultural museum" across the street. The story of the battle would be relegated to the museum's basement. The Alamo Cenotaph monument, erected on the centennial of the battle in 1936, would be moved away from the mission. The plan does not recreate the look and feel of a battleground. As Glenn Effler put it, "Alamo Plaza becomes an aquarium with nothing to see."[52]

The project's master planner, the non-Texan George Skarmeas, defends deemphasizing the battle, arguing that "the events of 1836 were just one small chapter in 10,000 years of history," and "we cannot single out one moment in time."[53] But the reason people care about the Alamo is because of the battle that took place there, the human drama, outsized personalities, and noble sacrifice. It is what made the Alamo "The Alamo." It's like saying that Gettysburg needs to focus less on the Civil War, or that D-Day was just another day at the beach.

LINCOLN AND GRANT AT WAR—AGAIN

Not even Abraham Lincoln—the man most credited with freeing the slaves, the president who preserved the Union and was martyred at the moment of victory—has escaped the vandals. Shortly after the Charlottesville incident, the Lincoln Memorial in Washington, D.C., was tagged with red spray paint, "F—k law," and *Vice Magazine* scoffed at "Abe Lincoln squatting on his (recently vandalized) throne."[54] Around the same time, a century-old bust of Abraham Lincoln in Chicago's West Englewood neighborhood was "covered in tar, wrapped in roofing paper, and set on fire." Alderman Ray Lopez blamed President Trump for giving people "a path to come out and be as anger-filled as they want to be." But local resident Christopher Jackson said mistreating the statue was "f—— up, honestly," adding, "You'd think people would appreciate it. Abraham Lincoln is Abraham Lincoln. He's one of the people who helped us. He freed the slaves. That's a big one."[55]

Yet not everyone agrees that Lincoln did free the slaves. For some progressives, the Great Emancipator was neither great nor an emancipator. It seems absurd to have to defend the anti-slavery bona fides of the man who said, "I hate it because of the monstrous injustice of slavery itself."[56] But since the 1960s, revisionist historians have told us that not only did Lincoln not free the slaves, he was a racist who wanted to ship freed blacks to Africa.

"Lincoln must be seen as the embodiment, not the transcendence, of the American tradition of racism," wrote *Ebony* magazine's executive editor, the historian Lerone Bennett Jr.[57] His book *Forced into Glory: Abraham Lincoln's White Dream* argues that far from being an abolitionist, Lincoln was in fact a white supremacist who had a dim view of blacks, and who did his best to prolong slavery so he could put together a plan to deport all the eventually freed slaves to Africa or the Caribbean. Bennett wrote that myth-making after Lincoln's assassination turned "a conservative White Supremacist" into "a national symbol of racial tolerance and understanding."[58]

Bennett transforms a stale truism about the political limitations of the Emancipation Proclamation (namely, that it did not actually free anyone) into a conspiracy theory about repatriation. But emancipation was politically risky, and Lincoln could not realistically have done more than he did.[59] Hard-core abolitionists despaired of him as a moderate and a compromiser, while Southern firebrands, appalled at the election of an extremist "Black Republican," started to secede before he even took office. Lincoln was forced to chart a difficult political course, attempting to placate various wings of his coalition, of which abolitionists were only one part, while also leading the Union in one of the most momentous wars in history. Maintaining the Union was a necessary precondition for ending slavery, since if Lincoln proclaimed the slaves free but lost the war, he would in fact have achieved nothing.

Those like Bennett who rush to condemn Lincoln ignore this sensitive political balancing act. "Lincoln's torments are well known, his vacillations were facts," Martin Luther King Jr. said in a speech honoring the centennial of the Emancipation Proclamation. He noted Lincoln was called "the 'Baboon President' in the North, and 'coward,' 'assassin,' and 'savage' in the South." However, "when Abraham Lincoln signed the Emancipation Proclamation it was not the act of an opportunistic politician issuing a hollow pronouncement to placate a pressure group," and through it "Lincoln achieved immortality."[60] When King gave his famous "I Have a Dream" speech on the steps of the Lincoln Memorial a year later, it wasn't because he thought Lincoln was a white supremacist.

However Lincoln felt about the slaves, he is also on the progressives' hook for his treatment of Indians. In 2016, the indigenous student organization Wunk Sheek staged a die-in at the University of Wisconsin at Madison to protest the mass execution on Lincoln's watch of thirty-eight Dakota men who had participated in the Sioux Uprising of 1862, which left up to eight hundred settlers dead. Of the 303 captured Indians who were condemned, Lincoln pardoned 264, knowing his pardon would be politically unpopular. Another Indian was later reprieved, and the rest were hanged simultaneously, the largest such execution in American history.

The protest took place around a campus statue of Lincoln erected in his centenary year of 1909, a copy of a monument in Lincoln's birthplace in Hodgenville, Kentucky, cast by the same sculptor, the famed German-born artist Adolph A. Weinman. Over the years it has been a fixture at the school, a good luck totem, and the background for innumerable graduation photos.[61] The protesters hung a sign around the statue's neck describing Lincoln's alleged crimes and saying #DecolonizeOurCampus.

"Everyone thinks of Lincoln as the great, you know, freer of slaves," Wunk Sheek member Misha told the student newspaper. "But let's be real: he owned slaves." (Just to be really real, Lincoln did not own slaves.) "As natives, we want people to know that he ordered the execution of native men," Misha continued. "Just to have him here at the top of Bascom is just really belittling."[62] A year earlier, a group affiliated with Black Lives Matter, About Race UW, suggested removing the Lincoln statue. The demand was tabled as "too extreme within the black community at the event," but why it was suggested in the first place was unexplained.[63] In the spring of 2017 the student government approved a resolution to educate the community about "Lincoln's oppression," an expression that in past decades was only used by unreconstructed Confederates.[64]

Even Ulysses S. Grant, leader of the victorious Union army and a two-term president, is being forced to atone for his sins. In the wake of the Charlottesville incident, New York City began a drive against "symbols of hate."[65] It was a wide-ranging review of practically every monument, plaque, bust, painting, park, school, and anything else in the city connected to history. Mayor Bill de Blasio explained, "we're trying to unpack 400 years of American history here—that's really what's going on."[66] And one of the suggestions was to tear down Grant's Tomb.

The General Grant National Memorial in Upper Manhattan's Riverside Park was built in 1897 to serve as the final resting place for the former president, who died in 1885, and his wife Julia Dent Grant, who passed away in 1902. Since 1958 the site been overseen by the National Park Service. The tomb has undergone cycles of decline and refurbishment over the years, and in the early 1990s the structure was so dilapidated that Illinois state lawmakers threatened to push for the Grants' remains to be moved to his adopted home state. Substantial repair and maintenance since then have returned the tomb to its former glory.

The condition of Grant's reputation is another matter. He was the only Republican president to have owned a slave, however briefly. That was a matter of family politics. Grant's parents strongly opposed slavery. But young Ulysses fell in love with Julia Dent, his West Point roommate Fred Dent's sister, who was from a pro-slavery family in Missouri. Grant's father was so upset over the match that he skipped the wedding. Later, Fred Dent transferred a slave named William Jones to Grant's farm. Grant freed Jones, even though he was down on his luck and could legally have sold him and kept the proceeds. But Grant did not want to profit from slavery in any way.[67] And Grant not only freed Jones, his armies freed tens of thousands of slaves during the war. As Grant told German Chancellor Otto von Bismarck during a European tour after leaving the presidency, once the Civil War commenced, it was his feeling that when the fighting was over, "slavery must be destroyed. We felt that it was a stain to the Union that men should be bought and sold like cattle."[68] His record as president reflected this, since he vigorously enforced laws to implement the postwar constitutional amendments against slavery and loosed the newly-formed Justice Department on the KKK.[69]

Another point of contention is General Order 11, which Grant issued on December 17, 1862, expelling all Jews from his area of responsibility in the Department of the Tennessee. Upset over what he saw as illicit Jewish trading, particularly in cotton, he believed expulsion was an expeditious solution. Jewish groups immediately protested, and when word got back to Washington, President Lincoln immediately revoked the measure.

But by then the damage was done. The Senate voted to censure Grant, and the order became an issue in the 1868 presidential race. Grant, however, repudiated his own action, saying he had no enmity for Jews or people of any other faith. Grant's contrition was accepted by the community, and he won the majority of Jewish votes that year. He later became the first president to attend a synagogue service. A rabbi served as one of his honorary pallbearers, and because it was the Sabbath he chose to walk the entire seven-and-a-half-mile funeral route.[70]

Professor Jonathan Sarna of Brandeis University, the chief historian of the National Museum of American Jewish History and the author of a book on General Order 11, believes that it would be "ignorant" for New York to punish Grant by removing his tomb. "Instead of trying to tear down monuments to all those with blemished records," he wrote, "citizens would be better served by more intense study of the lives of those whom past generations revered. We may find that there is much to learn even from flawed heroes' mistakes."[71]

The seventeenth-century director-general of the colony of New Netherland Peter Stuyvesant is also being criticized for being "an extreme racist who targeted Jews and other minorities including Catholics and energetically tried to prohibit them from settling in then New Amsterdam," now New York.[72] There is also the matter of the sidewalk plaque honoring the World War I hero Marshal Philippe Pétain of France, who received a ticker-tape parade in 1931. By 1940, he was collaborating with the Nazis as head of the Vichy government after France fell to the Germans in World War II.

A group of protestors calling themselves the Monument Removal Brigade splashed James Earle Fraser's equestrian statue of Theodore Roosevelt outside the American Museum of Natural History with blood-red liquid. Their statement condemned the statue as an emblem of "patriarchy, white supremacy and settler-colonialism" and demanded that the museum "rethink its cultural halls regarding the colonial mentality behind them."[73] The protestors noted that the statue features a Native American walking on one side of Roosevelt's horse, and an African tribesman on the other, symbolizing, they claim, the white-centric social hierarchy. Much more relevant to that point is the nine-foot-high painting in City Hall of former New York Democratic Governor Horatio Seymour, who ran against Grant for president in 1868 using the slogan, "This is a White Man's Country; Let White Men Rule."[74]

Ultimately Mayor de Blasio's special commission recommended moving only one statue. Dr. J. Marion Sims, the nineteenth-century father of modern gynecology and founder of New York City's first women's hospital, developed his groundbreaking surgical techniques by experimenting on twelve enslaved women in Alabama in the 1840s. His statue in Central Park, which was defaced in August 2017, will be moved to his burial site at Green-Wood Cemetery in Brooklyn.[75]

Like Yale University, New York City chose not to delve into the history of the person behind its name. New York was named for James Stuart, Duke of York, who commanded the Royal Navy during the Second Anglo-Dutch War (1665–1667), which gave England possession of New Amsterdam. In 1685, he ascended the throne as James II, ruling until 1688, when he was overthrown in the Glorious Revolution. While still Duke of York, he served as the governor of the British Royal African Company, a mercantilist slave trading enterprise operating in West Africa. People captured by the company were branded on their chests or foreheads "DY," for Duke of York.[76] But for now New York has decided not to rebrand itself.

GOODBYE, COLUMBUS

The most controversial subject of New York's monument review was Christopher Columbus. The seventy-six-foot-high monument to the Genoese mariner at Columbus Circle was erected in 1892 for the four hundredth anniversary of his famous voyage. While Mayor de Blasio originally said that this statue was "on the table" for removal, the commission decided to let it remain. "I think Columbus did some things that were deeply troubling," the mayor said afterwards, but noted that his memory "became wrapped up in the larger history of Italian-American people," and that was something that could not be "unwrapped."[77]

Columbus—"patient zero" for the plague of European culture that was loosed on the unsuspecting New World—has long been a target of the revisionist Left. Howard Zinn opens his influential *A People's History of the United States* (1980) with a chapter slamming the heroic version of Columbus's story. "To emphasize the heroism of Columbus and his successors as navigators and discoverers," he writes, "and to de-emphasize their genocide, is not a technical necessity but an ideological choice. It serves—unwittingly—to justify what was done."[78]

Columbus is under attack around the country that once idol-ized him. A marble statue on the waterfront in Boston's Italian North End was splashed with red paint, and "Black Lives Mat-ter!" was spray-painted on the pedestal.[79] A bronze statue in Houston's Bell Park was also given a red-paint bath.[80] A vandal in Detroit put an axe in the forehead of a Columbus bust.[81] In Baltimore, the oldest Columbus monument in the country was attacked with a sledgehammer by a group calling itself the "Pop-ular Resistance," which posted a video of the attack on YouTube. The forty-four-foot obelisk was erected in 1792 by the French consul and friend of Thomas Jefferson Chevalier d'Anemours, who was instrumental in forging the patriot alliance with France during the Revolution. One of the vandals held a sign reading "Racism, tear it down."[82]

San Jose, California, voted to remove from its city hall a Columbus statue that was a gift from the Italian-American com-munity in the 1950s.[83] Previously in San Jose a statue honoring the nineteenth-century mayor Thomas Fallon, who led the force that captured the city in 1846 during the Mexican-American War, spent years in crates because Hispanic groups said it glori-fied imperialism. The statue was eventually erected elsewhere, and City Park Plaza, where it was to have been displayed, was renamed Plaza de César Chávez.

Students at the University of Notre Dame, not yet woke to the whole "Fighting Irish" donnybrook, have focused instead on censoring a series of murals in the Golden Domed Main Building that depict Columbus's life and voyages. Painted in the 1880s by Luigi Gregori, the founder of Notre Dame's art department, the murals were a labor of love for the artist, who worked portraits of friends and fellow faculty members into the scenes.[84] But to the 340 students, faculty, and staff who signed a letter calling for the murals to come down, they depict a "highly problematic vision of Western triumphalism, Catholic militarism and an overly romantic notion of American expansion." The letter decries the "renewed rise of dangerous nationalism," and says that "it is time for Notre Dame to remove its own version of a Confederate monument."[85]

Columbus-hating is still a fringe view. He topped an ABC News-CNN "greatest of the millennium" poll in the field of exploration—Lewis and Clark came in a distant second—and his voyage was listed as the third-greatest human achievement after medical advances and the moon landing.[86] A 2017 Marist poll showed Columbus with a 56 percent favorable rating, double the number of unfavorable, and 76 percent believed that it was more proper to judge historical figures by the standards of conduct during the time they lived than by today's standards.[87] Italian Americans are especially sensitive to suggestions that their greatest national hero be purged. The recognition of Columbus and his achievements was a symbolic aspect of the acceptance and Americanization of Italian Catholic immigrants, who were viewed skeptically by nineteenth-century nativists. Erasing Columbus blots out the cultural contributions made by Italian Americans that honoring him was intended to highlight.

October 12 has been celebrated in the United States since the eighteenth century, and Columbus's voyage was the centerpiece of the World's Columbian Exposition held in Chicago in 1893. One of the stars on Chicago's city flag honors this event—and a statue cast by Moses Ezekiel for the Exposition was recently defaced.[88] Many states adopted October 12 as a holiday in the early twentieth century, and President Franklin Roosevelt first declared it a federal holiday in 1934. It was not just a celebration of the man, but also of the momentous consequences of his voyage. Yet progressives object to both, and their alternative, as Howard Zinn said, is to focus "not on the achievements of the heroes of traditional history but on all those people who were the victims of those achievements."[89] "Indigenous People's Day," which began as a 1970s protest, was widely popularized when the Venezuelan socialist dictator Hugo Chávez instituted the "Day of Indigenous Resistance" in 2002.[90] Since then a number of U.S. states and localities have either added Native American recognition to Columbus Day or chucked the observances altogether.

Seattle made it city policy to "participate in the annual Indigenous People's Day celebrations and activities," to encourage school and business recognition of the holiday, and "to promote the well-being and growth of Seattle's American Indian and Indigenous community." Washington State already recognized Native American Heritage Day on the day after Thanksgiving, but the Seattle resolution was not a positive affirmation of Native American culture so much as a slap at Columbus for the European invasion of North America.[91]

Mayor Ed Murray, deflecting criticism from Italian American groups, denied that the resolution was anti-Columbus and insisted that it would "add new significance to the date without replacing the Columbus Day tradition."[92] Yet the resolution's co-sponsor Bruce Harrell suggested that Seattle cannot reach "vibrancy as a city...until we fully recognize

the evils of our past."[93] (Or as Orwell might have put it, Guilt = Vibrancy.) And socialist councilmember Kshama Sawant, indigenous to Pune, India, scoffed at the bruised pride of locals of Italian heritage. Columbus, she charged, "played such a pivotal role in the worst genocide humankind has ever known." They ought to "celebrate Italian American social-justice activists" instead.[94]

Mr. Harrell said he makes "no excuses for this legislation," but then again he doesn't pay a price for it either. The resolution states that "Seattle is built upon the homelands and villages of the Indigenous Peoples of this region," which is tantamount to admitting the city's collective guilt. The lands were taken from the Duwamish and other tribes, and uber-woke Starbucks corporate headquarters occupies the city's Greater Duwamish District, the traditional tribal heartland. This resolution and others like it are simply consequence-free virtue signaling. Why don't the people of Seattle return these tribal lands if they feel so strongly about it? Even a few dozen downtown blocks of sacred soil would provide ample compensation.

Also, like Yale and New York, Seattle might want to reexamine its name. The city's namesake, Suguampsh and Duwamish Chief Seathl, owned slaves and avoided conflict with the settlers. His tombstone says he was a "firm friend of the whites." He was later reimagined as an environmentalist hero by virtue of an 1850s speech in which he supposedly said, "The earth does not belong to man; man belongs to the earth"—a line that was invented for a 1972 movie poster. Records of what the chief actually said are sketchy.[95] So maybe Seattle progressives should think about renaming their city for a more resistance-minded

Native American who fought against its founding, not a big sellout like Seathl.

Mount Rushmore National Memorial in South Dakota's Black Hills is also on the progressive chopping block. *Vice News* senior editor Wilbert Cooper wrote that the monument "obscures the multifaceted nature of these old dudes, transmogrifying them from individuals with a capacity both for greatness and evil into pure American deities." He said that he would "probably be onboard" with a proposal to demolish the monument, and not even to replace it with other presidents because "every single one has at least been partially complicit in horrific atrocities," including Barack Obama and, presumably, Calvin Coolidge. He also acknowledged President Trump's argument that getting rid of monuments is a slippery slope, but asked, "Would that be such a bad thing?"[96]

Destroying Mount Rushmore is an easy call for progressives. The four presidents it honors—Washington, Jefferson, Lincoln, and Theodore Roosevelt—are all bad guys in the left-wing universe. The location of the monument in the Black Hills, sacred to the Sioux (as it was to the Kiowa before the Sioux ejected them), is another blow. And it was carved in the 1920s and '30s by Gutzon Borglum, whose previous project was the bas-relief at Stone Mountain, Georgia, depicting Jefferson Davis, Robert E. Lee, and Stonewall Jackson. The Georgia site was chosen in part because it was where the modern incarnation of the Ku Klux Klan was founded in 1915. (As you might guess, there are also calls for the Stone Mountain carvings to be destroyed.[97]) Borglum had left the project, which is the largest such work in the world, because of personality conflicts with the sponsors. But the link to Stone

Mountain has inspired a conspiracy theory that Mount Rushmore—even with Lincoln on it—is somehow tied to the KKK.

A more positive response to Mount Rushmore is the nearby Crazy Horse Memorial, conceived in the 1930s by Lakota Chief Henry Standing Bear and others, designed by Borglum's assistant Korczak Ziolkowski, and begun in 1948. Carved on Thunderhead Mountain, the memorial depicts a mounted Crazy Horse pointing to where his people lie buried. Chief Standing Bear wrote that the tribal leaders "would like the white man to know that the red man has great heroes, too." The co-located museum has displays of Native American artifacts that rival any in the country. The massive project (the Mount Rushmore sculptures could fit easily on the side of Crazy Horse's head) will be the world's largest sculpture when completed, though there is still much to be done. Yet it is a good example of how history is better served by adding rather than subtracting from the American story.

Those who are more interested in destruction, however, might take notes from Taliban leader Mullah Mohammed Omar, who dynamited two massive fourth- and fifth-century Buddhist statues carved into a mountainside in Afghanistan's Bamyan valley in 2001. He considered the majestic and serene figures at the UNESCO World Heritage Site un-Islamic and blasphemous and dismissed the appeals of foreigners to preserve the Buddhas as "deplorable."[98]

FOUR

TAKING A KNEE

The last place you would have expected an assault on American identity was pro football. For decades, the NFL built its brand around an all-American, rough-and-tumble image. But in the history of bad business decisions, the League's choice to back protestors kneeling during the national anthem should rank right up there with NBC's and CBS's passing on Monday Night Football in 1970 and handing the gold-mine to ABC.[1] Defending the kneelers convinced a solid portion of the NFL fan base to spend any given Sunday not watching football.

The controversy started in 2016 when San Francisco 49ers' backup quarterback Colin Kaepernick began sitting out the pre-game playing of the national anthem; when he got some attention, he began kneeling. He explained at the time that he was "not going to stand up to show pride in a flag for a country that oppresses black people and people of color." He added that "there are bodies in the street and people getting paid leave and getting away with murder," referring to police shootings of African Americans.[2] The issue simmered through the 2016 season, at the end of which Kaepernick became a free agent and no team picked him up.

The protests spread in 2017, partly in support of the unemployed Kaepernick. But they exploded after a series of statements from President Trump, the most memorable of which he uttered at a political rally: "Wouldn't you love to see one of these NFL owners, when somebody disrespects our flag, you'd say, 'Get that son of a bitch off the field right now. Out! He's fired.'"[3] The following weekend 368 players knelt, sat, or were absent during the anthem, while 777 players locked arms or raised their fists. Altogether, some 70 percent of all the players engaged in some form of defiance.[4] NFL Commissioner Roger Goodell criticized the president for being "divisive" and for his "unfortunate lack of respect for the NFL." Goodell insisted that "the NFL and our players are at our best when we help create a sense of unity in our country and our culture," but those who protested during the national anthem were doing the opposite.[5] GQ magazine named Colin Kaepernick its "Citizen of the Year" because "he has become something more than a man—he's now a movement."[6]

Sports are supposed to be fun and inspiring, but the NFL protests are disruptive, distracting, and pointless. They are a public relations nightmare that the League has been unable to stop. Most fans prefer their football free of guilt-tripping toxic politics, and they are tuning out the NFL in droves.[7]

AMERICA'S GAME

"Of all our sports organizations," the New York Times columnist Dave Anderson wrote in 1973, "the National Football

League projects the most patriotic image."[8] It is an identity the League has nurtured for decades. Professional football, founded in the 1920s and rooted in a working- and middle-class fan base, flourished after World War II. The game's growth in popularity in the 1950s and '60s was due to a clear strategic vision, business savvy, the advent of television, and the inherent thrill of the game. Many point to the Baltimore Colts' dramatic televised overtime win over the New York Giants in the December 28, 1958, NFL championship game—dubbed the "greatest game ever played"—as the start of the League's dominance of professional sports.

According to Gallup, baseball was the leading spectator sport in 1961 by a 14 percent margin over football. By 1972 these numbers were reversed, and football had a 15-point edge.

This was no accident. For sixty years the NFL enjoyed the leadership of highly capable commissioners. Bert Bell (1946–1959), Pete Rozelle (1960–1989), and Paul Tagliabue (1989–2006) understood the game and its fans. The NFL benefited from the built-in drama of the possibility that, as Bell put it, "on any given Sunday, any team can beat any other team." The franchises promoted their larger-than-life athletes and profited from revenue-sharing and sales of licensed merchandise. NFL films produced by Ed Sabol recapped the weekly struggles set to symphonic scores that made even mundane games into epic gladiatorial bouts. The films were so effective that Sabol was eventually inducted into the Pro Football Hall of Fame.

Much of the credit for the NFL's success belongs to Rozelle, who "never lost sight of the fact that the product the NFL was selling was the game itself." During the turbulent 1960s, the NFL "served as a kind of social touchstone which recognized and honored" the "eternal verities of hard work, dedication, respect for authority, and community."[9] The game was sold as an all-American pastime, sporting a red, white, and blue shield.

Professional football consciously wove itself into the American story. During the 1976 Bicentennial, the NFL sponsored a high school essay contest with the theme "The Role of the NFL in American History." Humorist Dick West offered a few suggestions, such as when in 1861, Abraham Lincoln proclaimed all players free agents, which "prompted the 11 teams in the Southern division to withdraw from the NFL and form the new Confederate Football League." But Lincoln had to recapture these teams because "professional football could not stand divided."[10]

The Super Bowl, first played in January 1967, between the champions of the NFL and the rival American Football League (the two leagues merged in 1970) evolved into a national holiday. Super Bowl III put the game on the map when the AFL's underdog New York Jets, led by charismatic "Broadway Joe" Namath, shocked the favorite Baltimore Colts with an upset win. Super Bowl television commercials became some of the most expensive in TV. The move toward ads produced specifically for the game started with Apple's famous 1984 commercial with its Orwellian overtones.[11] And while celebrities had been involved in the game since Bob Hope hosted a pregame ceremony in 1969, the blockbuster halftime shows started with Super Bowl XXVII, which featured Michael Jackson. "Super Sunday" has become America's biggest annual entertainment extravaganza and a point of national pride. As of 2018, nineteen of the twenty most-watched television events in U.S. history were Super Bowls. (The exception, ranking ninth, is the 1983 series finale of *M*A*S*H*.) NFL games regularly win weekly ratings races, and the sport is so popular that millions of people tune in just to see the NFL draft.[12]

For many people football represents an escape from the increasingly strident political scene. Tim, a lifelong Oakland Raiders fan, summed up this perspective: "Football had become my break and my escape from the rest of the world. No matter what was going on everywhere else in the world, I could tune into a game on Sunday, turn the dial to sports radio or skip the other sections of the newspaper and go straight to sports. Sports could be my little oasis away from it all."[13]

That's what sports should be all about, harking back to the ancient Greeks, who set aside their conflicts for the thrill of the Olympic games. Pro football's nationalism had an appeal that transcended politics. The League was a celebration of the best in America. The only colors that mattered in the stands were team colors, and fans of every race and creed were united behind a single all-American passion—winning.

POLITICAL FOOTBALL

A sport as popular as football naturally mixed with politics. Some NFL athletes launched political careers after retiring. Jack Kemp went to Washington as a Republican congressman after quarterbacking the Buffalo Bills in the 1960s. NFL Hall of Famer Steve Largent played fourteen seasons with the Seattle Seahawks before going to Congress to represent his native Oklahoma.

Presidents loved football. John Kennedy made it part of his public image and appointed the former NFL halfback Byron

"Whizzer" White to the Supreme Court. Richard Nixon called a play during a Redskins game. Gerald Ford was a center and linebacker for the Michigan Wolverines during two undefeated seasons, and turned down NFL offers after college to pursue a law degree (while coaching football) at Yale. Ronald Reagan also played college football, and his supporting role as George Gipp in the 1940 film *Knute Rockne, All American* was the source of his enduring nickname, "the Gipper." Super Bowl XIX fell on the day Reagan was sworn in for his second term, and the Gipper performed the game's coin toss via satellite from the Oval Office.

Super Bowl parties at the White House are commonplace, with phone calls from the president to the winning team, often with an invitation to visit Washington. With rare exceptions, partisanship has not overwhelmed the thrill of the game. "No matter your political or demographic persuasion, the one thing you could find to talk about with someone was football," the sports blogger Will Leitch wrote. "Richard Nixon and Hunter S. Thompson bonded over football, for crying out loud."[14] Nevertheless, so many members of the Super Bowl LII champion Philadelphia Eagles team chose to boycott the planned 2018 White House celebration with President Trump that the event had to be canceled.

There have always been unavoidable links to the business end of politics. Teams have used political pull to obtain taxpayer-funded subsidies for their stadiums, for example. For many years the Sports Broadcasting Act "gave the NFL a limited exemption from antitrust law" to negotiate television contracts.[15] And the New Orleans Saints franchise owes its existence to a deal struck by Pete Rozelle and Congressman Hale Boggs and Senator

Russell Long of Louisiana in exchange for their support in Congress for the NFL-AFL merger. Professional football has also struggled with the same social issues as American society at large. The League at one time banned African American players and later instituted quotas, but now the majority of its players are black.

Football's all-American image didn't appeal to everyone. As the NFL clung to an explicitly nationalist identity, liberals denounced its "jingoistic military bullshit" and "militarized civic rituals."[16] The comedian George Carlin contrasted the pastoral pastime of baseball and mechanistic, industrial-age football: "In football the object is for the quarterback...to be on target with his aerial assault, riddling the defense by hitting his receivers with deadly accuracy in spite of the blitz, even if he has to use the shotgun," he said. "In baseball the object is to go home! And to be safe!" Other critics focused on the inherent violence of the sport and the growing severity of damage to the players, especially traumatic brain injury.

When the Goodell era began in 2006, the League faced a number of off-the-field public relations crises, including Michael Vick's dog-fighting scandal. Goodell was tough on player misconduct, instituting a Personal Conduct Policy and suspending players who violated it. In subsequent years the League promoted various social initiatives, such as breast cancer awareness (expanded to all cancer in 2017).[17] In 2010 the NFL invested ten million dollars in a marketing campaign aimed at women, since by then 40 percent of the League's fans were female.

The NFL faced blowback in 2014 for mishandling domestic-abuse charges against former Baltimore Ravens running back Ray Rice, who was captured on video knocking out his then-fiancée, Janay Palmer. The former FBI director Robert Mueller was brought in to investigate whether the NFL had prior knowledge of the videotape, and the National Organization for Women called for Goodell to resign, "saying the league 'has a violence against women problem.'"[18] In response Goodell hired three high-profile domestic violence experts to serve as League advisors.[19]

But while the League was becoming more socially conscious, it still frowned on players expressing opinions on the field that were not specifically sanctioned. Cleats honoring heroes of the September 11, 2001, attacks were discouraged, as were decals honoring slain Dallas police officers in 2016. Wide receiver Brandon Marshall was fined for wearing green shoes to highlight mental health issues, and running back DeAngelo Williams was not allowed to wear pink beyond the allotted breast cancer awareness month, even though his mother had died of the disease.[20] New Orleans Saints rookie running back Alvin Kamara was fined six thousand dollars for wearing bright red cleats during a Christmas Eve game.[21]

The owner of the Dallas Cowboys, Jerry Jones, explained the problem with these symbolic gestures: "There are tons of things out there that need to be recognized. Once you open that Pandora's box, how do you ever stop?"[22] Players could wind up kneeling for social justice, praying for the unborn, wearing socks against law enforcement, cleats for military heroes, and helmet decals for every cause imaginable.

So when Colin Kaepernick decided to kneel during the national anthem, fans might have expected he would be disciplined, or at least told to knock it off. This had nothing to do with the game, and for those who saw sports as a refuge from politics it was an unwelcome intrusion. And unlike breast cancer awareness, highlighting an important issue that can touch any family, many found Kaepernick's protest to be downright offensive. When he was allowed to continue, the controversy took off.

Some likened Kaepernick to the American sprinters Tommie Smith and John Carlos, who raised black-gloved fists on the podium at the 1968 Olympics in Mexico City. But Smith and Carlos were dismissed from the team the next day, and Smith, who was a soldier, was discharged from the army. Less well remembered is the event ten days later when the teenage California heavyweight George Foreman mauled the Soviet strongman Ionas Chepulis with a second-round TKO to win the gold medal in boxing. After the decision was announced, he ceremoniously bowed to the cheering crowd, holding aloft a small U.S. flag. "In those days, nobody was applauded for being patriotic," Foreman later said. "The whole world was protesting something. But if I had to do it all again, I'd have waved two flags." John Carlos remarked, "a lot of people on the left thought, 'Oh, George, he disrespected us,' or 'he hurt us,' or 'he didn't stand up for us.' Totally wrong. George was a tremendous individual during that time in '68, and he's even greater in life today."[23]

"Foreman dared to be different," the sports writer John L. Paustian noted, "and most Americans appreciated his sentiment." Paustian observed that Americans "were almost apologetic about being patriotic during the rebellious '60s," and many people were "intimidated by the radicals." But he felt that fans were "becoming less and less tolerant of those whose 'freedom of expression' is badly misdirected."[24]

In those days there was more respect for the flag and the anthem, not only in sports but in general. At the 1972 Munich Olympics, gold medalist eight-hundred-meter runner Dave Wottle, who made a dramatic dash from last place to first in the final three hundred meters of the race, inadvertently left his trademark white golf cap on during the playing of the anthem at the award ceremony and afterwards faced pointed press questions. "It was a mistake but the people at home might not realize that," the Ohio native said firmly. "I'll apologize to the American people right now—write that down."[25] When another Olympic runner did his warm-ups during the anthem at a meet in Michigan in 1973 he was booed. An observer noted, "He could've done it under the stands. Athletes keep demanding 'respect' these days. But to earn it, they must respect values, too. One of them is the Anthem."[26]

Later in 1973, then-Washington Redskins running back Duane Thomas turned his back on the flag during the anthem at pre-season opening day in Buffalo's new Rich Stadium. When fans later taunted him for the display, he threw his helmet at them and attempted to leap into the stands. Fans asked Commissioner Pete Rozelle to fine Thomas, but he said it was up to the club to take action, and the Redskins downplayed the incident. It was not repeated.[27]

Some defended Kaepernick's sideline protests as an expression of American values, invoking the First Amendment and tradition of dissent to argue it was just as respectful to kneel as to stand. The American Legion veteran's organization responded that "having a right to do something does not make it the right thing to do," and that while "there are many ways to protest, the national anthem should be our moment to stand together as one UNITED States of America."[28] Comedy Central's *South Park* spoofed the "patriotic kneeling" idea in its season 20 opener, when a stadium announcer asked the game day crowd to "please rise—or sit—or take a knee—in order to honor America!" The cartoon Kaepernick was so confused he didn't know what to do.

But kneeling for the anthem is not a First Amendment issue; employers can regulate speech in the workplace. The NFL's personal conduct policy says all employees "must refrain from conduct detrimental to the integrity of and public confidence in the NFL," which these protests surely are.[29] The Constitution does not require fans to pay to be the audience for an athlete's free expression, which he can do more effectively on his own time. And as noted above, the League has had no problem banning symbolic speech on the field in the past. The sideline protests have no greater First Amendment protection than dancing in the end zone.

As the protests spread they took on confusing symbolic meanings. Members of the Baltimore Ravens and Jacksonville Jaguars appearing at London's Wembley Stadium chose to dishonor the U.S. flag on foreign soil. Showing that they had *some* manners, they stood for "God Save the Queen," unaware, apparently, that it was the anthem of the former colonial masters of much of Africa. Raiders running back Marshawn Lynch sat during the national anthem at an exhibition game in Mexico City but stood for the Mexican national anthem.[30] And in a related twist, at the 2018 Olympics in PyeongChang, South

Korea, the African American speed skater Shani Davis boycotted the opening ceremony because he lost a coin toss to bear the flag. He called the toss "dishonorable" and invoked Black History Month, but his stance confused the media narrative since he was upset about being *excluded* from a patriotic display.[31]

"NO FANS LEFT"

Most people have disapproved of the protests at athletic events. A September 2017 poll showed that 64 percent of respondents thought NFL players should stand and be respectful during the national anthem. Half of the respondents said the protests made them less likely to watch the NFL, and 80 percent believed there should be less politics in sporting events.[32] A poll in October 2017 showed a wide racial divide over the issue; white respondents disapproved by 60 percent, while blacks approved at 79 percent.[33] Another survey showed that while half of white Americans thought the protests showed disrespect to the flag, 88 percent of blacks said the main point was to call attention to unfair policing.[34] But the most shocking poll from the NFL's point of view might have been the one that showed pro football had the highest unfavorable rating of any major sport, and baseball had regained the title of most popular.[35]

Fan discontent was most evident in sagging television ratings and increasingly empty stadiums. Many people simply tuned out. Ratings fell 10 percent in the 2017 season, following an 8 percent decline in 2016.[36] Declines were particularly strong among young viewers (ages eighteen to thirty-four), whites, and women.[37] In the post-season, ratings for the first four playoff games were down between 10 and 21 percent.[38] Total division-round viewership dropped 16 percent from the previous year, shedding more than twenty-three million collective viewers. And while President Trump was able to declare victory in Super Bowl LII because there were no protests, the audience for the championship game was the smallest in nine years.[39] In fact, after peaking in Super Bowl XLIX, ratings have slipped in every game since. The latest drop was the most dramatic, down 7 percent—that's eight million fewer viewers than a year before.

Some argued that there was no link between the protests and the ratings sag, citing the evolution of the fractured television market, new technologies in which audiences are more difficult to measure, cable-cutting, and other factors affecting the industry. Yet pro basketball has faced the same technical challenges, and its ratings have been up. Over the 2017 Christmas weekend, traditionally big for football, NFL ratings were down 9 percent, while the NBA, with a smaller viewership overall, nevertheless enjoyed a 20 percent spike from the previous year.[40]

Resellers began to offer tickets at bargain-basement prices. In December 2017, the Baltimore Ravens, fighting for a playoff berth and having sold out every home game since the team arrived in the city in 1996, resorted to taking out ads to implore fans to buy tickets. Meanwhile eighty-dollar seats were being resold by season ticket holders for twenty-nine dollars. Diehard Ravens fan Robert Harris observed that the feeling at the stadium was "not as intense as it used to be" and came up with a telling metric for fan disengagement: "I remember it would be wall-to-wall people," he said. "You couldn't even go to the bathroom. Now you can go to the bathroom whenever you want."[41]

A New Orleans Saints season ticket-holder, Lee Dragna, tried to get a refund on his eight-thousand-dollar tickets, and when the Saints refused he took them to court. He argued that the "rowdy, angry reaction" of fans to the protesting players made the stadium environment "borderline dangerous" and that the tickets were basically unusable. He blamed the players and especially the Saints leadership, who "created that behavior by condoning it." Dragna maintained that he and other fans were victims of a bait and switch: "If you sell tickets to a gaming event for entertainment, you should not be allowed to turn it political." And though his case had little chance of succeeding, he pledged that "one way or another they'll pay."[42] The Saints management maintained they "believe strongly in honoring our flag and the national anthem and what it represents," but encouraged the contrary. And former Saints fan Denise La Grange Fox publicly burned her team memorabilia, saying the team had "ruined and taken the fun out of sports."[43]

A boycott movement had been growing since the kneeling protests began in 2016. Some were boycotting in support of Colin Kaepernick after he was not signed to a new team; a #NoKaepernickNoNFL petition on Change.org attracted more than 176,000 signatures from people who "pledged not to watch any games until the free agent quarterback is signed to a contract."[44] But by far the most active and vocal boycotters were those who felt betrayed by the NFL for coddling the kneelers.

Longtime Steelers fan Jim Coletti wrote in a letter to the team management that he thought kneeling during the national anthem was "quite possibly the worst way to go about 'protesting'" and "an insult to every serviceman who has served or has passed away defending this country." Coletti added, "I realize that we live in a free country where people have the freedom to not participate in the national anthem. I also have the freedom to not spend another minute or dollar on your product." And "if you are truly that unhappy with the country, feel free to play for the CFL." [45]

Tim, the previously-mentioned Raiders fan, tuned out simply because the politicization of sports ruined his oasis. "If I went to the theater to watch a movie," he said, "and before the movie, during the movie and then after the movie I had to listen to PSAs regarding the actors'/actresses' political stances, I would quit going to movies, just like I am going to quit watching and reading about the NFL."[46] Kevin Williams, a veteran who opposes using the flag in protests but supports the right to do so, was even more blunt. "I hate politics," he said. "It's all over social media, television.... I can't even go out anymore without overhearing people having heated political discussion. Football used to provide me an escape from all that crap. Now politics has infiltrated something I used to love."[47] And Ed Clayton said, "I never thought I would be forced to choose between my love of pro football and fidelity to the patriotic traditions I was raised on, but now that it comes to that, it's a very easy choice. The NFL loses."[48]

Kevin Carlson, a pastor in Mesa, Arizona, finds the demonstrations jarringly out of place. "Football used to be a place where people of all races, religions and political views could come together," he wrote. "Not anymore. ... It just seems like a weird business model to actively try and run off half your audience, then be stunned when the audience begins to shrink. I want to keep watching. I love football. ... I guess I just miss the days when sermons were limited to church."[49]

The League had already been suffering from a perceived decline in player respectability. Former fan Juliette Akinyi Ochieng, who grew up watching the NFL with her father, noticed her own creeping disgust at the way players behaved and their ingratitude for the advantages they enjoyed. Juliette wrote that "as the character quality of NFL players seemed to descend, my interest in being entertained by them" did as well. Eventually she gave up on the NFL, and her father followed.[50] Fans also complained that ticket prices were too high, the game was too slow and had too many commercials, and in general supporting the League had become not worth the effort. The joke among the boycotters was that NFL stands for "no fans left."

President Trump took aim at the hypocrisy of players protesting against a country that has given them the opportunity to use their talents to become wealthier than most fans could ever hope to be. If an athlete wants to make millions of dollars in pro sports, he tweeted, "he or she should not be allowed to disrespect our Great American Flag (or Country) and should stand for the National Anthem." Kathy Barnette, an African American veteran and political commentator, wrote an open letter to NFL players on Thanksgiving suggesting the players "pause for a few moments to express your patriotism and love for our great nation when our national anthem is played and our flag flies before thousands of people who have paid good money to see you run around a field chasing a little ball."[51] Taking a knee is cheap; making a positive difference requires more time and effort.

Police—many of whom are football fans—were appalled by the protests. When Colin Kaepernick started denouncing law enforcement, a California police union called for a boycott of 49ers games. When Miami Dolphins players kneeled, a Florida police union asked deputies not to escort players from the stadium. When the Cleveland Browns management sided with the protestors, the city police union denounced the move strongly. "It's just ignorant for someone to do that," Cleveland Police Patrolmen's Association president Steve Loomis said. "It's hypocritical of the Browns management and ownership to want to have an armed forces first-responder day, and have us involved in it, when they allow their players to take a knee during the national anthem.... [T]hat's as offensive as it can get."[52]

But those who backed the protesters argued that the movement was an important response to a police brutality crisis. "In football, they are using a really visible way to get across that more than 800 unarmed people have been killed this year by police," explained Jim Corbett, coauthor of the adult coloring book *I Am So Sick of White Guys.* "It is outrageous."[53]

That number would be outrageous if it were accurate, but it is wildly inflated. In the 987 fatal police shootings recorded in the *Washington Post* database for 2017, only sixty-eight of those shot were unarmed.[54] Of those, twenty—less than a third—were African American, eleven of whom were shot while fleeing the scene of a crime, a situation in which police are uncertain whether they are armed. The remaining nine cases represent less than 1 percent of police uses of deadly force, and it is wrong to assume they were senseless, racially-motivated executions. One of the dead was a forty-two-year-old Haitian immigrant, Jean

Pedro Pierre, who attacked sheriff's deputy Sean Youngward, dragging and kicking him while Youngward implored Pierre to settle down and explain what was going on. Officers tried to subdue Pierre with a Taser and a baton before resorting to side-arms. The killing was a needless tragedy, but also a last resort.[55]

A foreseeable if unintended consequence of the high-profile protests is a rise in anti-police violence, which has deterred officers from protecting urban communities. A 2017 FBI study on violence aimed at law enforcement officers found that "assailants inspired by social and/or political reasons believed that attacking police officers was their way to 'get justice' for those who had been, in their view, unjustly killed by law enforcement." Officers believe that this socially acceptable anti-police hostility is "the new norm," and it has "had the effect of 'de-policing' in law enforcement agencies across the country, which assailants have exploited."[56]

In the end this hurts those same at-risk communities. In Baltimore, for example, alleged de-policing after the riots sparked by the death of Freddie Gray in custody in 2015 has led to spiraling crime rates. Mordantly dubbed "Bodymore," the city suffered a record per-capita homicide rate in 2017.[57] "What we have seen is that the police have distanced themselves, and the community has distanced themselves even further," said the Reverend Kinji Scott. "So the divide has really intensified, it hasn't decreased."[58]

Ultra-violent Chicago offers another example. In 2016, the year Colin Kaepernick began his protest, police scaled back patrols, and arrests dropped 28 percent. But crime rates increased: 4,334 people were shot in Chicago that year, "one person every two hours. Almost all the victims have been black. The police

have shot 25 people, virtually all armed or otherwise dangerous—less than .6 percent of the total."[59] Nevertheless, "Black
Lives Matter activists [continue] to claim that it's the cops who
are the biggest threat facing Chicago's young black men today."[60]

And in another telling statistic, a 2017 survey asked children
under the age of twelve what they want to be when they grow
up. "Athlete," the number-one response in 2015, had fallen to
number eight. "Policeman," which had been number ten, soared
to number three.[61]

Veterans were also offended by the protests. Military color
guards routinely appear at NFL games during the anthem, and
many viewed the kneelers' disrespect as an insult to the men and
women in uniform, who have been a loyal part of the NFL fan
base.

This issue was highlighted in a September game when the
Pittsburgh Steelers tried to sidestep the kneeling controversy by
staying in the tunnel while the anthem played. But Alejandro
Villanueva, an offensive tackle and veteran Army Ranger who
had served three tours in Afghanistan, stepped out of the tunnel
to show respect for the flag anyway. His NFL jersey became an
overnight best-seller, and the rest of the team were booed when
they emerged.

Villanueva later apologized for inadvertently making the
team look bad. "Man, these are divisive times in the United
States," commented Steelers Head Coach Mike Tomlin, who is
African American. "We are not politicians, we're coaches and
professional athletes. If those of us or individuals choose to participate in politics in some way, I'm going to be supportive of
that, but when we come out of locker rooms, we come out to

play football games. To be quite honest with you, I didn't appreciate our football team being dragged into politics this weekend."[62] Steelers quarterback Ben Roethlisberger supported "the call for social change and the pursuit of true equality," but said that his team should stand for the national anthem to show "solidarity as a nation, that we stand united in respect for the people on the front lines protecting our freedom and keeping us safe. God bless those men and women."[63]

There are many longstanding ties between the NFL and the military: flyovers and on-field displays, the ubiquitous recruiting ads, and the League's "Salute to Service" campaign, which maintains that "honoring the military is part of the fabric of the NFL." Since 2011, "the NFL has raised more than $17 million for its military non-profit partners."[64] The League says it "takes pride in supporting military personnel and remains committed to raising awareness for the sacrifices they make on our behalf."[65]

But these gestures have not impressed the NFL boycotters, who targeted the 2017 Veteran's Day weekend "Salute to Service" games out of "solidarity with veterans around the country, as football players have continued to disrespect the national anthem, the American flag, and everything our nation stands for."[66] NFL teams had planned a number of pro-military events for that November 12. The Minnesota Vikings, for example, carried a flag onto the field that had been flown at a forward base in Afghanistan.[67] The League issued a statement that it would not change its anthem policies in the face of the boycott, but did pledge to give five dollars to its veteran partner organizations every time someone used the hashtag #SalutetoService on social media.[68] For his part, Colin Kaepernick visited the African American Civil War museum in Washington, DC, to "pay homage and acknowledge our forgotten heroes."[69]

Yet while the League sought to dampen the idea that the protests were anti-military, left-wing critics fueled the fire. Many referred to a 2015 report, "Tackling Paid Patriotism," prepared by Arizona Senators John McCain and Jeff Flake. It showed that the Defense Department spent fifty-three million dollars between 2012 and 2015 on marketing and advertising contracts with professional sports organizations. More than ten million dollars went to major sports leagues. The government underwrote "taxpayer-funded DOD marketing gimmicks" such as "on-field color guard, enlistment and reenlistment ceremonies, performances of the national anthem, full-field flag details, ceremonial first pitches and puck drops." The Senators concluded that "this kind of paid patriotism is wholly unnecessary and a waste and abuse of taxpayer funds."[70] The NFL wound up returning almost three-quarters of a million dollars to the DOD.[71]

The report later inspired the hard-left outlet *ThinkProgress* to comment that "rather than organic, wholesome expressions of patriotism, the tradition of players standing for the national anthem is a recent tradition that may have coincided with a marketing ploy meant to sell cheap, manufactured nationalism."[72] "This anthem thing is a scam," the actor-activist Jesse Williams declared. "This is not actually part of football. This was invented in 2009 from the government paying the NFL to market military recruitment to get more people to go off and fight wars to die."[73]

Williams, however, is mistaken. The national anthem has always been part of the NFL pregame. It was televised at the legendary 1958 championship game. In the 1960s the League issued guidelines on proper player alignment and behavior during the anthem. This issue arose because players were seen goofing around during the pregame anthem when the country was in mourning two days after President John F. Kennedy was assassinated. In the 1970s, Minnesota Vikings Coach Harry "Bud" Grant, a World War II Navy veteran, paid special attention to drilling players on how to stand and how to hold their helmets during the anthem. One of his players said, "For our first exhibition game, we didn't have time to get our punt-return play in, but we were ready to stand at attention for the National Anthem."[74]

So the idea that NFL national anthem ceremonies are a product of a Defense Department marketing effort for the War on Terrorism is false. If anything, the NFL has done less to promote the anthem in the past two years than it did decades ago. But for those who believe that patriotism, honoring veterans, and football go hand in hand, the Army-Navy game remains one of the country's oldest and proudest football traditions, and you won't see any kneeling except perhaps in prayer.

THE NFL FUMBLES

Any industry facing a public relations meltdown on this scale would quickly find a way to get out of it, placating dissatisfied customers and somehow changing the subject. But the NFL did none of these things. At first the League and the media denied there was a problem. Reports on declining NFL television ratings during the 2016 season rarely if ever mentioned the kneeling protests as a source of the sag. When President Trump made it impossible to ignore the issue in 2017, the protest was recast as part of the "resistance," as though the president had started the problem and the boycotters were accused of being divisive. By the time the League finally banned sideline kneeling during the anthem in the spring of 2018, it was seen as too little, too late.

Not all teams were involved equally in the protest movement. The Seattle Seahawks and San Francisco 49ers had the most active protestors. The Dallas Cowboys, Minnesota Vikings, Carolina Panthers, and Tampa Bay Buccaneers had hardly any.[75] But the protests had besmirched the reputation of the League as a whole, and teams were feeling the impact. The Baltimore Ravens team president, Dick Cass, wrote a letter to season ticket holders noting the increased number of no-shows, even with a strong Ravens season, and acknowledged that the protests were a factor.[76] The owner of the Miami Dolphins, Stephen Ross, said he initially supported the protests, but when the message was interpreted as anti-military, he began to oppose it. In the 2018 season, he stated flatly, "all of our players will be standing."[77]

Former NLF running back and Heisman Trophy winner Herschel Walker blamed Commissioner Goodell for not nipping the problem in the bud. "Guys, let me tell you this," he said. "Our flag is very special, and black lives matter, but what we should do is go to Washington after the season and protest there instead. We have young men and women fighting for the flag. And we have to respect the White House."[78] (Walker started his pro career in the USFL with the Trump-owned New Jersey Generals.) Former NFL safety Burgess Owens responded to the protests by saying he stands "against the sanitizing of our history. The Left has already done so within the black community, resulting in the lack of gratitude seen on today's NFL sidelines." Owens said it was "time to Stand Up, Man-Up and defend our country and culture. This will only occur when patriotism is valued over popularity, profit and politics."[79]

The African American writer and filmmaker Shelby Steele believed that the failure of the "forced and unconvincing" protests to motivate people marked the end of "an era in which protest has been the primary means of black advancement" in American life. "The oppression of black people is over with," he wrote. "This is politically incorrect news, but it is true nonetheless. We blacks are, today, a free people. It is as if freedom sneaked up and caught us by surprise."[80]

The singer Joy Villa thought the protest was misdirected. "If they really want to protest something in the black community, they need to protest black-on-black crime," she said. "They need to protest the lack of education within their community. They need to protest single moms who are stuck on welfare for generations and keep having kids." She echoed Steele's observation that "what's happening unfortunately is we're losing our quality as Americans, as unifiers and as people who should be joining together to solve the issues in the black community."[81] To add more perspective, according to the FBI there were 7,881 black murder victims in 2016. In the cases where offender data were reported, 90 percent of the killers were also black. And there were only two reported cases of anti-black murders defined as hate crimes—as opposed to five white hate-crime murder victims.

The NFL could have done what the NBA did when faced with a similar situation in the 1990s. During the 1995–1996 season, the Denver Nuggets point guard Mahmoud Abdul-Rauf remained seated during the national anthem, violating the league rule that players should stand in a "dignified fashion." A Muslim convert, Abdul-Rauf (formerly Chris Wayne Jackson) said that the American flag was a "symbol of oppression" and "tyranny." "You can't be for God and for oppression," he explained. "It's clear in the Koran. Islam is the only way."[82] The NBA took a zero-tolerance approach to this protest and suspended Abdul-Rauf without pay until he agreed to abide by the rules. Abdul-Rauf defiantly said he would rather give up basketball than compromise his beliefs, but he called off his nonviolent jihad after sitting out one game.

The NFL, by contrast, chose a typically bureaucratic response to the kneeler problem, agreeing to donate almost one hundred million dollars to social justice causes over seven years. An initiative of this magnitude, however, will become an institutionalized reminder of a problem that will never go away. Everyone involved, from League administrators to those receiving the money, will have an incentive to keep "awareness" of the issues alive. The result will be a grievance bureaucracy whose full-time job is to highlight the problems that the NFL says it will help creatively solve, which will keep these issues in the public mind, taking the focus away from sports and further eroding the brand.

The plan may not even placate the protestors. Eric Reid, a 49ers safety, said the deal was a "charade," since the initiative would simply move "funds that are already allocated to breast cancer awareness and Salute to Service," harming those programs but making it easier for the owners to agree to the plan. The NFL denied this.[83]

Depending on how the money is donated, the NFL is also courting a political backlash that could threaten its privileged status among lawmakers and fans. The public might be less willing to support massive taxpayer subsidies for stadiums. Congress might decide to investigate how much the League has known about the degenerative brain disease endemic among players and whether it has knowingly put players at risk by ignoring it the way the tobacco industry ignored evidence of the link between smoking and cancer. The Occupational Safety and Health Administration might review the health consequences of playing professional football and issue a blizzard of new regulations. The Federal Communications Commission might examine whether the League engages in monopolistic behavior negotiating television deals. And the anthem protests could start a useful debate over why the billionaire team owners and millionaire players need all the subsidies, legal loopholes, and other public support that keeps their expensive sports entertainment business afloat.[84]

Not content with needlessly politicizing pro football, the NFL is encouraging social activism at the college level too. In February 2018 the League cohosted a three-day "Advocacy in Sport" workshop at Morehouse College in Atlanta, Georgia, designed to train "the next generation of athletes who wish to use sport as a powerful platform for advocacy," according to the NFL executive vice president of football operations, Troy Vincent. "Our partnership is designed to equip athletes as influencers and community leaders with the mechanics to develop their advocacy platform."[85] Although the workshop is "a direct extension of Colin Kaepernick's activism," the college says it "will not support or promote kneeling during the national anthem." Which is more than pro football can say. And the New England Patriots' owner, Robert Kraft, hardly helped win back the traditional fan base by lending the team jet to student anti-firearm activists to fly to Washington, DC, to protest against the Second Amendment.[86]

One could ask, what in the name of Lombardi does having athletes "develop their advocacy platform" have to do with football? Programs like this may only produce a more militant generation of future player-protesters. The more the league drags politics into sports the worse it will get.

COMBAT FOOTBALL

Since the NFL seems determined to institutionalize identity politics in pro football, maybe it should go all the way. In 1973, the science fiction writer and futurist Norman Spinrad published "The National Pastime," a story about what happens when football embraces America's national divisions and makes them part of the game.[87] The "Combat Football League" comprises six teams organized around key social-demographic categories: a black team, a Hispanic team, one for "frustrated Middle Americans," one for "hippies and kids," one for gays, and "a team for the motorcycle nuts and violence freaks." In this way the sport becomes a more accurate reflection of divided America, and also allows groups to work out their frustrations by proxy on the field. The rules of football are altered to allow more open violence (the ball carrier may slug defenders for example), and protective gear like helmets and shoulder pads are discarded. The result is a bloody, on-field national catharsis in the guise of a sporting event. And when the violence on the field begins to be replicated in the stands, the Combat Football League simply coopts it, reporting official scores of both weekly team play and fan casualties. The sport becomes so popular that the NFL is forced to adopt combat football rules or go out of business.

Spinrad said the story was inspired by British soccer hooligans, "very violent yobs who went to the games to get into fights with each other." He said even though "American football on the field is the most violent sport," American sports fans are "seldom violent, at least so far." But when you have "the left versus the right, the center versus the coasts, cops versus Black Lives Matter, Christians versus metrosexuals, getting down to men versus women," some type of conflict is "potentially just a shot away."[88] A dystopian future football league might also borrow from the 1975 film *Rollerball* and cut back on rules and time limits in the post-season to make it that much more interesting—and violent.[89]

Maybe Vince McMahon would consider the combat football model for his XFL reboot. Granted, he has mandated that in his league there will be no on-field politics, and players will be judged by "the quality of human being they are"—no criminal records allowed. But won't left-wing critics charge that those are hopelessly old-fashioned American ideas that have no place in these increasingly "woke" times?

No one wants a future like the one Spinrad imagined in "The National Pastime," but if we want to avoid sliding in that direction, stop with all the politics, salute the flag, and get on with the game.

FIVE

LAND OF THE FREE AND THE HOME OF THE SLAVE

The NFL kneelers were hardly the first protesters to go after the American flag. The Stars and Stripes is a powerful symbol that has long been targeted by those who think America has not lived up to its ideals. As far back as 1856, the radical abolitionist William Lloyd Garrison rejected the flag as an emblem of slavery. "I disown the American flag as the symbol of unequalled hypocrisy and transcendent oppression," he said, "and, casting it into the broad Atlantic, defy all the waters thereof to wash out its bloody stains."[1]

Protestors scoff that the flag is just a piece of cloth, but it sure gets under their skin. To them it is not the banner of liberty, not Old Glory, but the flag that flew over Japanese internment camps in World War II, the flag of Jim Crow and segregation, of imperialism, capitalism, racism, and exploitation. They don't see it flying to honor a free people but waving from the mast of every American slave ship.

Progressive disgust with the flag was illustrated vividly when the American Civil Liberties Union tweeted out a picture of a cute toddler wearing an ACLU onesie that sported a crying cartoon baby and the caption "free speech." The message read, "This is the future that ACLU members want." But the child was white, blond, and holding an American flag. An ACLU Twitter follower responded with a skeptical, "A White kid with a flag?!" and the organization lamely answered, "When your Twitter followers keep you in check and remind you that white supremacy is everywhere."[2] The knee-jerk condemnation of a three-year-old with a flag as a symbol of white supremacy only shows how anti-American the Left has become. The ACLU lost an opportunity to teach a lesson about unity and patriotism, and instead caved in to the angry left-wing narrative that the flag is racist—or the little white kid holding it is.

BURNING OLD GLORY

The flag means many things to many people. Most love and revere it, but some despise it. They either condemn the flag as a symbol of a country that hypocritically preaches liberty but practices the opposite or oppose the American experiment altogether. But the flag, a powerful, instantly recognizable symbol of freedom and what America stands for, can also inspire. As the nineteenth-century clergyman Henry Ward Beecher wrote, "A thoughtful mind, when it sees a nation's flag sees not the flag only, but the nation itself; and whatever may be its symbols, its insignia, he reads chiefly in the flag the government, the principles, the truths, the history which belong to the nation that sets it forth.... It is the Banner of Dawn; it means Liberty."[3]

The American flag is a revolutionary banner. When it was unfurled in 1777, its thirteen stars announced a "new constellation" to the world. And the flag and its constellation have evolved as the country has expanded. "Each added star has its story to tell," wrote Colonel James Alfred Moss, who founded the United States Flag Association in 1924, "of struggle and toil, of danger and hardship, of suffering and privation, to win a State from the wilderness and present it to the Union."[4] The nickname "Old Glory" originated with a Massachusetts-born ship's captain named William Driver, whose mother gave him a large flag as a gift when he first went to sea in 1824. The flag accompanied him on voyages around the world. "It has ever been my staunch companion and protection," he wrote. "Savages and heathens, lowly and oppressed, hailed and welcomed it at the far end of the wide world. Then, why should it not be called Old Glory?"[5] The Yankee sailor was fifty-eight and living in Nashville when the Civil War began. Being a Unionist in rebel territory, he sewed the flag into his comforter and slept under it. When the city was occupied by Union troops he insisted that "Old Glory" be raised over the state house, and when the flag's story was retold the nickname stuck.[6]

The American flag and motifs based on it have a secure place in advertising, marketing, and civic display. It flies from every public building and from many homes and businesses. A Pew survey showed that more than 60 percent of Americans display the flag in some fashion, at their home, at work, or on their car. Support for the flag cuts across lines of age, education, sex, and region.[7] Another poll showed that 52 percent completely agree and 31 percent mostly agree with the statement, "It is important to publicly show support for your country by doing things such as displaying the flag."[8]

The flag is also an important emotional touchstone in times of crisis. After the September 11, 2001, attacks, flags sprouted everywhere, symbols of unity and defiance. Thomas E. Franklin's photo of three firemen raising the flag amidst the rubble of the World Trade Center towers evoked Joe Rosenthal's image of Marines raising the flag on Iwo Jima and conjured the same emotions of pride and determination.

Traditionally the flag was treated with respect. A century ago the Daughters of the American Revolution published a U.S. Flag Code, noting that it "is the symbol of the brotherhood of man. It stands for courage, for chivalry, for generosity and honor. No hand must touch it roughly, no hand shall touch it irreverently."[9] But this notion has fallen by the wayside for some. Flags used to be burned only as honorable retirement after long service had left them unfit for display. But in the 1960s, flag burning became a fashionable way to score political points.

One of the most noted flag burnings took place on April 25, 1976, at a baseball game at Dodger Stadium. William Thomas and his young son ran into center field with a flag, doused it in lighter fluid, and held a match to it. But Rick Monday, a Chicago Cubs center-fielder, dashed over and snatched the flag as if he were fielding a grounder. The organist struck up "God Bless America" and twenty-five thousand fans sang along. The scoreboard flashed "Rick Monday—You Made a Great Play."

UPI sports editor Milton Richman wrote, "Rick Monday isn't one of those super-patriots. He's just an ordinary guy. Ordinary in the sense he doesn't get up on a soap box making speeches but still appreciates all the opportunities this country offers over so many others."[10] Sparky Anderson, manager of the Cincinnati Reds, concurred: "A guy like Monday embarrasses others because he's so plain, so down-to-earth and so good at what he does. I'm not a flag-waver, but I think what he did in Los Angeles is a perfect example of the kind of men our country has always been known for, men who would defend the flag."[11]

Monday was modest about what happened. "I don't feel I did anything that millions of others wouldn't have done," he said. A fifteen-year-old Dodgers fan whose older brother had died in Vietnam was in the stands that day. He later told Monday that when he saved the flag and the crowd started singing, his parents burst into tears. The boy's family talked about what happened on the way home, and how "for the first time [it] put some meaning in what their son had done," Monday recalled. "It was a very moving conversation and I have never forgotten it. I don't think I ever will."[12] Meanwhile the would-be burners got a fifty-dollar fine and a year's probation.

James Roark's photo of the event, "This Is Our Flag," was nominated for a Pulitzer Prize in sports photography. Jim Murray of the *Los Angeles Times* called it "the most famous picture of its kind since the flag-raising at Iwo Jima."[13] Rick Monday kept the rescued flag and used to fly it at his home, but in recent years has had to keep it indoors because extremists have tried—again—to burn it.

Opinion polls have consistently shown majority opposition to flag burning and support for laws, and even a constitutional amendment, to protect Old Glory. The amendment debate has its roots in 1984, when a member of the Revolutionary Communist Youth Brigade, Gregory Lee Johnson, burned a flag at the Dallas City Hall during the Republican National Convention, chanting "red, white, and blue, we spit on you!" Johnson was convicted under a Texas law against desecration of venerated objects. The Supreme Court eventually ruled five-to-four in *Texas v. Johnson* that flag burning is protected speech under the First Amendment, invalidating flag-protection laws in forty-eight states.

Congress responded with the Flag Protection Act of 1989, which the high court struck down in *United States v. Eichman* (1990). Dissenting, Justice John Paul Stevens wrote that the central issue was not the statute's suppression of ideas, since those ideas can be expressed many other ways, but the government's "legitimate interest in preserving the symbolic value of the flag" without regard to the content of speech. Stevens said the flag "is a reminder both that the struggle for liberty and equality is unceasing and that our obligation of tolerance and respect for all of our fellow citizens encompasses those who disagree with us." First Amendment rights are not absolute, and some symbols are worth protecting. But since the 1990s flag burning has lost much of its drama. These days you'll get more attention burning a Koran.

Protesters burned Confederate flags in response to the horrific church shooting in Charleston, South Carolina, in 2015, and some American flags were immolated along with them. In

Denver, protesters outside the Colorado state capitol not only burned both flags but denounced the Founding Fathers and called for the removal of the Colorado Civil War Memorial. The memorial features a statue of a dismounted Union cavalryman and a list of battles in which Coloradans fought, including the Sand Creek Massacre of November 29, 1864, in which scores of Cheyenne and Arapaho men, women, and children were gunned down. The statue is mistakenly believed to be of Colonel John M. Chivington, who led the raid and whom a review panel later charged with cold-blooded murder. A plan is underway to add a memorial to the Sand Creek victims on the capitol grounds, but some still would like to see the Union cavalryman go.[14]

In Brooklyn, a group called Disarm NYPD hosted a "Burn the American Flags" event, declaring on their Facebook page that "both the Confederate flag, and the American flag are symbols of oppression." They stated that they "do not believe the ideals of America are anything to be revered." Burning the flag is a first step to dismantling "our stunted, cynical expectations of what is possible" and shows "a commitment to building a better world. A world better than America."[15]

The half-dozen Brooklyn flag-burners scattered when locals noticed what was going on and moved to stop them. John Carroll of Queens, who pulled a flag from a small grill, called the radicals "losers looking for a few minutes of fame." New York State Senator Martin Golden (R-Brooklyn) praised those who broke up the demonstration and said it was sad to watch "this despicable act of hatred take place on sacred Brooklyn ground." Even Mayor de Blasio released a statement saying the flag burning was "a divisive, disrespectful way to express views, and does not reflect the values of our city."[16] Commenting on the protest, Fang Wong, an Asian-American Vietnam veteran and a former national commander of the American Legion, observed that "it's a cowardly way of showing what you believe in."[17]

Flag desecration is also an easy way to make a splash in the art world. In 1996, a flag art display in Phoenix featured, alongside some patriotic displays, a flag stuffed in a prison toilet bowl, a flag spread out on the ground to walk on, and a flag made of strips of human skin ("obtained through 'legal channels,'" according to the exhibit catalogue). Navy veteran Robert Reinhardt thought the display was "disgusting, degrading, not art but mostly trash that insults all those who have fought and died for America," and added, "you don't entertain or teach anybody anything, by making a flag of human skin, like Hitler's people did in concentration camps."[18]

The "flag on the floor" installation by Dread Scott (Scott Tyler) was first shown in 1989, and entitled "What Is the Proper Way to Display a U.S. Flag?" It features a photo-montage of various uses of the flag and a notebook on a shelf in which visitors can offer their thoughts on flag display—but they have to tread on Old Glory to get there. The work has appeared in several art galleries over the years, and some veterans have expressed their view by folding the flag and putting it on the shelf. Scott was also involved in the flag-burning incident at the U.S. Capitol that gave rise to the 1990 *Eichman* Supreme Court case. One of Dread Scott's latest works, "On the Impossibility of Freedom in a Country Founded on Slavery and Genocide," is a performance piece that features the artist struggling against the blast of a fire hose, evoking the hosing of anti-segregation protesters in Birmingham, Alabama, in 1963, and inspired by the 2014 protests in Ferguson, Missouri. He describes his work as "revolutionary art to propel history forward."[19]

Recent racially-charged flag protests on campuses include such themes as stand on the flag, drag the flag, and "F-ck Your Flag." These events don't even pretend to have artistic merit and are simply anti-American. In April 2015, a photo of Eric Sheppard, a member of the New Black Panthers Party, walking on a flag at Valdosta State University in Georgia went viral on social media. The photo spawned the #EricSheppardChallenge, in which others were encouraged to post pictures and videos of their own flag desecrations. Sheppard, a self-described "terrorist towards white people," was later arrested on gun charges.[20] During the protest an Air Force veteran, Michelle Manhart, stepped in to save a flag, and when protestors claimed she was stealing their property she responded, "This flag actually belongs to the entire United States."[21]

A "stand on the flag" protest at UCLA was disrupted when a disabled veteran confronted the group, getting in their faces and shouting, "People are dying for your stupid ass!" Nearby students applauded.[22] At Wright State University in Dayton, Ohio, veterans responded to a "stand on the flag" event with a larger counter-demonstration. Some veterans knelt and prayed next to the flag as protestors stood on it. A retired black sergeant-major confronted a white hipster protester, calling him a "maggot" and saying, "Dude, if you know my heritage, I guaran-damn-tee you, we'll set you straight."[23] One demonstrator, Tommy DiMassio, later admitted he thought the demonstration would "ruffle some feathers," but "did not anticipate how tense the backlash would become."[24]

At American University, distraught progressives gathered on campus the day after Donald Trump won the 2016 presidential race to burn flags and scream their discontent. "This is a representation of America!" one radical screamed, "We are going down in flames!" "F— white America!" another shouted. Even on this liberal campus, students were shocked by the outpouring of raw anger. One sophomore who voted for Hillary Clinton said she was "definitely uncomfortable" at the demonstration, "more in shock than anything, that a fellow student at my university would be willing to burn our nation's flags and be happy about it."[25] And in 2018 at the University of Washington in Seattle, a speech and prayer rally by a dozen Republican supporters of the president was disrupted by leftist protestors who tore up and burned American flags, in addition to shouting, swearing, spitting, and throwing punches.[26]

Even flags honoring the anniversary of the September 11, 2001, terror attacks aren't safe. At Columbia University, students stuck scores of flags in the ground as part of a 9/11 commemoration, and an aging hipster plucked them out and threw them in the trash. When confronted, the vandal just laughed, and a campus public safety officer opined wrongly that the man was "well within his rights to protest." Student organizers of the memorial retrieved the flags from the trash and replaced them, and other passing students pitched in to help.[27]

A similar incident happened at Occidental College, where "vandals crushed, snapped, and threw in the garbage" 2,997 memorial flags and put "posters and flyers up that shamed the victims of 9/11." Students replaced the flags, and when more were uprooted, the organizers issued a statement asking that their display be respected, promising "if you try to destroy it, we will rebuild it."[28] And at Saddleback College in California, Professor Margot Lovett tore down students' 9/11 memorial posters, saying the students were outside the school's restrictive "free speech zone." Lovett, a gender studies and humanities professor who chairs the history department, probably disapproved of the posters' content. Shortly after the terrorist attacks in 2001, she distributed a statement from the Black Radical Congress asserting that "U.S. imperialism has brought genocidal levels of death and destruction to people around the world" and that "true anti-racism may require us to put ourselves at risk physically in order to defend Arabs and Muslims from unwarranted attacks."[29]

Some schools have tried to ban the flag as an "offensive symbol." The student senate at the University of California, Davis rescinded a longstanding rule that a flag be present at their meetings because it "represents capitalism, colonialism and the genocide of indigenous people." The author of the polarizing and divisive measure said it was intended to start a conversation about "how polarized our society is, and how divided we are." Michael Gofman, a member of the student senate who opposed the measure, said his parents "saw this country as completely different, where they were able to do what they want with their future, and I see a flag as representing all of that—freedom, liberty and opportunity." Since his parents were Soviet émigrés, they knew a thing or two about freedom.[30]

At UC Irvine, the student government voted to remove the "triggering" American flag from a building lobby. A nationwide letter of support signed by hundreds of professors noted that "U.S. nationalism often contributes to racism and xenophobia, and that the paraphernalia of nationalism is in fact often used to intimidate." But the executive committee of the student government overturned the measure and restored the flag. "Our campus is patriotic and proud," said the student government president, Reza Zomorrodian. "We did something right for our campus."[31]

An art teacher in the Santa Rita School District in California told a thirteen-year-old student who was drawing an American flag with the words "God Bless America," "You can't draw that, that's offensive!" It was unclear whether the teacher was agitated by the flag, the reference to God, or both. But the teacher had praised a student's drawing of Barack Obama.[32] Around the same time, Live Oak High School in Morgan Hill, California, banned students from wearing American flag t-shirts or other symbols on Cinco de Mayo because they are "incendiary" and could cause violence by offending Hispanic students. The school could have used the tensions creatively, as an opportunity to teach respect for the American flag among the Hispanic kids, especially since Cinco de Mayo is a minor, local holiday in Mexico that became prominent in the United States only because of a 1980s beer marketing campaign. Instead, school administrators gave in to the "heckler's veto" and rewarded hot-headed bullies at the expense of the rights of patriotic students.[33]

The incident spawned litigation that reached the Court of Appeals for the Ninth Circuit, which in 2015 upheld the restrictions. This decision was at odds with precedent set by the Supreme Court in the 1969 case of *Tinker v. Des Moines Independent Community School District*, in which high school students successfully defended their right to wear black armbands to protest the Vietnam War. "It is ironic," the law professor and blogger

Eugene Volokh noted in an amicus curiae brief, "that the student expression censured in this case involved a showing of respect for the American flag," since previous courts had ruled that students could not be compelled to salute it. "Likewise," he concluded, "the government cannot prohibit schoolchildren from displaying the flag, either."[34] The Supreme Court declined to hear the case, so for now the decision of the Ninth Circuit stands.

But sometimes school administrators can be persuaded to see reason. Rocori High School in Cold Spring, Minnesota, announced that students were "not allowed to display flags or banners from their vehicle" while parked in the school parking lot. The blanket ban was intended to prevent the display of the Confederate flag, not exactly a widespread practice in Minnesota. Students responded by filling the parking lot with cars and trucks flying the stars and stripes. "I'm here to support my son who's making a stand," Don Ihrke declared. "This is his truck and he's proud of his truck, and he's proud of his American flag. He has a sister who's a sergeant in the Marine Corps, and he's proud of his sister."[35] Superintendent Scott Staska explained that the "issue wasn't with the American flag," but with "people being disrespectful to other people." After the students rallied round the flag, the school rescinded the rule, but it still bans symbols that cause others to feel "threatened, uncomfortable or unsafe"—though that is exactly how Old Glory makes some skittish progressives feel.[36]

THE "RACIST ANTHEM"

Our national anthem, "The Star-Spangled Banner," is facing as much criticism these days as the flag it honors. In

Baltimore in September 2017, an elaborate monument to Francis Scott Key was splashed with red paint and "racist anthem" was spray-painted on its base.[37] Months later another Baltimore monument, erected for the anthem's centennial, was also painted red, and "racist anthem" was painted on the pavement in front of it. The monument, which was paid for by contributions from school children, depicts a boy and girl holding a scroll with a dedication to the anthem and citizens who "stood ready to sacrifice their lives in defense of their homes and their country."[38]

The anthem's challenging vocal range is part of the song's suspense. *Slate* music critic Carl Wilson noted that "the drama at any major event is who's going to sing the anthem...and whether they will master the 'Banner' or it will defeat them." Think of Robert Goulet flubbing the anthem at the start of the second Muhammed Ali–Sonny Liston bout in 1965, Rosanne Barr butchering it at Jack Murphy Stadium in 1990, or the mess the pop singer Fergie made of it at the 2018 NBA All Star Game. "The anthem is communal property," Wilson wrote, "but all the great performers make it their own and then return it intact, with luck without letting it hit ground."[39]

More singable alternatives are "America the Beautiful," "God Bless America," "This Land Is Your Land," and "America" ("My Country, 'Tis of Thee"). The latter is set to the tune of the British national anthem, "God Save the Queen," which could cause confusion at Olympics award ceremonies. George London, a famous baritone and the first artistic director of the John F. Kennedy Center for the Performing Arts, suggested "The Battle Hymn of the Republic"—or "Dixie."[40]

But no song will please everybody. The *New York Daily News* columnist Gersh Kuntzman penned a diatribe against Major League Baseball's post-9/11 practice of singing "God Bless America" at the seventh-inning stretch. The song, he complains, embodies some of America's worst features: "self-righteousness, forced piety, earnest self-reverence, foam." Acknowledging that Kate Smith's famous renditions of the Irving Berlin song became "as much a symbol of post-war patriotism as the flag, the space program and all the white people moving to the suburbs," he contends the song is now "divisive": 84 percent of those who describe themselves as "very liberal" dislike it, as do 88 percent of Kuntzman's fellow atheists. He suggests fans not rise to honor "a song that is not the national anthem of a nation that is not uniquely blessed by some deity that doesn't exist anyway."[41]

Most critics of the national anthem prefer more spirited, homegrown tunes, such as Lee Greenwood's 1984 country hit, "God Bless the U.S.A." In the 1940s, the journalist Westbrook Pegler noted that the United States had "produced more music, by volume, than all the other [countries] combined from the beginning of time." He suggested finding an alternative by Irving Berlin, George M. Cohan, or John Philip Sousa, "men who possessed and couldn't help expressing the living spirit of their country."[42] But one editorialist from Texas countered that the living spirit of the country was already embodied in a song that custom and tradition had sanctified. "It is not the melody or the words that really makes a song sink into our hearts, it is the courage, the valor and everything else that is good and right, symbolized into an anthem and a flag," he wrote. "Wouldn't we feel just a little unpatriotic never again standing in respect to the words, 'O'er the land of the free and the home of the brave?'"[43]

Not everyone buys into the anthem's patriotism. Progressive critics focus on the song's supposed glorification of war, arguing that when Woodrow Wilson adopted it by executive order in 1916 he was trying to whip up enthusiasm for America's entry into World War I.[44] In a debate in 1935, the New York assistant superintendent of schools said the anthem should be excluded from high school programs because it was "too militaristic [and] really has no significance." Mrs. S. Lyman Otis, a regent of the Daughters of the American Revolution, replied that if he thought "bombs bursting in air" was too much for kids, then they should just skip it.[45] More recently *The Progressive* denounced the anthem as "a terrible song, with racist and militaristic overtones. It needs to be replaced.... [W]e need a new anthem, one that celebrates peace, social justice and diverse expression."[46]

This brings us to the charge, widely accepted on the Left, that "The Star-Spangled Banner"—its third stanza, to be precise—is racist, a charge that does not hold up to scrutiny. To be sure, Francis Scott Key's record on race was mixed. He owned slaves, but he also offered pro bono legal representation for other slaves petitioning for their freedom. In 1835 he prosecuted Arthur Bowen, a Washington, DC, slave accused of threatening his female owner, Anna Thorton. But when a riot ensued over the incident, Key stood in front of Bowen's jail cell and faced down a mob bent on lynching him.

In the third stanza of his poem about the defense of Fort McHenry, Key mocks British troops who three weeks before the battle burned Washington and looted Alexandria. The Redcoats had in mind a similar fate for Baltimore and other coastal cities but were dramatically beaten back. Key taunted this "haughty host" as "the hireling and slave." Ignoring the obvious meaning of Key's phrase, the revisionists maintain that the "hireling" is the regular British soldier, while "slave" referred to the British Second Corps of Colonial Marines, composed of former slaves who had been encouraged to escape bondage and fight alongside the British.[47] According to this line of thinking, the slave-owning Key had been upset by the idea of marauding freed blacks wreaking havoc on Southern coastal cities and was so gratified by their defeat he inserted this line into his poem.

However, this is speculation. There is no evidence that Key was referring to the Second Corps of Colonial Marines or that he even knew that the unit existed, or cared if it did. In fact, the expression "hireling and slave" was a well-established rhetorical device of the day that had nothing to do with black slaves in the United States. It was an all-purpose insult that could be used to refer to enemy troops, foreign leaders, corrupt politicians, or anyone else in need of a put-down.

For example, an Annapolis newspaper defended the "war for justice" in 1812 because it would not be "a war such as is engaged in Europe, where the military hirelings or slaves are ready to obey the commands of their master."[48] Another article from around the same time denounced French raids on American ships, asking "how long are the American people, who shed their blood for Independence, to be insulted with impunity, by the hireling slaves and minions of a blood-stained and inexorable tyrant?" The tyrant in question—Napoleon—was likewise mocked in an allegorical poem of the day: "from a hireling and a slave, Thou art a King."[49] Radicals protesting bread prices in London in 1800 asked how long people would "quietly and cowardly" suffer to be "half-starved by a set of mercenary slaves and government hirelings?"[50] And in 1795, long before the Second Corps of Colonial Marines existed, a dispatch from Baltimore condemned the "the Hireling Slaves" of King George III.[51]

Key's use of "the hireling and slave"—a rhetorical jab at the chastened British troops—accords with the standard usage of his time with no implication that it referred literally to American former slaves. "Slave," moreover, is a convenient rhyme for "grave," and he was, after all, writing a poem.

Before the recent ruckus, no one who sang the anthem thought it sent a racial message. If anything, people believed that the anthem promoted unity. And few Americans know the anthem's words beyond the first stanza anyway. Recall the story from the Battle of the Bulge, when German infiltrators disguised as U.S. troops were dropped behind the lines to engage in sabotage. GIs would ask suspected spies to sing the second (or third or fourth) verse of "The Star-Spangled Banner." If they *didn't* know the words, they were assumed to be genuine Americans.[52]

Antipathy to the national anthem goes well beyond the third stanza, however. Before the Civil War, abolitionists mocked the hypocrisy of the "land of the free and the home of the slave." And the *New York Times* columnist Brent Staples notes that many blacks long ago rejected "The Star-Spangled Banner" in favor of "Lift Every Voice and Sing," the unofficial "black national anthem." James Weldon Johnson wrote the words in 1900 to celebrate Abraham Lincoln's birthday. His brother, J. Rosamond

Johnson, later provided the music. The song "spread rapidly through black America in the early 1900s," writes Staples, "reflecting a growing sense that the promise of full citizenship in the nation's canonical texts simply did not apply to African-Americans." Singing "Lift Every Voice and Sing" in place of "The Star-Spangled Banner" was "a quiet act of rebellion against the racist status quo." And the actual national anthem was viewed as "a loyalty test and an excuse for people who called themselves patriots to harass and beat people who dissented from the song's message."[53] The Reverend Joseph Lowery quoted "Lift Every Voice and Sing" in his benediction at President Barack Obama's inauguration, and some NBA teams have begun playing it at games during Black History Month.[54]

In a much different vein from the melodic "Lift Every Voice and Sing," the rapper "T.I." came up with his own "New National Anthem," a song that "serves as a sprawling rumination addressing police brutality, systemic racism, gun culture and a laundry list of other social problems currently plaguing the U.S."[55] The chorus goes:

> Home of the brave and free (well damn officer what did I do?)
> Free just to murder me (Naw hold up man don't shoot, I live over there)
> Land of the beautiful (ay, ay man what you doin?)
> Cursed by the hate we throw (you trippin' dawg)
> Is this the new national anthem? (how many times has that ever happened to you, what the f—- do you know about being a black man in America?)

Is this the new national anthem?(And you wonder
why we walk around with straps)

So what is the answer to the anthem that begins with a question? Is this no longer the land of the free and home of the brave? Has the twilight's last gleaming finally faded? Will the dawn's early light never arrive? Will the answer to the question "Does that star-spangled banner yet wave?" ever be no?

It is sad that progressives promote the idea that unifying national symbols like the flag and the anthem represent racism and other evils. This bitterness only promotes further anger and division and achieves nothing productive. It has not always been this way. Back in 1941, on the eve of the U.S. entry into World War II, Detroit Post 135 of the Jewish War Veterans sought to "knit a closer relationship between all racial groups in the city" by presenting an American flag to the city's Phillis Wheatley Home. Founded in 1895, the Phillis Wheatley Women's Clubs were named for a Revolutionary War–era slave who published a book of her own poetry and was an admirer of George Washington. "We are brought together by our loyalty to our flag," Rabbi Leon Fram said, "a symbol of hope and courage, a hope that America shall always remain the land of true democracy." The president of the Phillis Wheatley Association, William Headers, accepted the flag and affirmed that African Americans have "always stood loyal to the United States" and were "ready and willing to do [their] share now." The ceremony, conceived by Ben Davidson, the chairman of the JWV's Committee on Americanism, was also attended by African American posts of the American Legion.[56]

How would such a sincere gesture of racial and national harmony be received today? It would certainly be controversial. Progressives would view it as an insult. Protestors might show up to disrupt the ceremony, and that flag might not survive the day. But no one should believe that our current state of national division is a sign of progress or civic health. The angry activists who despise the flag and think it worthy of burning should remember that Martin Luther King Jr. and his marchers carried it before them at Selma, and when they reached the statehouse in Montgomery, Alabama, they sang "The Star-Spangled Banner."

SIX

NO NATION
UNDER GOD

Americans for the most part are a people of faith, and the quest for religious liberty has been central to the nation's story. So it didn't look good when delegates to a major political party's convention publicly rejected God.

During the platform debate at the 2012 Democratic National Convention, former Ohio Governor Ted Strickland offered an amendment to insert a passing reference to God and to restore the promise President Obama made (and did not keep) to recognize Jerusalem as the capital of Israel. The platform committee had removed these two items, but the party leadership felt it would not play well in the heartland, so they had to go back in. By the time the leadership noticed the omission, however, convention rules required an amendment. The chairman of the convention, Los Angeles Mayor Antonio Villaraigosa, tried to rush the embarrassing motion through on a voice vote requiring two-thirds ayes. He failed twice. On the third attempt the no's were just as loud, but Villaraigosa ruled in favor of the aye's anyway. The hall erupted in shouting.[1] Video of delegates loudly shouting "No!" and jeering at the outcome led to the irresistible headline, "Democrats boo God."[2]

Inserting the minor phrase "God-given potential" into the platform was hardly worth the black eye the party took over the booing incident. Hillary Clinton's 2016 platform sought to make up for the 2012 debacle by tossing in the phrase three times instead of one.[3] But these brief nods to God were a far cry from the 2004 Democratic platform that affirmed dedication to "faith and family, duty and service, individual freedom and a common purpose to build one nation under God."[4] And Democrats had moved light years from their 1996 platform that said, among other things, "Americans have a right to express their love of God in public, and we applaud [President Clinton's] work to ensure that children are not denied private religious expression in school."[5] That Democratic Party is long gone.

The booing incident underscored how religion has become a dividing line in American culture. Religion does not have the influence it once did. Questioning the role of faith, even belief in a supreme being, is much more common than it used to be. *Time* magazine caused a ruckus with its 1966 cover story, "Is God Dead?" because at the time many people found even asking the question offensive. The folk singer Bob Dylan commented, "If you were God, how would you like to see that written about yourself?"[6] Today the question would hardly be noticed—though it would be brave indeed for a mainstream publication to host a debate over the future of Islam under the headline, "Is Allah Dead?" Nevertheless, most people still concur today that "God shed his grace" on America. One recent poll showed that 62 percent agreed either mostly or completely with the statement "God has granted America a special role in human history."[7]

In the 2016 election, each party could point to solid support from various denominations. Protestants, white Catholics, Mormons, and Evangelicals were in Donald Trump's camp. Hillary Clinton found support from Hispanic Catholics, Jews, and several smaller groups including Muslims. This support was vital in such a close election. White, "born-again" or evangelical Christians, strong in rural areas and accounting for 26 percent of the electorate, went 81 percent for Trump. The religiously unaffiliated, mostly urban and 15 percent of the electorate, voted 68 percent for Clinton.[8] And the leadership in the various denominations tended to be even more politically committed than their congregants.[9]

But more telling than voters' religious affiliation is how observant they are. In general, more religiously committed people tend to vote Republican.[10] Fifty-six percent of those who attend services weekly—a third of the electorate—voted for Trump. Among those who attend monthly, Trump had a three-point edge. Among those who attend only a few times a year, the vote was split. But Hillary Clinton dominated among the 22 percent who never go to services, winning 62 percent of their votes, twice the support given to Trump.[11] Atheists, agnostics, and those who claim to be "nothing in particular" also skew heavily Democratic.[12]

Republican dominance among the religiously observant is illustrated by the Jewish vote in the 2016 election. A pre-election poll of Jewish voters showed that Hillary Clinton led by 64 percent among Reform Jews and by 28 percent among Conservatives, but she lost among highly observant Orthodox Jews by 29 percent.[13] On Election Day, some districts in Brooklyn's Orthodox Jewish Borough Park neighborhood voted Trump by over 80 percent.[14] One sympathetic local compared them to "Rust Belt voters. They are hardworking people, not college educated."[15] And like many working- and middle-class Trump voters, they are very religiously observant.

Orthodox Rabbi Daniel Lapin has noted the challenges that creeping secularization have posed for people of faith, and in particular for American Christians. He said there is a war "against those who regard the Bible to be God's revelation to humanity and the Ten Commandments to be His set of rules for all time." Rabbi Lapin says the secularists are trying to "make Christianity, well, sort of socially unacceptable. Something only foolish, poor and ugly people could turn to." As if to confirm his observation, Joy Behar, a co-host of ABC's *The View*, criticized Vice President Mike Pence's Christian faith by saying that hearing from Jesus is evidence of "mental illness."[16] If Christianity's "benign influence on the character of America" is lost, the rabbi continued, it will be replaced by "a sinister secularism that menaces Bible believers of all faiths." And "once the voice of the Bible has been silenced...we shall see a long night of barbarism descend on the West." Thus "without a vibrant and vital Christianity, America is doomed, and without America, the West is doomed." Rabbi Lapin warns, "You are under attack. Now is the time to resist it."[17]

THE NEW JERUSALEM

"Reason and experience," said George Washington in his Farewell Address, "both forbid us to expect that national morality can prevail in exclusion of religious principle. And it is substantially true, that virtue or morality is a necessary spring of popular government."

Religious principle was traditionally an important part of American public life. There was no notion that the government would try to exclude it. Matters of faith were left to local communities, not federal judges, a policy rooted in the history and development of the country. England had a state religion, and the intersection of faith and politics was a source of political instability, especially during the seventeenth-century English Civil War. Religious conflicts had wracked continental Europe as well, and the New World was a magnet for religious dissenters and others who faced persecution, official sanction, even execution. This freedom to worship was what brought the Pilgrims to Plymouth, as well as the Puritans who followed. They established communities that became working expressions of their theology. And at times they became as oppressive as the governments they fled.

When dissent arose, as it inevitably does, people left (or fled) to found new communities in line with their own ideas, whether religious or secular. The dissident Puritan preacher Roger Williams founded the Providence Plantation on the principles of separating church and state, liberty of conscience, and fair dealing with Native Americans. Members of The Religious Society of Friends (Quakers) were harshly mistreated by the Puritans, who executed four of them, most famously Mary Dyer in 1660.

The Quakers later became well established in the Delaware Valley and in Pennsylvania. And there have been other examples of religious bias and persecution in the country, against Mormons, Catholics, Jews, and others.

But as the colonies and the country grew, the tradition of open-mindedness and acceptance of religious differences took root. The religious warfare of Europe, the state-sanctioned inquisitions and pogroms, had no place here. As George Washington wrote in his famous letter to the Hebrew Congregations of Newport, Rhode Island, the government of the United States "gives to bigotry no sanction, to persecution no assistance." He invoked the biblical vision of a New Jerusalem where "every one shall sit in safety under his own vine and fig tree, and there shall be none to make him afraid."[18] And the view of America as Zion was so prevalent that Benjamin Franklin and Thomas Jefferson initially proposed that the Great Seal of the United States feature scenes from Exodus, with Moses leading the Israelites into the wilderness towards the Promised Land.

The First Amendment's guarantee that "Congress shall make no law respecting an establishment of religion, or prohibiting the free exercise thereof" reflects this basic American live-and-let-live attitude. The federal government was prohibited from making any sect the official state faith and from banning any religion, assuring, as Justice Joseph Story wrote in his famous commentaries on the U.S. Constitution, that "the Catholic and the Protestant, the Calvinist and the Arminian, the Jew and the Infidel, may sit down at the common table of the national councils, without any inquisition into their faith, or mode of worship."[19] But this did not mean that faith was excluded from all aspects of public life. The Founders, in their usual practical way, left it up to states and communities to find the balance between religion and government.

The United States became a patchwork of faiths according to local traditions, patterns of settlement, the backgrounds of immigrants, intermarriage, and innumerable other factors. Various community standards evolved, and they changed as communities changed. People were free to reject religious affiliation or to cluster in communities in which a religiously informed way of life predominated. Sometimes conflicts arose between such religious communities and the broader political order, as when Old Order Amish, practicing their faith-based traditional way of life, objected to state laws forcing their children to attend public high schools. The Amish believed this was disruptive and dangerous to their traditions. The Supreme Court ruled in *Wisconsin v. Yoder* (1972) that Amish religious conviction and the right to practice their faith outweighed the state's interest in compulsory education, and there was no evidence that going to high school would make the Amish youth better citizens. In fact it would probably harm more than help.

Historically, the government recognized faith as both a source of law and a fact of American life. James Wilson, a signer of the Declaration of Independence, a delegate to the Constitutional Convention, and one of the original justices of the Supreme Court, believed that "far from being rivals or enemies, religion and law are twin sisters, friends, and mutual assistants," and that "the divine law, as discovered by reason and the moral sense, forms an essential part of both."[20] Congress opens its sessions with an invocation, a tradition reaching back to when Benjamin

Franklin called for daily prayers at the Constitutional Convention. Franklin was convinced that "God governs the affairs of man," and noted that the Continental Congress had asked for "Divine protection." With the Revolution over, he asked, "do we imagine we no longer need His assistance?"[21]

Religious symbolism is well in evidence in Washington. In the Senate chamber are the inscriptions "In God We Trust" and *Annuit Coeptis* ("He has favored our undertakings"). On the House side, a marble relief portrait of Moses hangs on the gallery wall, facing the Speaker's chair. A painting in the Capitol rotunda by John Gadsby Chapman depicts the baptism of Pocahontas. When the cornerstone of the Washington Monument was laid in 1848 a Bible was placed inside it, and the obelisk's aluminum cap, the highest point in the District of Columbia, is inscribed with the words *Laus Deo*, "Praise God."

Marble friezes in the courtroom of the Supreme Court—where each session begins with the invocation "God save the United States and this honorable court"—feature eighteen lawgivers from the ancient world, among them Moses, Confucius, and Mohammed. The friezes are the work of Adolph A. Weinman, the sculptor of the abused Lincoln statue at the University of Wisconsin. The eastern pediment of the building is decorated with Hermon Atkins MacNeil's elaborate sculpture "Justice, the Guardian of Liberty," at the center of which sits an imposing figure of Moses, with the two tablets of the Ten Commandments.

A clear majority of Americans believe that the Bible is either inspired by God (47 percent) or the literal word of God (24 percent).[22] Throughout American history, the government's respect for religion was simply taken for granted. In 1892, the Supreme

Court ruled in *Church of the Holy Trinity v. United States* that it was impossible for a law to be interpreted in a way to substantially harm religion because it would never be the intention of the legislature to do that.[23] Justice David Josiah Brewer wrote that "no purpose of action against religion can be imputed to any legislation, state or national, because this is a religious people. This is historically true." He recognized that "American life, as expressed by its laws, its business, its customs, and its society," shows "everywhere a clear recognition of the same truth."

We find the same thought in *Zorach v. Clauson* (1952), upholding a New York law that allowed children, on written request by their parents, to attend religious instruction off campus during "released time" for one hour a week during the school day. Justice William O. Douglas, an arch-liberal, who championed many controversial ideas in his years on the bench, nevertheless argued that Americans "are a religious people whose institutions presuppose a Supreme Being." Douglas said there is "no constitutional requirement which makes it necessary for government to be hostile to religion and to throw its weight against efforts to widen the effective scope of religious influence," because that would be to take sides with "those who believe in no religion over those who do." The 2018 Supreme Court ruling in favor of Christian baker Jack Phillips, who had been punished by the Colorado Civil Rights Commission for refusing to make a cake for a same-sex wedding, hinged on the finding that the commissioners had demonstrated "an impermissible hostility toward religion."[24]

Maintaining local religious freedom became more difficult when the Supreme Court began to apply the First Amendment's

establishment and free exercise clauses to state and local governments in the 1940s. As federal courts overturned longstanding
community standards, religion began to be aggressively pushed
out of the public space. Nativity scenes and monuments to the
Ten Commandments on public property, prayer in schools, and
any sort of government recognition of the people's faith came
under increasing scrutiny by courts. In the 1960s, the Supreme
Court made a radical departure from the old norms and wiped
most traces of religion from public schools. Madalyn Murray
O'Hair, the founder of American Atheists, made a habit of bringing antireligious lawsuits after her success in 1963 in ending Bible
reading in Baltimore's schools. (Note however that recent polls
consistently show public support for prayer in school by wide
margins.[25]) O'Hair overreached when she pushed a case that
maintained that judicial oaths ending in "So help me God" systematically excluded non-believers from the judiciary, a view
which the U.S. Court of Appeals for the Fifth Circuit said
"approaches absurdity." She even confronted NASA when Apollo
astronauts were saying prayers, a case which also failed. Astronauts in particular might feel they should get right with God—
they are heading in his direction but don't want to visit before
their time.[26]

Congress pushed back against judicial encroachments on
religious practices with the Religious Freedom Restoration Act
of 1993, sponsored by Republican Senator Orrin Hatch of Utah
and Democratic Representative (later senator) Chuck Schumer
of New York and signed into law by President Bill Clinton back
when bipartisanship was possible in Washington. Responding to
judicial decisions that upheld restrictions on traditional American

Indian religious practices, the act forbade government infringements on religious conduct without a compelling state interest. RFRA was the basis for a 2017 lawsuit filed by the Archdiocese of Washington challenging the DC public transportation authority's rule against advertisements promoting "any religion, religious practice or belief."[27] The Church lost the case in its initial rounds on the grounds that its ads—showing a silhouette of shepherds in the field and a guiding star, entreating people to "Find the perfect gift" during the holidays—rather obviously promoted religion. The question the judges should have addressed is, why should the government be allowed to actively discriminate against religious groups buying ad space in the marketplace of ideas?

THE CRUSADE AGAINST CROSSES

The cross is ubiquitous in Western art and culture and used widely in American monuments, especially those honoring the dead. Although the cross is the preeminent Christian symbol, it is not always erected for a specifically sectarian purpose. Take for example the Peace Cross in Bladensburg, Maryland, a forty-foot concrete monument erected in 1925 by the American Legion and others to commemorate the forty-nine soldiers from Prince George's County who were killed in World War I. The monument stands on the site of the Battle of Bladensburg, where in 1814 American forces attempted and failed to stop British troops marching on Washington. The cross was acquired by the Maryland–National Capital Park and Planning Commission in 1961, and in 2015 was placed on the National Register of Historic Places.

But a war broke out over the Peace Monument. In 2017 the U.S. Court of Appeals for the Fourth Circuit ruled that the memorial "has the primary effect of endorsing religion and excessively entangles the government in religion."[28] Since the cross was erected for a clearly secular purpose, it is hard to see how it endorses religion or entangles the government in religion. This anti-cross decision could also threaten the Canadian Cross of Sacrifice and the Argonne Cross, both in Arlington National Cemetery and likewise erected to honor the dead of World War I.

The Supreme Court earlier addressed a similar question in *Salazar v. Buono*, which involved the cross on Sunrise Rock in the Mojave National Preserve. The original wooden cross (later replaced with concrete-filled metal pipes) was erected in 1934 by members of the Veterans of Foreign Wars, like the other crosses to honor the dead of the First World War. When the National Park Service announced in 1999 its plans to remove the cross, Congress intervened, first by defunding the removal effort and then by privatizing the land on which the cross stood. The Supreme Court's highly technical decision ruled in favor of letting the cross remain, though remanded the case to a lower court to re-examine the land swap. Justice Anthony Kennedy noted that "the goal of avoiding governmental endorsement [of religion] does not require eradication of all religious symbols in the public realm."[29] But shortly after the decision, vandals took it upon themselves to eradicate the cross. Subsequent efforts to place a new cross on the site have been resisted. Justice Clarence Thomas archly observed, "If a cross in the middle of a desert establishes a religion, then no religious observance is safe from challenge."[30]

Privatization failed at Sunrise Rock but worked elsewhere. The Mount Davidson cross in San Francisco was erected in the 1920s, though the first wooden crosses were burned down by arsonists. The current 103-foot concrete cross, in honor of the California pioneers, was completed in 1934. President Franklin Roosevelt illuminated the cross by telegraph using a solid gold telegraph key given to Western Union by George W. Carmack, one of the men who started the Klondike Gold Rush. In the 1990s San Francisco lost a lawsuit over the cross and auctioned it off along with almost a half-acre of parkland on which it stood. The Council of Armenian American Organizations of Northern California, having won the auction with a bid of twenty-six thousand dollars, placed a plaque on the cross commemorating the victims of the 1915 Armenian genocide in the Ottoman Empire, but the plaque was stolen by someone who wanted to erase that tragic history.

The Ground Zero cross at the National September 11 Memorial and Museum faced a challenge from atheists who said they suffered physical and emotional damages from its very existence, including "dyspepsia, symptoms of depression, headaches, anxiety, and mental pain and anguish." The crossed steel beams that the ironworker Frank Silecchia found amid the rubble days after the attack had become a symbol of hope and healing for many. When the beams were pulled up from the World Trade Center pit, the Franciscan priest Father Brian Jordan, who had been offering Masses for Ground Zero workers, began conducting his services at the cross. This was one reason the atheists argued that the "rubble that resembles a cross" was a "Christian icon" that represented "an impermissible mingling of church and state."[31]

But the Second Circuit Court of Appeals rejected this argument, saying that regardless of the shape of the cross or even the fact that it has been used as an object of veneration, "displaying The Cross at Ground Zero has always been secular: to recount the history of the terrorist attacks of September 11, 2001, and their aftermath."[32] Preserving that history and all that the cross represented for the people affected by that national tragedy was more important than an atheist's tummyache.

BREAKING THE TABLETS

"The fundamental basis of this Nation's law was given to Moses on the Mount," President Harry S. Truman said. The Ten Commandments, among the most important documents in world history, form one of the pillars of Western law. "The fundamental basis of our Bill of Rights comes from the teachings which we get from Exodus and St. Matthew, from Isaiah and St. Paul," Truman added. "I don't think we emphasize that enough these days."[33]

Not everyone agrees. In 2014, Michael Tate Reed rammed his car into a 4,800-pound Ten Commandments monument on the grounds of the Oklahoma capitol. In 2017, Arkansas installed a similar monument near its capitol. Within twenty-four hours, Reed rammed his car into that monument too. Reed, who has been diagnosed with schizoaffective disorder, told investigators he is a Christian, but that he firmly believes in the separation of church and state. Then he asked the public for funds to help repair his car.[34]

Decalogue monuments sprouted across the country in the 1950s for a very secular purpose—movie advertising. In 1956, the filmmaker Cecil B. DeMille, working with Minnesota Judge E. J. Ruegemer and the Fraternal Order of Eagles, erected monuments across the country to promote DeMille's epic movie *The Ten Commandments*. Judge Ruegemer had begun a personal crusade to raise awareness of the Commandments years earlier when a young boy appearing in his court had no idea what the Commandments were. Over five years, the judge and the Eagles distributed more than seven thousand framed copies of the Ten Commandments to schools, churches, and courts.[35] Working with DeMille, the group dedicated more than one hundred of the granite monuments across the country. Some of the dedication ceremonies featured the film's stars Charlton Heston and Yul Brynner.[36]

Over the years, other groups and communities followed this example. And in time the Decalogue monuments and similar displays became magnets for court cases and vandalism. A Decalogue monument outside the Indiana statehouse was vandalized in 1991. It was repaired and sent to the Eagles Lodge in Anderson, Indiana, where it was hit again.[37] In 2003 a federal judge ordered the city of La Crosse, Wisconsin, to remove a Ten Commandments monument from a public park, and when the city attempted to privatize the land around it, the activist judge denied that move too.

In *Stone v. Graham* (1980), the Supreme Court struck down a Kentucky law requiring that the Ten Commandments be posted in every public school classroom. In 2005 the Court also eliminated Ten Commandments displays in Kentucky county courthouses. But the key case that year came from Texas. In 1961 the Eagles had erected a six-foot-high Decalogue monument outside the capitol in Austin, which was eventually joined by thirty-seven other markers and monuments on the capitol grounds. Forty years later Thomas van Orden sued, saying the monument violated the First Amendment's Establishment Clause. But lower federal courts sided with the state, and in *Van Orden v. Perry* the Supreme Court affirmed their judgments.

In the majority opinion, Chief Justice William Rehnquist noted the many representations of Moses and the Ten Commandments in and around public buildings in Washington, and even at the Supreme Court. Such "passive" monuments, he wrote, required nothing but reflection from those so inclined, and did not violate the constitutional prohibition on establishment. He also recognized "the role of God in our Nation's heritage." And he denied the idea that a monument was incompatible with the Constitution by virtue of "having religious content or promoting a message consistent with a religious doctrine." Justice Clarence Thomas added that recognizing the religious aspect of the monument was critical, since he believed the Court's past attempts to avoid that issue were confusing and at odds with the facts.

So the Texas monument remained, but the lawsuits have kept coming, and cities have experimented with means to erect monuments and avoid lawsuits. Somersworth, New Hampshire, balances its Decalogue monument with a rotating series of flags bearing social and political messages at what they call the Citizens' Place. For example, the town has flown an atheist flag and a flag for ecumenical peace.[38] This approach fosters dialogue and communication rather than litigation and strengthens community bonds rather than letting distant jurists muse on the matter in remote chambers.

Another response has been to set up competing monuments. The Satanic Temple proposed donating a bronze statue of Baphomet, a goat-headed occult deity, with two children gazing at it, to "complement and contrast" the Ten Commandments monument on the Oklahoma capitol grounds. The Supreme Court has ruled that governments are under no "free speech" obligations to accept donated monuments, and the Satanic Temple lost interest when the Oklahoma Supreme Court ruled that the Decalogue monument (which was repaired after Michael Tate Reed rammed it) had to be removed.[39] The Baphomet statue ended up on display in Detroit, prompting the Baptist minister Dave Bullock to lament, "The last thing we need in Detroit is having a welcome home party for evil."[40]

"KEEP GOD'S COMMANDMENTS"

Judge Ruegemer sentenced the young boy who didn't know the Ten Commandments to learn them and live by them. Yet advising people to obey the Commandments has become the center of yet another dispute over religion in the public space.

Nelson County, Virginia, south of Charlottesville, was named for Thomas Nelson Jr., a signer of the Declaration of Independence and the fourth governor of Virginia. The county was the home of the writer Earl Hamner Jr., whose early experiences during the Great Depression in the town of Schuyler formed the basis for his novel *Spencer's Mountain*, which he later developed into the television series *The Waltons*. The Nelson County Circuit Courthouse in Lovingston (formerly Loving's Gap) was dedicated in 1809 and is rich with history. Thomas

Jefferson designed the attached jail, which is now used as office space. In the mid-nineteenth century the courthouse doubled as a house of worship for several denominations, and during the Civil War it was a hospital.[41]

During recent renovations, restorers uncovered the painted-over words "Virtus—Keep God's Commandments—Veritas" at the base of the balcony in the main chamber of the courthouse. The uncovered words may be from an instruction from Moses in Deuteronomy. Perhaps the phrase was inspired by a famous sermon on the theme by old Williamsburg's Reverend Adam Empie. Or maybe it was just good advice. It's unclear when the words were painted over—they were under at least four coats of paint—but they were mentioned in the courthouse's 1973 nomination form for the National Register of Historic Places. Yet rediscovering the words started an immediate debate over what to do about them. The expression was part of the heritage of the building, but it was still a working courthouse and the slogan was overtly religious. Country supervisor Thomas Bruguiere Jr. said, "You can't change history. I think we should leave it up, leave it alone. It shouldn't offend anybody." And the board chairman, Tommy Harvey, vowed that the county was "not going to back down from a fight." Douglas Laycock of the University of Virginia Law School predicted that whether the slogan was displayed or covered up, "someone's going to challenge this."[42]

Sure enough, the Wisconsin-based Freedom From Religion Foundation sent a letter demanding the words be concealed and threatening legal action. The town estimated that defending the slogan could cost up to half a million dollars, a price that Lovingston could ill afford.

Religious imagery and slogans are not unknown at other courthouses. In addition to the sculptures of Moses at the Supreme Court, the E. Barrett Prettyman Federal Courthouse in Washington, DC—home of the secretive FISA Court—is adorned with a bronze plaque with the tablets of the Ten Commandments, a Torah scroll, and Moses blowing a shofar. The Trylon of Freedom sculpture in front of the building, depicting various freedoms guaranteed by the Constitution, features a woman kneeling in prayer and a man standing before a cross and tablets of the Decalogue. The Ten Commandments are etched in glass over the vestibule doors at the Dauphin County, Pennsylvania, courthouse, and etchings below illustrate the Commandments' admonitions. And an inscription above the entrance to the Santa Barbara County Courthouse reads, "God Gave Us the Country, the Skill of Man Hath Built the Town."

Henderson County, Tennessee, came under fire for a Bible verse on the cornerstone of its fifty-year-old county courthouse. The engraving is from Psalm 89:14 and reads, "Justice and judgment are the habitation of thy throne: Mercy and truth shall go before thy face." The Freedom From Religion Foundation threatened to sue unless the verse was removed. Mayor Dan Hughes refused, and said he wanted to up the ante by adding Psalm 33:12, "Blessed is the nation whose God is the Lord; and the people whom he hath chosen for his own inheritance." A local resident thought the inscription should stay, adding, "It's a big Bible Belt around here, and you know, if they don't like it, they don't have to read it."[43]

The most common reference to God at courthouses is the national motto, "In God We Trust." Derived from the fourth stanza of "The Star-Spangled Banner," it was first used on currency during the Civil War but did not become the official national motto until 1956. In 1959 the state of New York encouraged courts to display plaques with the new national motto, and it is engraved on the walls behind judges' benches. A U.S. Court of Appeals ruled in favor of the motto's use on public buildings in 1970, but it has not been reviewed by the Supreme Court.

The motto graces many other courthouses around the country. Thurston County, Nebraska, and Watauga County, North Carolina, both added it to county courthouses. The Hot Spring County Courthouse in Malvern, Arkansas, erected a rock with the motto on it, which caused little controversy. Shortly after it went up vandals visited the town, but they targeted the local veterans' monument. "I'm gonna be honest with you," County Judge Bill Scrimshire said, "I'm surprised it was that one."[44] And Macon County, North Carolina, has placed the motto on several official buildings as well as on all the county police cruisers.[45]

These and other religious references have figured in recent court cases. The Anderson County Courthouse in Clinton, Tennessee, erected black granite plaques carved with "In God We Trust." The day after the first plaque went up, Kenneth Darrin Fisher, who was being tried for attempted first-degree murder of his wife, moved that the case be dismissed because the motto violated his freedom of worship. Fisher claimed Cherokee descent, and his attorney said the inscription converts the building into a "temple of fundamentalist Christianity."[46] The motion was later withdrawn, and Fisher was convicted and sentenced to eighteen years.

The convicted murderer Rudolph Roybal's 1992 death sentence in California was overturned twenty-five years later when a judge ruled that San Diego County Deputy District Attorney

James Koerber engaged in "egregious misconduct" by quoting the Bible during the penalty phase. Koerber had quoted Numbers 35:16, that "the murderer shall surely be put to death." U.S. District Judge Jeffrey Miller contended that Koerber erred by encouraging jurors to "vote for death because it was God's will, and not that the imposition of the death penalty complied with California and federal law."[47] Elsewhere the Connecticut supreme court unanimously rejected the murderer Pedro Miranda's appeal that his conviction be overturned because one of the witnesses said he "asked God for direction" in picking him out of a photo array. The Supreme Court's decision relied on the trial judge's having told the jury to disregard the comment.[48] Miranda was serving a life sentence for killing a thirteen-year-old girl.

So what is the fate of the exhortation to keep God's Commandments at the Nelson County courthouse? The board of supervisors, noting that the county could ill-afford to mount a legal defense, voted to put a removable cover over the words that would be in place during court proceedings and could be taken off to display the words at other times. Larry Saunders, the sole dissenting voice on the board, said he was less concerned about facing judges in litigation over the inscription than he was about giving an account to "the Big Judge." "I'm not in favor of covering it up," he said. "I'm in favor of restoring it and being proud of it. I know I'll be outvoted, but…I'm proud to say that I'm in favor of keeping it uncovered."[49]

HOLY DIVERSITY!

Attacks on religious imagery go beyond the First Amendment. A coalition of sixteen Muslim groups requested that the image of Mohammed on the Supreme Court frieze depicting famous lawgivers be sandblasted off because the image of the Prophet amounts to idolatry and the sword in the figure's hand promotes the idea that Muslims spread their faith by the sword. The request was rejected since, among other reasons, the image was part of a well-intentioned effort to portray famous lawgivers of history and removing Mohammed "would impair the artistic integrity of the whole."[50]

A complaint was filed with the Washington, DC, Office of Human Rights on behalf of Muslim students at the Catholic University of America complaining that the prevalence of Catholic symbols on campus hinders the Muslims from practicing their faith free of distractions. Crucifixes in classrooms, Catholic literature, pictures of the pope, and the presence of the massive Basilica of the National Shrine of the Immaculate Conception all allegedly contribute to an anti-Muslim environment. The complaint sought to have the university provide sanitized worship spaces.[51] It is unclear why these students hadn't suspected Catholic University might have a Christian flavor when they applied to go there—the name is a clue—or why they can't simply "celebrate diversity" like their Christian classmates.

Muslim students at the Jesuit Loyola University in Chicago complained that holidays such as Eid were not as prominently celebrated on campus as Christmas. Muslims make up approximately 5 percent of the student body, and Loyola energetically promotes non-Christian holidays, while secularizing Christmas—Happy Holidays!—to make it more inclusive. Nevertheless, while the campus is festively decorated during the Christmas season and offers many holiday-themed activities, it offers

Over twenty-five cities have removed or relocated monuments dedicated to the Confederacy. Here, a statue of Robert E. Lee in New Orleans is prepared for removal. *Infrogmation of New Orleans*

Protesters defaced the Jackson and Lee monument in Baltimore before its removal in 2017. The statue "Madre Luz," of a pregnant black woman with a baby on her back, replaced the previous monument and was also vandalized. *Ryan Patterson*

In the outcry over Confederate images, retailers pulled rebel flags from their shelves and Warner Bros. stopped making toy versions of the 1969 Dodge Charger "The General Lee" from the 1980s television series *The Dukes of Hazzard.* *Wikimedia Commons*

The Founding Fathers are also under attack. This plaque honoring George Washington at the church he attended in Alexandria, Virginia, was slated for removal, along with a similar plaque honoring parishioner Robert E. Lee, because they make some in the ultra-liberal congregation "feel unsafe." *James S. Robbins*

Progressives object to all four presidents on Mt. Rushmore. That and its location in the Black Hills, which is sacred to the Sioux, has led some to call for the national monument to be blown up, Taliban-style. *Graphic by James S. Robbins*

The "Early Days" section of the Pioneer Monument in San Francisco was slammed for its "offensive imagery." The only politically correct aspect of the monument is that the *vaquero* and priest are Spanish speakers. *Beyond My Ken*

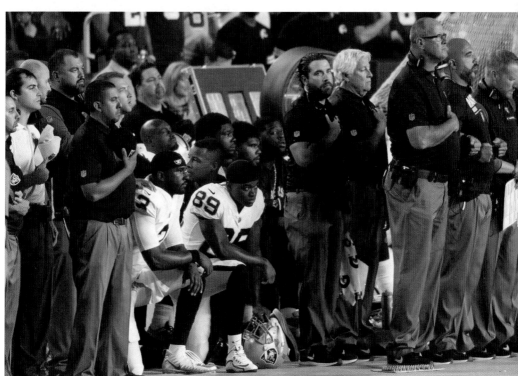

NFL football players kneeling during the National Anthem to protest racism and law enforcement offended large numbers of fans, and has caused the League to lose millions of television viewers. *Keith Allison*

Progressives erroneously charge that "The Star-Spangled Banner" contains racist lyrics, which has led to attacks on monuments to Francis Scott Key, like this one in Baltimore. *Ryan Patterson*

The U.S. Court of Appeals for the 4th Circuit has ruled that the Peace Cross in Bladensburg, Md., honoring local World War One casualties, excessively entangles the state in religion and must come down. The ruling threatens similar cross monuments in Arlington National Cemetery. *Ken Firestone*

Renovations at the historic Nelson County Circuit Courthouse in Lovingston, Va. uncovered the painted-over words, "Virtus—Keep God's Commandments—Veritas." The town was immediately threatened with a lawsuit, and must keep the words covered during court proceedings. *James S. Robbins*

Ten Commandments monuments, like this one on the Texas State Capitol grounds, have become magnets for litigation and vandalism. The Supreme Court struck down a challenge to this monument, noting "the role of God in our Nation's heritage." *Daderot*

President Trump actively fought back in the War on Christmas, saying "we say Merry Christmas, again, very, very proudly." The president's activism has caused some progressives to be afflicted by what the liberal *Washington Post* calls "Trump Christmas brain." *The White House*

Progressive agitators protesting an appearance by Milo Yiannopoulos at the University of California, Berkeley declared war on free speech. The protesters smashed windows, ignited Molotov cocktails, and threw rocks at police, causing the event to be cancelled. *Pietro Piupparco*

Progressives, like these protestors in Central Park in New York City, seek to erase American nationality by eliminating the country's borders and doing away with immigration and citizenship laws. *Rhododendrites*

Feminists promote wearing the traditional Muslim hijab as a symbol of freedom. In fact, the liberty America offers Muslim women is the freedom to remove the hijab if they choose, an action that would land them in prison in many other parts of the world. *Pixabay*

Increasing divisions in American politics have led to the potential for heated confrontations. Here at a 2017 "March 4 Trump" rally at the Minnesota capitol, a Trump supporter tells a counter-protester, "Get a job!" *Fibonacci Blue*

Violent progressives in "black bloc" groups like Antifa seek to take their fight for power to the streets, using the same fascist tactics they claim to oppose. *Mobilus In Mobili*

If a new Civil War broke out along political lines it might initially look like this map of the 2016 election results. Pro-Americans would control the nation's heartland while progressives would be holed up in urban areas. Such a conflict would be devastating regardless of the outcome. *Ali Zifan*

President Trump's campaign slogan "Make America Great Again" was met with predictable howls from progressives, since a majority on the Left says the country was never great to begin with. However, most Americans want to feel good about their country and its amazing history. *Gage Skidmore*

nothing comparable for Muslim holidays. More should be done to promote these holidays, insisted the discontented students.[52] And according to the Simmons College "Anti-Oppression Library Guide," even saying "God bless you" when someone sneezes is an "Islamophobic microaggression" that invokes "oppressive systems of religious/Chrisitan [sic] hierarchy."[53]

Similar political sensitivities prompted the College of the Holy Cross in Worcester, Massachusetts, to dump the name of its student newspaper, *The Crusader*. The change was prompted by a letter signed by fifty faculty members noting "the rising tide of xenophobia in the American political sphere and the fact that *The Crusader* shared a name with a KKK-sponsored newspaper." The paper's staff also determined that being associated with the "massacres" and "conquest" of the medieval Crusades was problematic.

The paper was first named *The Crusader* in 1955 after the longstanding team nickname. Alumnus and Democratic Senator David I. Walsh had said years earlier that "Crusaders" was an "admirable" team name that "interprets the traditions and customs and all that Holy Cross stands for."[54] The newspaper had previously been called *The Tomahawk*. The earlier name, dating to 1925 and now of course highly politically incorrect, evoked the Nipmuc Indian village Pakachoag that was at the school's location on Mount Saint James. The paper's staff back then referred to the newsroom as the highly un-PC "Wigwam."[55]

The new newspaper name, *The Spire*, evokes "the twin spires that dot the top of Fenwick Hall" in the center of campus.[56] But those spires have a troubling history of their own. The original Fenwick Hall burned down in 1852 and was rebuilt using a donation from the family of the school's first valedictorian, James Healy. The donation money was raised by selling slaves from the family's Georgia plantation. (Healy himself was of mixed race, though he identified as Irish.)[57] Apparently that history does not trouble the staff enough to uninspire them.

The Spire's editors assured readers that the new name was "most certainly not about appeasing faculty or creating 'safe spaces,'" which it most certainly was.[58] Jack Fowler, a Holy Cross alumnus and the publisher of *National Review*, predicted wryly that "in 10 years *The Spire* will be *The Minaret*."[59] Holy Cross may transform into Holy Crescent. Meanwhile, the "Crusaders" mascot was reviewed by school administrators and found to be acceptable, even though the era of the Crusades was "among the darkest periods in Church history." Previously depicted as a knight in armor, the Crusader is being reimagined as a social justice warrior.[60] Yet since the Holy Cross chair of New Testament Studies teaches that Jesus was a "gender-fluid drag king" who had "queer desires," maybe these naming controversies are the least of the school's problems.[61]

The San Domenico School in San Anselmo, California, founded in 1850 as the first Catholic school in the state, is erasing most of its heritage in the name of inclusion. In 2017 the school removed 90 percent of its icons and statues, including a beloved statue of the Virgin and Child in the school's courtyard that had been the focus of an annual "May crowning" ceremony for many years. This statue and others were "pitched in the basement." One parent complained that the headlong pursuit of "inclusion" has meant "letting go of San Domenico's 167-year tradition as a Dominican Catholic school and being both afraid and ashamed to celebrate one's heritage and beliefs." Another charged that those running the school are "intentionally eroding their Catholic heritage. They're trying to be something for everyone and they're making no one happy." The head of the board of trustees dismissed these complaints, saying "people have a hard time with change."[62]

This is the sort of typical, high-handed response from bureaucrats that people who value history and tradition have come to expect. Those who discard longstanding customs in favor of the latest fads usually demean their critics as old-fashioned, out-of-date, uneducated, narrow-minded, and intolerant. But turning churches into bland, preachy, left-leaning therapy centers is also killing them off. For example, Father Dwight Longenecker believes that Catholicism has divided into two churches. One is a "politically correct, essentially humanistic" older liberal elite church that runs much of the official apparatus but has no message and struggles with shrinking congregations. The other is a more vibrant, "lean, energetic and entrepreneurial" grassroots Catholicism made up of "folks who believe in angels and demons, the reality of the spiritual battle, [and] subscribe to traditional views on worship and the sacraments."[63] These are the people who understand that in religion, as in society in general, too many compromises with social trends mean losing your identity, and with that the power to inspire. Awe-inspired worship is replaced by a social-activist self-help program in which the Bible is reduced to a reference book and God is optional.

Courts are responsible for much of God's erasure in the public space. But court rulings are often inconsistent. Their precedents are hard to comprehend, and anyone who claims to be offended essentially has standing to sue. Since the system rewards those who conjure up cases, radical cranks wage endless "lawfare" on expressions of faith. As Justice Thomas wrote in *Perry*, the system "elevates the trivial to the proverbial 'federal case.'" He argued for bringing more order to the system by returning to an interpretation of the First Amendment that the Founders would have recognized. "Every acknowledgment of religion would not give rise to an Establishment Clause claim," he wrote. "Courts would not act as theological commissions, judging the meaning of religious matters. Most important, our precedent would be capable of consistent and coherent application."

A return to the founding principles, shifting questions of religion and politics away from federal courts and back to communities, would do much to correct the balance between the people and the government. And as President Ronald Reagan warned, "if we ever forget that we're one nation under God, then we will be a nation gone under."[64]

SEVEN

UNHAPPY
HOLIDAYS

"We're getting near that beautiful Christmas season that people don't talk about anymore," President Trump said at the 2017 Value Voters Summit. "They don't use the word 'Christmas' because it's not politically correct.... Well guess what? We're saying 'merry Christmas' again."[1] In his 2017 video message to the troops, the president said, "I just want to wish everybody a very, very Merry Christmas. We say Merry Christmas, again, very, very proudly."[2]

Winning the war on Christmas is part of the president's MAGA agenda, but critics say it's a concocted issue. "There is no evidence of an organized attack on Christmas in the United States," sniffs the *New York Times*.[3] Others point out that President Obama also said "Merry Christmas" and that the expression was never officially banned in the White House. The *Washington Post* charges that President Trump has in fact made things worse by transforming "Merry Christmas" into a political statement.

People—mostly liberals—afflicted with what they call "Trump Christmas Brain" are hesitant to use the traditional greeting because it might look like they are siding with the president.[4]

Some critiques are harsher. *The Atlantic* insists that Trump's emphasizing "Merry Christmas" has turned "the holiday into a tool of demagoguery. ... It is an homage to an era when the nation was Christian and any other religion was second-class, and when whiteness meant unquestioned authority."[5] That is, they decode Trump's secret message as "May all your Christmases be *white*." CNN's Don Lemon jumped on the bandwagon, announcing that Trump's Christmas message was "a dog whistle to the base."[6] *Newsweek*'s Cristina Maza, under the bizarre headline "How Trump and the Nazis Stole Christmas to Promote White Nationalism," asserted that "the fight to end the war on Christmas is exclusionary politics at its most flagrant."[7]

Progressives also charge that emphasizing the religious aspects of Christmas encourages Islamophobia, though it isn't really a "phobia" when ISIS says it is out for "Christmas blood."[8] The Bangladeshi immigrant Akayed Ullah, an admirer of the Islamic State, didn't help matters when he attempted to blow himself up in a New York City subway passenger tunnel on December 11, 2017. Ullah said he was triggered—as was his bomb—after seeing a Christmas poster. The detonator on his homemade IED, which fortunately did little damage except to him, used, appropriately enough, a Christmas tree bulb.[9] Later that month, we learned that saying "Merry Christmas" can be hazardous to your health when a Salvation Army bell-ringer was viciously attacked outside a Walmart after offering the traditional greeting.[10]

THE WAR ON CHRISTMAS

The expression "Merry Christmas" was popularized by Charles Dickens's *A Christmas Carol*, first published in the United States in 1844. When the curmudgeonly miser Ebenezer Scrooge finally and sincerely wishes a "Merry Christmas" to his clerk Bob Cratchit, it marks his redemption as a human being. Use of the greeting increased steadily into the mid-twentieth century, declined through the 1960s, and has since rebounded. "Although it's been said many times, many ways," "Merry Christmas" remains the preferred greeting for the season. According to a 2017 CBS poll, 67 percent prefer to say "Merry Christmas" (up from 56 percent in 2005), and 25 percent favor "Happy Holidays" (which has dropped from 41 percent).[11] Almost 90 percent said it was okay to say "Merry Christmas" to spread holiday cheer regardless of their own preference, with a mere 11 percent saying it should definitely be avoided.[12]

"Happy Holidays" initially spread as a way for retailers to be able to greet customers without fear of offending them. The public is about evenly divided on whether this is a good idea, but there are strong partisan differences. Two-thirds of Democrats say stores should use the generic greeting, and two-thirds of Republicans say they should not.[13] Another survey revealed that "Happy Holidays" was actually the more offensive greeting—a third of those polled were bothered by hearing it, as opposed to only 3 percent being irritated by "Merry Christmas."[14] Some respond to "Happy Holidays" with "Merry Christmas" just to make a point.

The Christmas issue has been a conservative rallying point since John Gibson's 2005 book *The War on Christmas: How the Liberal Plot to Ban the Sacred Christian Holiday Is Worse Than You Thought.*[15] There was a time in the seventeenth century when the celebration of Christmas was banned outright; the Puritans objected to its popish roots and believed it led to far too much merry-making. And when German immigrants brought their Christmas tree with them, Americans viewed it suspiciously as a pagan peculiarity. But Christmas observance and American traditions grew in the nineteenth century, especially after the publication in 1823 of the poem "A Visit from St. Nicholas," better known as "The Night Before Christmas." December 25 was established as a federal holiday in 1870, and no serious effort has been made to remove it. Over time Christmas evolved from a purely Christian observance into a national season of festivity. Today, 90 percent of Americans celebrate Christmas. Of those, 46 percent plurality see it as a religious holiday, while one-third view it as only cultural. And a 51 percent majority attend religious services on Christmas Eve or Christmas Day.[16]

Gift-giving is an important part of the season and critical to the American economy. Many small businesses make most of their yearly profits during the holidays, and "Black Friday" and "Cyber Monday" have become part of the cultural landscape. The commercialization of Christmas has led many Christians to caution people to remember "the reason for the season" and prompted nostalgia for the days when the holiday was less about gifts and more about faith.

But every generation since the 1800s has made the same complaint. In Harriet Beecher Stowe's story "Christmas; or, the Good Fairy," the wealthy, jaded young Ellen Stuart notes that Christmas is approaching. She has to "think up presents for everybody" but doesn't know what to get them, since all her friends and family are similarly well-off. Her aunt comments that times were simpler when she was a girl, and "presents did not fly about in those days as they do now." Auntie convinces Ellen that if she really wants to make a difference she should be a "good fairy" and give practical gifts to the less fortunate.[17]

The commercialization of Christmas encouraged the celebration of Hanukkah in America. Many Jews who came to the United States in the late nineteenth and early twentieth centuries saw the exchange of gifts at Christmastime as part of what it meant to be an American. Joining in the Yuletide festivities was a strain on their faith, but there was a handy solution: Hanukkah. A minor, non-religious Jewish holiday, it usually falls around Christmas, affording American Jews a way to join in the gift-giving of the season without compromising their religious identity. Hanukkah grew in significance after the establishment of the state of Israel in 1948, when the struggles of the young Jewish nation gave a new resonance to story of the Maccabean Revolt against Israel's Greek occupiers.[18]

The war on Christmas opened with lawsuits over crèches at city halls, the singing of Christmas carols at schools, and Christmas parties in government offices, all based on the same view of the First Amendment that fueled the Ten Commandments litigation.

Two-thirds of Americans believe that Christian symbols like nativity scenes should be allowed on government property, either alone or combined with other symbols like menorahs. Republicans are somewhat more in favor (79 percent) than Democrats (60 percent), but there is majority support on both sides. Even those unaffiliated with a religion support the displays at 50 percent, and only about a quarter of Americans are completely opposed to them.[19] Nevertheless, many judicial decisions have gone against holiday observances, with some important exceptions. In *Lynch v. Donnelly* (1984), the Supreme Court upheld seasonal display in Pawtucket, Rhode Island, of a Santa Claus house, Christmas tree, and crèche, all under a banner reading "Season's Greetings," finding no "purposeful or surreptitious effort" on the city's part to advocate a particular religious view and ruling that the Constitution "affirmatively mandates accommodation, not merely tolerance of all religions, and forbids hostility toward any."[20]

As with the Ten Commandments monuments, this issue is better left to local governments than to the courts. But sometimes the results of unwarranted judicial interference in community life are surprising. The town of Wadena, Minnesota, had displayed a nativity scene in a public park for more than forty years until the Freedom From Religion Foundation threatened a lawsuit. The city sold its crèche to a group of local ministers who moved it to private property. But townsfolk were upset that they had lost their familiar display and began erecting nativity scenes across Wadena. Soon the nativity scene figures outnumbered the town's six thousand residents. "The whole community has come out to support this," said city councilman Gillette Kempf, who owns a local bookstore. "It's an expression of who we are as a community and what we believe. We believe in the Nativity."[21] The threat of a suit encouraged believers to take action instead of simply leaving the outcome up to the government. It was a very American response.

DECONSTRUCTING THE HOLIDAYS

The Wadena case is typical of the First Amendment-driven challenges to Christmas that have been going on for decades. Recently, however, the assault has become more comprehensive and virulent, no longer based on a (mis)interpretation of the Constitution but driven by identity politics. This has expanded the battleground beyond questions of the use of public property to Christmas traditions in general.

Christmas music is being deconstructed to show its "troubling" origins. Take for example the beloved ditty "Jingle Bells," the first song sung in space thanks to a prank by Gemini VI astronauts in December 1965. But don't enjoy it too much, progressives warn, because it is a "prime example" of nineteenth-century popular music whose "blackface and racist origins have been subtly and systematically removed from its history." The song's composer, Songwriters Hall of Fame member James Lord Pierpont, wrote music for minstrel troupes, as did Stephen Foster and other songwriters of the period. "Jingle Bells" is no innocuous children's tune about a happy sleigh ride, revisionists tell us, but a satire of "black participation in northern winter activities." Never mind that Pierpont's father was a well-known New England abolitionist preacher and Pierpont himself played the organ at his brother's abolitionist-leaning Unitarian church in Savannah, Georgia. The "laughing and singing" celebrated in the song are "a predictable and stereotyped feature to racialize the performance."[22] Thanks, revisionists.

University of Virginia students were induced to take a stand against Irving Berlin's classic "White Christmas," made famous in 1942 by Bing Crosby, and the largest-selling single in history.

As an experiment, Media Research Center reporter Dan Joseph asked UVA students to sign a petition to ban the song, charging that it was "laced with micro-aggression" in that it "'perpetuates the idea that white is naturally good' and ignores 'other kinds of snow,'" while leaving unaddressed the problem of climate change. Many students were willing to sign up to "stop white supremacy in the holiday season."[23] Meanwhile in Britain, University College London tweeted about an impending snowfall, asking students if they were "dreaming of a white campus." The "offensive" tweet sent snowflakes swirling. "You know who else dreamt of a white campus?" one person griped, "Hitler, that's who!" The college retracted the tweet, which drew additional charges of "pandering" and making the situation worse. Parody becomes impossible when sullen progressives are looking for new ways to be offended.[24]

Cultural commentators at the University of Alberta raised objections to a number of holiday tunes. Perry Como's 1951 hit "It's Beginning to Look a Lot Like Christmas" features gender-stereotyped toys, where boys get boots and pistols, and girls get "dolls that will talk and will go for a walk." But "wouldn't it be fun to see Janice and Jen as budding engineers, disassembling the mechanical doll?" Eartha Kitt's mildly racy 1953 hit "Santa Baby" promotes "an exchange of sexuality for material goods," reflecting the backward norms of that era. These days it would be better to "leave some equal pay and reproductive rights under the tree, instead of a sable." And the 1979 novelty tune "Grandma Got Run Over by a Reindeer" by Elmo and Patsy was a product of "the conservative era of Reaganism" and resistance to the "second-wave feminist movement." Grandma, the victim of a hit and run by Santa, "is positioned as someone who gets in the way of male fun and so her death is something to celebrate."[25]

Katherine Timpf of *National Review* jokingly added that Nat King Cole's "The Christmas Song" ("Chestnuts Roasting on an Open Fire)" is a problem because it refers to "folks dressed up like Eskimos." "Winter Wonderland" also has an objectionable Eskimo lyric. The soaring "Do You Hear What I Hear?", a peace anthem written during the Cuban Missile Crisis, is insulting to people with hearing loss who "don't need some ableist song to remind them of that all holiday-season long." And "Santa Claus is Coming to Town" bringing a big bag full of his "white, male and Christian privileges," which makes him totally incapable of judging how people "handle adversity that you know nothing about."[26] But the problem with such satire is that today's goofy joke is tomorrow's strident progressive cause, so it's best not to give them ideas.

Frank Loesser's Academy Award-winning duet "Baby, It's Cold Outside" has faced persistent criticism for its alleged narration of date rape. In fact, it reflects courtship rituals of the 1940s, when a degree of coyness was expected before things got more serious. In the hookup culture version of the song the two would naturally already have had sex, so the lyric would be "I really can't stay" / "I'll get you a Lyft outside." The song is rightly infamous, however, for its link to radical Islamic terrorism. "Baby, It's Cold Outside" was playing in 1949 at a church dance in Greeley, Colorado, where an Egyptian student, Sayyid Qutb, was stunned watching the dancers in dimmed light as "arms circled waists, lips met lips, chests met chests, and the atmosphere was full of passion."[27] It sounds like a fun time, but this was the moment of Qutb's epiphany that decadent Western culture had to be destroyed, and upon returning to Egypt he launched the modern radical Islamic movement. Qutb's younger brother, Mohammed, lectured on his Sayyid's advocacy of violent jihad at King Abdul-Aziz University, where one of the students present was Osama bin Laden. But none of what followed was Frank Loesser's fault.

Christmas movies are also under fire. CNN's Carol Costello denounced the uplifting holiday staple *It's a Wonderful Life* for its supposed sexist content, because in the bleak alternative world with no George Bailey, Mary Hatch is a librarian instead of Mrs. George Bailey. "But seriously," Costello asks, "if gorgeous, brilliant Mary had never met her George Bailey, would she have ended up working in a library?"[28] Granted, if the movie had been all about women's empowerment, maybe Mary would have become a doctor, lawyer, or cable TV news anchor. But since the point of the film was that George Bailey had improved the lives of everyone he met in ways he didn't realize, it would not have made sense for Mary—the person closest to him—to be the only character to benefit from George never having been born. Nor does Ms. Costello explain why she thinks working in a library is particularly demeaning, or if she thought it was a less-than-wonderful life for Mary to be the mother of a stable, happy family. And it's worth noting that Mary helps save the day, so she wasn't a helpless bystander.

It's not just old-timey Christmas movies that progressives object to. Any flick that uses the holiday season as a framework to promote American values is likely to be found intolerable. *Slate* denounced the Hallmark Channel's "Countdown to Christmas" weekend movies as "42 hours of sugary, sexist, preposterously plotted, plot hole-festooned, belligerently traditional, ecstatically Caucasian cheer." All the Hallmark movies, sneers the reviewer, "depict a fantasy world in which America has been Made Great Again.... They brim with white heterosexuals who exclusively, emphatically, and endlessly bellow 'Merry Christmas' to every lumberjack and labradoodle they pass." And naturally all this harmless, holiday-themed escapism is the president's fault: "The Christmas-down-your-throat bombast, holly-jolly sexism, the characters' zaniness and unyielding impulsiveness—it's all very Trumpian behavior."[29]

But maybe that is why it is so popular. "Countdown to Christmas" attracted 17.6 million viewers in 2017, up 16 percent from the previous year. Hallmark's overall network ratings for 2017 were up 15 percent. The presentation of *The Christmas Train* had higher ratings than competing programs on the four broadcast networks. And in November, when the countdown began, Hallmark was "the most-watched cable network among 18- to 49-year-old and 25- to 54-year-old women."[30] Hallmark has produced 136 Christmas movies since 2008, and the franchise is a resounding success. And one of the movies, *The Twelve Trees of Christmas*, is about how a Manhattan librarian saves her local branch from demolition by a roguishly charming New York real estate developer. Maybe that's a librarian even the dour Carol Costello can take seriously.

YOU'RE A RACIST, MR. GRINCH

Kids' Christmas shows are also under attack. A CBS News poll found that America's favorite animated holiday specials are

Rudolph the Red-Nosed Reindeer, A Charlie Brown Christmas, How the Grinch Stole Christmas, and *Frosty the Snowman*.[31] The four programs emerged from a golden age of network television programming, 1964–1969, and viewing them has become a cherished American family tradition. Predictably, all four fail the PC test.

Rudolph the Red-Nosed Reindeer started as a Montgomery Ward giveaway children's book, then a number-one pop single by Gene Autry in December 1949. The author, Robert L. May, likened his story to "The Ugly Duckling," since Rudolph's nose is a source of his sadness and his redemption.[32] The sociologist James Barnett, author of a major mid-century study on how Americans celebrate Christmas, said it was the "only original addition to the folklore of Santa Claus in the century."[33] The Rankin/Bass stop-motion "Animagic" version of the story premiered in 1964 on NBC, pre-empting an evening episode of *Meet the Press*. A review of the TV special likened the Rudolph story to "the American dream of success—be good, be able, and you'll get a break and succeed."[34] It is also the story of Rudolph's overcoming his self-doubts about being different and Santa's and the other reindeer's finally recognizing the value of his uniqueness—as well as that of the other "misfits" Rudolph encounters along the way.

But the progressive take on *Rudolph*—as reflected in a flurry of tweets after the show's annual airing in 2017—is that it's "a parable on racism & homophobia w/ Santa as a bigoted exploitative prick." Santa's operation at the North Pole is "an HR nightmare and in serious need of diversity and inclusion training." The other reindeer are mostly jerks. Even the vindication at the end is offensive because Rudolph is valued only because he can be exploited in Santa's twisted gift-giving enterprise. In the progressive universe, *Rudolph* will go down in history as "the story of a xenophobic elf who bullies a reindeer and a transient prospector who commits attempted murder against a recently-tortured" abominable snowman.[35]

A Charlie Brown Christmas, which first aired on CBS in 1965, is a classic "true meaning of Christmas" movie that touches on commercialism, peer pressure, and faith, the latter being the source of controversy. In the show's most memorable scene, Linus takes center stage ("Lights, please") and recites the Gospel of Luke's narrative of the birth of Jesus, explaining, "That's what Christmas is all about, Charlie Brown." Charles Schulz put the soliloquy in the script, and his skeptical partner, the animator William Melendez, said, "There's never been any animation that I know of from the Bible. It's kind of risky." Schulz replied, "Well, if we don't do it, who will?"[36]

Charlie Brown's sad little tree was a parable for the special itself. Few thought the final product would amount to much. Neil Reagan, the brother of Ronald Reagan and the creative director of the McCann Erickson advertising agency—representing the sponsor, Coca-Cola—previewed the cartoon. He was not impressed. CBS executives thought the final product was a disaster, but they had already pre-empted *The Munsters*, and it was too late to change the schedule. Even the production team had their doubts. "We thought that it was maybe just too slow and we had failed poor Charlie Brown," said Lee Mendelson, the producer. "I remember one of the animators, Ed Levitt, stood up in the back and said, 'You guys are crazy, this is going to run a hundred years.'"[37] When the show aired, it attracted around half the people watching TV that night, an impossible feat these days. The Peanuts special won Emmy and Peabody awards, and Vince Guaraldi's jazzy soundtrack became an overnight sensation.[38]

Mendelson later called Linus's soliloquy "the most magical two minutes in all of TV animation."[39] Yet not everyone is comfortable with it. In 2015, an eastern Kentucky school cut the passage out of a live performance of the show. Audience members then spontaneously filled in the missing parts. The incident prompted Kentucky legislators to sponsor a bipartisan bill that spelled out students' rights to express religious beliefs in school and to have artistic and theatrical programs that further the understanding of cultural or religious heritage. It also clarified that the Bible could be used for the study of history and literature, but not for religious instruction.[40] Another test came when a middle school in Killeen, Texas, took down a nurse's aid's Christmas poster featuring Linus and a quotation from his soliloquy. A state court intervened and the poster was restored, with the proviso that it specify that it was "Ms. Shannon's Christmas Message."[41]

How the Grinch Stole Christmas is another "true meaning of Christmas" parable, in which the mountain-dwelling cynic undergoes a conversion through the example of the pure-of-heart Whos. Based on the 1957 book by Dr. Seuss (Theodore Geisel), the television special premiered on CBS in 1966. Like *A Charlie Brown Christmas*, it promotes an appreciation of the spiritual basis of the holidays.

It took a while for anyone to recognize the viciously racist subtext of Dr. Seuss's tale, but the film scholar Brady Hammond eventually discovered it. The character of the Grinch is an example of "greenface," a substitute for "blackface" that conveys the same nefarious racial messaging. Green-skinned characters "are presented as fantasy creatures" but actually "are proxies for black American stereotypes." The "redemption of the Grinch ultimately reinforces the racism of the film" because "it is not Whoville that changes to become more inclusive." Rather, "the Grinch decides that the whos of Whoville are indeed superior and it was him [sic] who was in the wrong." The Grinch is thus transformed into an Uncle Tom.[42] And we might as well tie in the narrator, Boris Karloff, most famous for his role in the 1931 horror feature *Frankenstein*, a monster often portrayed as green, and an infinitely flexible metaphor historically seen as both a comment on racism as well as racist itself.[43]

It's hard to understand the point of this critique. After all, the Grinch *was* in the wrong, wasn't he? And weren't the Whos genuinely forgiving and inclusive? Is there a more preferred politically correct ending other than the Grinch being honored at a feast? This resonates with the current left-wing critique of Theodore Geisel's work that was highlighted when Cambridge, Massachusetts, school librarian (Carol Costello take note) Liz Phipps Soeiro rejected a donation of ten Dr. Seuss books from First Lady Melania Trump. "Dr. Seuss's illustrations are steeped in racist propaganda, caricatures, and harmful stereotypes," Ms. Soeiro huffed.[44] But no one objected when First Lady Michelle Obama read Dr. Seuss's *Oh, The Things You Can Do That Are Good for You!* to school children, joined by the Cat in the Hat and Thing One and Thing Two.[45] And Ms. Soeiro herself had dressed up as the Cat in the Hat (though not in "catface") and tweeted out "Happy Birthday Dr. Seuss! K and 1 celebrated with a green egg breakfast!"[46] The National Education Association selected Theodore Geisel's birthday, March 2, for Read Across America Day, but this was before Trump derangement hit the Left, so what was laudable for Mrs. Obama was unconscionable coming from Mrs. Trump. It is a shame that the beloved Dr. Seuss has been targeted by the Orwellian Left for erasure. As David Burge observed on Twitter, "It was a surprisingly short journey from Robert E. Lee to Dr. Seuss."[47]

Christmas is being erased altogether these days in the name of "inclusiveness." The thinking goes that in increasingly diverse communities, openly celebrating Christmas is exclusionary because those who are not Christian will feel unwelcome or offended. The solution is to homogenize holidays and observances, reducing them to the lowest common denominator. Saying "Happy Holidays" is one example of this, but the concept has mushroomed uncontrollably in recent years.

This was the logic behind guidelines at the University of California, Irvine for "planning inclusive celebrations." The Office of Equal Opportunity and Diversity counseled that university departments and administrators should be "inclusive and sensitive" to "cultural and religious practices and celebrations," and that one way to do this is to completely eliminate all mention of them. For example, "focus on celebrating a special occasion, instead of a specific holiday. Consider having a 'Year-End Celebration' or celebrating seasonal themes such as Fall, Winter, or Spring." "Display diverse symbols representing a variety of faith traditions along with secular ones." And "ensure that office celebrations are not indirectly celebrating religious holidays." Yet the same guidance provided a helpful link to the "The Official Kwanzaa Website"—the only holiday the office promoted—because omitting it would apparently not be inclusive.[48]

The University of Tennessee's Office for Diversity and Inclusion issued a similar set of guidelines, titled "Best Practices for Inclusive Holiday Celebrations in the Workplace." The guidance warned, "ensure your holiday party is not a Christmas party in disguise." Decorations, food, and refreshments should "not be specific to any religion or culture." And of course, keep "Secret Santa" under wraps, and dreidel is strictly *verboten*. (Ironically, dreidel originated with Jews in Maccabean times illegally studying the Torah when the Greek occupiers were promoting their version of diversity and inclusion by wiping out Judaism.) The UT guidelines were so offensive that some of Tennessee's congressmen called for Chancellor Jimmy Cheek's resignation, even though he had nothing to do with the incident. Congressman John Duncan, a UT alumnus, denounced the "extremism" of those behind the idea, saying "the people on the far left who claim to be tolerant seem to be tolerant of everything except traditional Christianity."[49] The guidelines were quietly withdrawn.

Ole Miss, which used to hold a tree-lighting ceremony called "A Grand Ole Christmas," replaced that tradition with "Hotty Toddy Holidays." One presumes from the name that now it's the students getting lit. One administrator explained that the traditional name "connoted too much Christianity on campus," which of course it would since the event is a Christmas tree lighting. But like UC-Irvine and UT, Ole Miss wanted to have a more "inclusive" environment, so "Grand Ole Christmas" had to go.[50]

There are many other examples. The University of Minnesota's College of Food, Agricultural, and Natural Resource Sciences noted that "decorations, music, and food should be general and not specific to any one religion" during "neutral-themed" celebrations. Even "bows/wrapped gifts" are "not appropriate for gatherings and displays at this time of year." Actually, Christmas is the time of year when they're most appropriate.[51] The University of Maine banned "xmas trees, wreaths, xmas presents, menorahs, candy canes, etc.," on campus, but permitted "winter themes, snowmen, plain trees without presents underneath, decorative lights but not on trees, [and] snowflakes." The purported purpose of the ban, absurdly enough, was to make everyone "feel included and welcome on campus."[52] Missouri State cast the net even wider, cautioning against displays any time of year featuring crosses, nativity scenes, menorahs, stars of David, the Bible, the Koran, drawings of Jesus, or images of Mohammed (which would be doubly problematic). Santa Claus, however, somehow flew by the censors.[53]

In the Bethel School District in Oregon, Christmas has vanished, Halloween costumes are banned, Thanksgiving parties have become "harvest parties," and Valentine's Day has turned into "buddy day," with no exchanges of cards or candies allowed. The school board maintained that this is needed so that all students can participate in all celebrations. Middle School student Kayla Green was more sensible than the school board when she said, "changing the name of the holidays doesn't change the holiday, it just changes how people talk about it." She noted that no matter what the school board mandates, "Valentine's Day is still Valentine's Day; Christmas is still

Christmas. This is American culture, and those are American holidays.... Pretending it's something else doesn't change it."[54] In the city of Bloomington, Indiana, Good Friday and Columbus Day are now "Spring holiday" and "Fall holiday." Mayor John Hamilton declared that he was "proud of our diverse workforce at the city" and that the stripping our country's holidays of their meaning is "another way we can demonstrate our commitment to inclusivity."[55]

Of course, promoting diversity by eliminating it can be just as insensitive. Maryland's Montgomery County School District sought to be "inclusive" by changing the names of all religiously-based holidays to generic equivalents, in part out of concerns they might offend Muslims in the community. But the growing Muslim cohort simply wanted holidays like Eid al-Fitr and Eid al-Adha—which were already automatic excused absences for Muslims, as Rosh Hashana and Yom Kippur are for Jewish students—recognized on the school calendar alongside other holidays. One Muslim parent, Zainab Choudry, observed that "they would remove the Christian holidays and they would remove the Jewish holidays from the calendar before they would consider adding the Muslim holiday," making it look less like "promoting inclusion" and more like stamping out Eid.[56]

Some communities have pushed back against the homogenization drive. Some years ago, Roselle Park, New Jersey, had given in to political correctness and changed its town Christmas tree to a "holiday tree." But in 2015, the town council voted to change it back. Liberal councilwoman Charlene Storey initially resigned in a huff, saying she could not "in good conscience continue to be part of a council that is exclusionary or to work with a mayor who is such." She later rescinded the resignation and was made chairman of a new "diversity committee." Democratic Mayor Carl Hokanson, who spearheaded the renaming, said "people are offended that we use the word Christmas. Well, I feel offended when you tell me 'holiday.'"[57]

THE SPIRIT OF THE SEASON

The elimination of holidays by faceless bureaucrats in the name of diversity and inclusion is self-evidently absurd. Religious holidays—whether Christmas, Hanukkah, Eid, Diwali, or others—are important and meaningful for those who observe them and should not be considered offensive to those who do not. Chad Felix Greene, who is Jewish, writes of being insulted when an older coworker gave him a personalized Christmas card. He even complained to human resources about the "offense." But the next year the same woman gave him another card and said, "I hope you have a lovely holiday." He felt a pang of guilt at his past behavior, and over time realized that taking offense where none was intended was a matter of choice—and it was the wrong one. "Despite my cold and bitter temperament," he writes, "she tried to warm my heart with a small and simple gift every single year she had the opportunity to do so."

"It is so easy to be offended," Greene continues, "so easy to feel hostility and suspicion." He writes that "victimhood is attractive because it gives people permission to be judgmental without consequence and feel superior in doing so." The judgmental ones have "a sense of being special, enlightened, and above it all. But this merely traps people in a cycle of bitterness and loneliness as they fight the urge to simply enjoy the holiday season with every-one else." And these days he finds himself "loving Christmas and the cheer, colors, sounds, and small acts of kindness surround-ing" him, not because he is less Jewish, but because he has dropped his "heavy cloaks of victimhood" and concluded that "kindness matters."[58]

Americans have a right to celebrate holidays in whatever manner they wish and not to be shamed and bullied by the PC police. People are only driven further apart by being forced to walk on eggshells out of fear that someone will take offense at their innocent, heartfelt expressions of good cheer. This is the point President Trump is making by saying "Merry Christ-mas"—that despite what progressive censors say, it is okay to use this traditional greeting. People should say Merry Christmas—or Happy Hanukkah, Happy Diwali, Eid Mubarak, or any other holiday greeting proudly and happily and hope people will take it in the festive spirit in which it is offered. Americans can be joyful for each other. And they should leave it to the cynical progressive Scrooges to grumble about the "idiots" saying Merry Christmas who should be "boiled in their own pudding and buried with a stake of holly through their heart."

EIGHT

DON'T KNOW MUCH ABOUT HISTORY

*It might very well be that literally every word in the
history books, even the things that one accepted
without question, was pure fantasy.*
—George Orwell, *1984*

In Ronald Reagan's farewell address to the nation as president, he noted "the resurgence of national pride" in the country since the strife-torn 1960s and pessimistic 1970s. "This national feeling is good," he said, "but it won't count for much, and it won't last unless it's grounded in thoughtfulness and knowledge." Reagan said what the country needs is "an informed patriotism" and questioned whether "we [are] doing a good enough job teaching our children what America is and what she represents in the long history of the world." The Gipper noted that those who had come of age in previous decades "grew up in a different America. We were taught, very directly, what it means to be an American. And we absorbed, almost in the air, a love of country and an appreciation of its institutions." National pride was learned from the family, from neighbors, in schools, even in the popular culture, which "celebrated democratic values and implicitly reinforced the idea that America was special."

But by the late 1980s things had changed. "Younger parents aren't sure that an unambivalent appreciation of America is the right thing to teach modern children," Reagan said. "And as for those who create the popular culture, well-grounded patriotism is no longer the style." The American spirit was back, but it had not been re-institutionalized. Reagan believed it was important to get back to "some basics: more attention to American history and a greater emphasis on civic ritual." He warned that lacking this, we faced "an eradication of the American memory that could result, ultimately, in an erosion of the American spirit."[1]

Since Reagan left office with that warning, things have gotten worse. The eradication of American memory is well underway. The arbiters of popular culture have moved from ambivalence about patriotism to outright hostility. Civic ritual is under attack. And the spirit of America is no longer in the air but has gone underground.

It is important to know and understand American history, but many people don't see it as practical. In a 2013 Gallup poll on the most valuable fields of study, history came in fourth behind math, English, and science, with 8 percent. This middling ranking held across lines of sex, ideology, and education. But history outranked economics, social studies, and art and theater.[2] Many people are apparently over-confident in their knowledge of history. In a study by the American Revolution Center in Philadelphia, "89 percent believed they could pass a basic test on the American Revolution." But when actually tested on "the beliefs, freedoms, and liberties established during the Revolution," 83 percent failed.

The vast majority still agreed that "knowledge of the history and principles of the American Revolution is very important" and should be taught in schools.[3] If only it were.

TEACHING ABOUT AMERICA

American education has traditionally had a civic purpose. Schooling has been seen as necessary for the development not only of a well-rounded person but also of a strong society. Education is a pathway for people from every walk of life to live even better. An educated, informed electorate is fundamental to the health of the Republic. And there has always been a public benefit from inculcating American values. As Thomas Jefferson noted, "if a nation expects to be both ignorant and free in a state of civilization, it expects what never was and never will be."[4] He saw to it that the Northwest Ordinance of 1787 provided that "religion, morality, and knowledge, being necessary to good government and the happiness of mankind, schools and the means of education shall forever be encouraged" in the new western territories.

This view of education as a means of inculcating not only knowledge but also moral rightness, good living, and American values, held sway in this country for most of its history. However imperfectly the ideal was realized in the nation's schools at different times and in different places, the notion that educating the nation's children was "necessary to good government and the happiness of mankind" was never in question. And the education system was also a way for immigrants and their children to be introduced to the history and norms of the American experiment.

The traditional mission of schools was to teach basic skills, inculcate good citizenship, and prepare young men and women to be productive members of society.

Most states require some form of education in civics and history for elementary and high school students, but these requirements are not always met, and even when civics is taught, students do not all benefit equally. The 2014 National Assessment of Educational Progress survey of eighth-graders shows broad improvement since the 1990s in knowledge of American history. Overall, 18 percent of students scored above the proficient level, with 53 percent at basic level and 29 percent below basic. Achievement levels in civics education were similar to those in American history.[5] As in many other subjects, white and Asian children and those in higher-income areas do better on average than low-income and minority children. Some states are moving to require students to pass the same test given to immigrants seeking American citizenship before they can receive a high school diploma.[6] In higher education, history and civics get far less attention. Only 18 percent of colleges and universities require a course in American history or government.[7]

What should be taught in American history classes has been hotly debated since the 1990s, when revisionist curricula began to push out traditional, more patriotic courses. "Today's students can readily identify Sacajawea and Harriet Tubman but often can barely discuss Washington or Jefferson—except as slave owners," one national curriculum review noted. "The once well-known story of the growth and expansion of American democracy and human rights is barely perceptible in many state standards and curricula."[8] The famous historian Arthur M. Schlesinger Jr., an unabashed liberal, warned that the progressive push for more "inclusion" in the study of American history was "promoting the 'balkanization' of America by legitimizing divisive identity politics over the 'melting pot' metaphor."[9] In *The Disuniting of America*, Schlesinger argued that the country's traditional goal was "not to preserve old [foreign] cultures, but to forge a new American culture."[10]

A report published by the Thomas B. Fordham Institute illustrates the influence of diversity-centered education in the debate over what to teach kids about the terrorist attacks of September 11, 2001. The attacks provided an opportunity to focus on such questions as why the terrorists hate freedom, why they targeted the United States, and "how our forebears responded to previous attacks upon their country in particular and freedom in general."[11] Instead, teachers were more interested in discussing value-relativism and the possibility that Al-Qaeda had legitimate grievances against the "imperialistic" United States. The National Education Association's "Remember Sept. 11" lesson plans for 2002 asked teachers not to "purposely or inadvertently take one side over another" and suggested discussing "historical instances of American intolerance" such as the internment of Japanese Americans during World War II.[12] Any reasonably open discussion about the threat of radical Islamist ideology (as distinct from the Muslim faith) was impossible because of the risk of falsely being labeled a bigot.

THE COSMOPOLITAN AGENDA AND COMMON CORE

American history seems to be losing its national purpose altogether. A panel at the annual meeting of the Organization of

American Historians in 2014 discussed the "cosmopolitan" agenda in history, which would transcend the national framework and present the country in a much different context. Jane Kamensky of Brandeis University said American history needs to be "rescued from not only the national but from the nationalist framework." She recommends contextualizing the story as indigenous people's "freedom struggles against imperial masters." Other panelists said that the future study of "what used to be called the United States" should focus more on issues such as imperialism, "global, gendered analysis," "entanglement with the planet, people, and nations," and transcending the idea of "American history."[13]

The framework for post-American history was set in 2000 with the OAH's *La Pietra Report*, recommending an effort to "connect American history more strongly to historical themes that are not exclusively American." The authors believe the history of the country should be rewritten to "incorporate an awareness of larger, transnational contexts, processes, and identities." The aim is not to "have United States history thus erased," they write, but "to deepen its contextualization and to extend the transnational relations of American history."[14]

This approach ties into the Common Core objective of making American students into "competent global citizens." The Common Core Initiative, which was instituted in 2009, began as an effort to establish minimum state education standards but soon became a wedge for the federal government to take control of curricula, textbooks, and testing, promoting a decidedly liberal agenda. A Project Veritas undercover interview with Kim Koerber, a former marketing executive for leading textbook publisher

Pearson Education, confirmed the suspicions about Common Core. Ms. Koerber said that the reason for pushback against the program was that "there's a bunch of Republican people, conservatives that don't like being told what to do by people they don't agree with." When the AP U.S. History agenda was set, she noted, "Texas got upset about it" because "they wanted [the] Founders in it, they wanted to pound the Founders into it," she said, pounding her hand for emphasis. "And it's like—come on, the dead white guys did not create this country."[15] Continually changing textbooks happens to be a bonus for publishers, who have a government-mandated market. "The textbooks have to change, and the school district has to adopt the new ones," Ms. Koerber said, "that's profitable."

Not all educators want to remove America from American history. Some historians recognize the necessity of nurturing the civic myths that bind the country, which is especially important with immigration at record levels. Robert Paquette of the Alexander Hamilton Institute for the Study of Western Civilization warns that "the United States cannot survive as a nation if the traditions and principles that made it cohere as a prosperous and distinctive country are distorted and marginalized."[16] Professor Paquette echoes Ronald Reagan's warning that "we've got to teach history based not on what's in fashion but what's important," like the country's founding and our national achievements. "If we forget what we did," Reagan said, "we won't know who we are."[17]

Progressives counter that what we did was evil, and who we are is not worth knowing. Yet tearing down traditional history and civics education leaves kids lacking basic knowledge of

American identity and confused about what Americanism means. An education system that no longer teaches or values the fundamentals and scorns the past strikes at the heart of American character and pride. If young people are taught only that America's history is one of exploitation, slavery, imperialism, racism, and other bad things, why would they care about a country founded on these evils?

In some cases, the hostility to expressing a positive view of the country verges on violence. When New York Public School 90 pulled the song "God Bless the USA" from a graduation ceremony, Republican Congressman Robert L. Turner organized a group of kids to sing it in front of the school. Angry adults showed up to heckle and bully the kids and organizers, shouting, "You all burn in hell! Shame on you! Shame on you!" and "You Republicans go to a Republican area and do that. We don't do that here!"[18]

THE WAR ON AMERICAN VALUES

It is not only the facts of history and their meaning that are under siege but fundamental American values as well. For example, the 1992 Democratic platform hailed "the basic American values that built this country and will always make it great: personal responsibility, individual liberty, tolerance, faith, family and hard work."[19] But by 2016 "personal responsibility" and "individual liberty" were written out of the Democratic platform, and the only "hard work" it hailed was Barack Obama's.

This was not an incidental oversight. Those who move in progressive circles and espouse traditional values are the target of vitriol, as Professor Amy Wax of the University of Pennsylvania Law School and Professor Larry Alexander of the University of San Diego School of Law learned in August 2017 when they penned a thoughtful essay on the "breakdown of the country's bourgeois culture." They noted that in the mid-twentieth century the cultural script reinforced a variety of traditional norms. "Get married before you have children and strive to stay married for their sake," they wrote. "Get the education you need for gainful employment, work hard, and avoid idleness. Go the extra mile for your employer or client. Be a patriot, ready to serve the country. Be neighborly, civic-minded, and charitable. Avoid coarse language in public. Be respectful of authority. Eschew substance abuse and crime." And even though society was not perfect, adherence to these norms made it better.

But in the 1960s, Wax and Alexander argued, a variety of factors "encouraged an antiauthoritarian, adolescent, wish-fulfillment ideal—sex, drugs, and rock-and-roll—that was unworthy of, and unworkable for, a mature, prosperous adult society." At the same time, blame-centered identity politics gave rise to a political and social "obsession with race, ethnicity, gender, and now sexual preference." And as these countercultural views progressed, "particularly among the chattering classes—academics, writers, artists, actors, and journalists—who relished liberation from conventional constraints," the idea of "condemning America and reviewing its crimes" became a "class marker of virtue and sophistication." The result has been increasing poverty and violence, dysfunctional single-parent families, drug abuse, and anti-assimilation views among ethnic groups. The cure, wrote Wax and Alexander, is for cultural arbiters to drop the "multicultural grievance polemics and the preening pretense of defending the downtrodden" and "return to the 1950s posture of celebrating" the traditional values that made America great.[20]

The professors had attacked too many sacred cows, and now they were gored. The Penn graduate student union GET-UP quickly denounced the "presence of toxic racist, sexist, homophobic attitudes on campus," even though the article had nothing to do with race, sex, or preference. "The kind of hate Wax espouses is an everyday part of many students' lives at Penn," GET-UP continued, "and we can and must fight against it." In an interview with the *Daily Pennsylvanian*, Professor Wax emphasized rightly that "bourgeois values aren't just for white people" and can help anyone succeed.[21] And of course, it is ridiculous to assert that Penn or any U.S. college is a hotbed of everyday hatred, unless you are a conservative. The most risky, punk thing any U.S. college student could do is walk across campus wearing a red "Make America Great Again" cap.

A Penn graduate student group called the IDEAL Council wrote a mind-numbing screed accusing Professor Wax of racism, homophobia, moral panic, white supremacy, eugenicism, and "queerphobic rhetoric," none of which was in her article. They demanded that the university impose new restrictions on speech, allow anonymous (and unprovable) grievances to be filed against professors, and establish a "Diversity & Inclusion office" that would provide "resources for students experiencing marginalized [sic] or discrimination at Penn."[22] (This kind of moral outrage always turns into a shakedown.)

Not to be outdone, five virtue-signaling Penn law professors published a commentary in the school paper arguing that endorsing traditional middle-class values is like a "defense of Confederate statues that ignores their promotion of white supremacy," and warning that "assertions of white cultural superiority have devastating consequences."[23] But the only consequences the article promoted were peace, stability, and prosperity. What these critics failed to do was address the case for bourgeois values on its merits, because it is difficult to argue against hard work, civility, personal responsibility, and having a good education.

The very foundations of knowledge are on the outs in some academic circles. A Syracuse University philosopher tells us that reason is a "white male Euro-Christian construction," which is somehow related to a "grotesque ideological exaggeration of freedom over equality" and by some means ultimately leads to the "trigger-happy practices of the police...on the streets of black America."[24] An article in the *Daily Iowan* explores "cognitive privilege," which is like white privilege for smart people. In this construct "the accident of having been born smart enough to be able to be successful is a great benefit that you did absolutely nothing to earn"—shades of Barack Obama saying "if you've got a business, you didn't build that." The *Iowan* article says intelligent people "have nothing to be proud of for being smart," a message that can do incalculable harm to efforts to promote student self-esteem through education.[25]

The *Journal of Urban Mathematics Education* tells us that meritocracy in math "functions as a tool of whiteness" because it "ignores systemic barriers and institutional structures that prevent opportunity and success."[26] And two progressive mathematics groups say that math education is "grounded in a legacy of institutional discrimination based on race, ethnicity, class, and gender."[27] It is hard to see how "math is racist" adds up to anything good for minorities, but these notions do bring to mind George Orwell's contention that "Freedom is the freedom to say that two plus two makes four. If that is granted, all else follows." Denying this truth simply multiplies our divisions.

Real-world application of these notions could have disastrous consequences. The head of Purdue University's engineering program, Donna Riley, argues that academic rigor is really all about "white male heterosexual privilege." She believes rigor has undeniable "sexual connotations" of "hardness, stiffness, and erectness," and reveals how "structural forces of power and privilege operate to exclude" all who don't fit the white patriarchal mold. Not only that, but "scientific knowledge itself is gendered, raced, and colonizing," and we need to do "away with [rigor] altogether so we can welcome other ways of knowing. Other ways of being. It is about criticality and reflexivity."[28] All of which prompted Roger Kimball of the *New Criterion* to caution, don't hire a Purdue engineer to build your bridge.

THE NEW SEGREGATION

To the progressives, reason, rigor, effort, personal responsibility, and other products of "white patriarchy" are definitely out of favor. Diversity is in. Diversity-mania was supercharged by the five-to-four Supreme Court decision in *Grutter v. Bollinger* (2003) upholding the University of Michigan Law School's affirmative action admissions policies based on a "compelling interest" in "promoting diversity." Such policies, common at many schools, were an attempt to get around the Supreme Court's earlier decision in *Regents of the University of California v. Bakke*, which struck down racial quotas as unconstitutional discrimination. Armed with their new compelling-interest exemption, academic administrators began branding admissions, hiring, promotion, on-campus activities, budgeting, and anything else they could wedge in as "promoting diversity."

The push for diversity in schools, in universities, and in society in general has seriously weakened our national unity. Diversity *by definition* requires focusing on differences, whether of race, sex, sexual orientation, or a multitude of other categories. It is therefore inherently divisive. And the diversity support system rewards those who exacerbate the differences and reinforce the divisions on which their favored status depends. This has led to some very un-American outcomes.

Owen Rickert tells how a focus on diversity broke the sense of community at the Blake School, a private college prep school in Hopkins, Minnesota. The student body was already a diverse group. "White. Black. Asian. Gay. Straight," Rickert said. "It never mattered before." Students accepted each other for who they were—not, one might say, for the color of their skin but the content of their character. He was excited to go to school. He had been attending Blake since kindergarten and got along with everyone. "It felt like one great accepting and unifying community," Rickert said. "No one had to teach us that, it just happened."

This sense of unity began to break down when he was in the ninth grade. The school instituted diversity-focused programming that sought not to celebrate community but to reinforce differences. The focus on "diversity" led to "classification and resentment that did not exist in us before."

Mandatory diversity lectures and similar events destroyed the organic sense of community at Blake and replaced it with division, suspicion, and blame. "All of a sudden the suggestion is put in front of every white person in this school that racism is inherent in them because of the color of their skin," Rickert said. "White privilege equates to shut-up; anything you say has no meaning because you are privileged." Education turned into indoctrination, and those who might have objected stayed silent for fear of "being seen as an enemy." And none of this divisive programming had anything to do with preparing students for college or making them productive members of society. The school Rickert had loved decayed to the point where he simply wanted to graduate and get out. He moved on to the University of Wisconsin, well prepared for the diversity-centered indoctrination he no doubt has encountered there as well.[29]

The old ideals of integration and assimilation are falling by the wayside. In the 1990s at the University of Tennessee at Chattanooga, white and black fraternities and sororities came together to participate in the African American tradition of step-dancing. Stepping is a form of dance with African roots that has long been a means of bonding and celebration of African American culture. The StepDown event at UTC grew into a major campus celebration and brought together white and black kids who might not otherwise have mingled.

But as the event grew and included not only stepping but other kinds of dancing, black students thought the original meaning was being lost. Tensions at the campus also ran high in 2016 when a white student and her friends wrote "Make America Great Again" and "Build That Wall" in chalk on a campus sidewalk. Their legitimate expression sparked outrage among some campus groups, leading to town hall meetings and other forms of collegiate group therapy. The startled student later explained that "she came from a small town and didn't understand how supporting Trump might be offensive." In any case, her sentiments were hardly outside the mainstream, as Donald Trump carried Tennessee by a 26 percent margin.[30]

Such were the circumstances under which UTC's black Greeks decided to reclaim their tradition from white "cultural appropriation" by withdrawing to step separately. UTC eventually canceled StepDown altogether, and the white Greeks replaced it with a lip-syncing event. The rise and fall of StepDown reflects America's transition from promoting unity to fostering division and segregation. The white kids at UTC could have stuck to Tennessee square dancing in the first place, though progressive scholars tell us that style of dance was part of a plot by Henry Ford to counter the popularity of jazz, and was originally appropriated from slaves anyway.[31]

These days segregation in the name of diversity is all the rage. The University of San Francisco has a blacks-only student orientation. An Evergreen State student publication has a "no whites allowed" opinion section, "a place where we can be us without it being overshadowed by the dark cloud that is living under white supremacy and having to see things from a white perspective."[32] Harvard University hosted a student-organized black-only commencement ceremony. Schools hold no-white retreats, establish no-white safe spaces, and use other segregationist methods Bull Connor would have approved of.

"Whiteness" is treated like some kind of disease. Stanford University is offering a course on "White Identity Politics" in which students "survey the field of whiteness studies" and look at political approaches, "including abolishing whiteness or coming to terms with white identity."[33] A University of Iowa education professor seeks to "dismantle whiteness" in her "curriculum, assignments and pedagogy."[34] Columbia University's Teachers College held a "Reimagining Education Summer Institute" conference featuring panels on "Whiteness in schools," "3 ways to face white privilege in the classroom," and "Deconstructing Racial Microaggressions."[35] Some students react to hostile hyper-identity on campus by withdrawing, simply not wanting to deal with it. But then they are accused of perpetrating the "invisibility microaggression." If on the other hand white students complain about being unfairly targeted in this dehumanizing environment, they are accused of "white fragility."

DIVERSITY DESPOTISM

The pursuit of diversity on campus has never included diversity of ideas. Quite the opposite. "Diversity" refers only to aspects of identity like skin color, sex, and choice of sexual partners. When it comes to ideas and belief systems—which in fact are more important facets of a person's identity—the rule is, the less diversity the better.

"Universities in the liberal arts were supposed to embody the best knowledge and ethics of the Western tradition and faithfully transmit them to the next generation," Professor Abraham H. Miller writes. "They were supposed to be a haven for open discourse, for tolerating ideas whose value was based not on whose identity they promoted but how well they could be defended against an empirical reality."[36] But the old notion of a university as a refuge for free thought and expression is dead. In the Orwellian world of the modern campus, diversity means conformity; students and faculty are forced to commit to a set of progressive beliefs, any deviation from which invites instant reprisals from the PC bureaucracy, or in some cases harassment by radical student enforcers.

Professor Miller notes that the advent of diversity on campus also required a bureaucracy to oversee and impose it. But "bureaucracies are like cancers; they constantly need to grow." The diversity bureaucracy became a progressive priesthood. "[S]teeped in the political correctness theme of the evil of white privilege and the sanctity of minorities that survived it, the New Class [is] on a mission to morally rearm the universities." The growing programs require more students, who have been "recruited irrespective of their qualifications." Some of them "experience academic frustration, and frustration leads to anger and militancy." But the militancy feeds the system, because "if there are no diversity issues on campus, there is no need for an identity-based bureaucracy, sensitivity sessions, and a shadow university's indoctrination sessions in the residence halls." So the self-perpetuating system expands in costlier directions, ever more divisive and underwritten by massive student loan debt and federal grants. The University of Michigan, for example, has more than two hundred employees devoted to "diversity, equity and inclusion."[37] Meanwhile non-political students "majoring in legitimate fields have neither the time nor energy to protest"—and would be smacked down if they did.[38]

Professors have too much to lose to rock the boat. Tenure, which traditionally was supposed to protect academics with unorthodox views, now acts as an impediment to new ideas. Academic freedom, which had been a sacrosanct professional norm, is now severely compromised. In the comedian Adam Carolla's documentary *No Safe Spaces*, Harvard law professor Alan Dershowitz says that in his fifty years of teaching at some of the top schools in the country, he has "never met a group of less courageous people in [his] whole life than tenured Harvard and tenured other professors. They are so terrified of their own shadow. They don't want to do anything that upsets a student."[39] And for good reason, since in the climate of victimization that they have helped bring about, even the most innocent, unintended transgression can be professionally fatal.

Erika Christakis, an instructor at Yale, was driven from the school over an email questioning campus guidelines on politically incorrect Halloween costumes. The university's Intercultural Affairs Committee, warning students against a variety of costume choices that might involve supposed stereotyping or cultural appropriation, reminded them that Yale "values free expression as well as inclusivity." Professor Christakis's open letter sought to generate a discussion on whether bureaucratic control over student costumes was better than having a reflective conversation among students themselves. She believed "the growing tendency to cultivate vulnerability in students carries unacknowledged costs," suggesting that the micro-managing guidelines—seeking to forestall any possible offense—went too far.

The result, of course, was outrage, as triggered students trembled with fear at even the suggestion that costume choice should be a matter of personal responsibility. "Nearly a thousand students, faculty and deans called for my and my husband's immediate removal from our jobs and campus home," Christakis writes. And in addition to demands for apologies and disavowal of her ideas, the self-important activists wanted "advance warning of my appearances in the dining hall so that students accusing me of fostering violence wouldn't be disturbed by the sight of me." Christakis, a registered Democrat, recognizes "the dizzying irrationality of some supposedly liberal discourse in academia these days" and believes this will continue until universities "declare that ideas and feelings aren't interchangeable."[40]

Dr. Rachel Brown, a former associate dean at the University of Missouri School of Medicine, sued after she was demoted for questioning policies that she believed imposed unconstitutional racial quotas on admissions. The school was responding to charges of insufficient diversity among students and faculty in the wake of African American protests in 2015 that led to the resignation of the university system's president. According to Dr. Brown's complaint, Mizzou med school administrators wanted to aggressively recruit out-of-state minority students rather than admit kids from Missouri because they saw the locals as "bumpkins, hicks and illiterates who lived in Hooterville."[41] But locals may not be interested in going to Mizzou anyway. The University of Missouri has faced declining fortunes since the protests; in 2017 enrollment dropped 7.4 percent, and around four hundred staff positions had to be trimmed because of a loss of $16.6 million in revenue. Administrators blamed the decline on demographic trends but did admit there were "public perception concerns" lingering after the 2015 protests.[42] This backlash against campuses that indulge student radicals has been dubbed "The Mizzou Effect."

Students and faculty have also been denied due process under Title IX proceedings, which deal with cases of sexual assault, stalking, and a hostile campus climate. Under the terms of the Department of Education's infamous "Dear Colleague" letter of 2011, the burden of proof in these cases was lowered from "clear and convincing" to "more likely than not."[43] In some instances, "creating a hostile climate" included publishing an article at variance with the politically correct viewpoint. Laura Kipnis, a professor at Northwestern University, faced a grueling investigation over an article in which she argued that codes banning professor-student dating "vastly increased the power of administrators over our lives." When she wrote another article about the unfair and intrusive investigation process, she was deluged with emails from other professors enduring similar inquisitions.

"I soon learned that rampant accusation is the new norm on American campuses," she wrote. "My inbox became a clearinghouse for depressing and infuriating tales of overblown charges, capricious verdicts, and frightening bureaucratic excess." She uncovered "an astonishing netherworld of sexual finger-pointing, rigged investigations, closed-door hearings, and Title IX officers run amok." And this world was mostly unknown because "campus bureaucrats have shrouded the process in demands for confidentiality and threats that speaking about it can lead to job loss or expulsion."[44]

Bureaucrats and activists have exploited the legitimate purpose behind Title IX to create a climate of fear. Any student can initiate a Title IX proceeding for practically any reason (since expressing any idea at all can make a climate "hostile" to panicky snowflakes), which explains Alan Dershowitz's comment that professors are "scared of their own shadow." Even the arch-liberal Justice Ruth Bader Ginsburg has said that some college codes of conduct are unfairly enforced, and Secretary of Education Betsy DeVos has rescinded the Obama-era Title IX guidance.[45] The collegiate star-chamber investigations, however, are unlikely to cease.

FREE SPEECH IS VIOLENCE

Free speech in general is frowned on in the academic environment. A poll of three thousand U.S. college students found that while by a slight majority students support the abstract notion of freedom of expression, they are much more in favor of "diversity and inclusion," which means excluding speech they don't like. Students "overwhelmingly favor free speech zones on campus," which really means they favor censorship zones everywhere else. And 37 percent say that shouting down speakers is sometimes acceptable, with 10 percent backing the occasional speaker beat-down if they feel triggered.[46] In the old days creeps like this would never be in college in the first place.

The paradox of free speech vs. diversity was illustrated recently at Brandeis University, where a martyr to the cause of freedom of expression was gagged once again. In 2016, Brandeis held a two-day conference called "Comedy and the Constitution" to herald the arrival of the papers of 1960s "sick comic" Lenny Bruce, who died of a drug overdose in 1966. Bruce's arrests on obscenity charges for his routinely vulgar routines became an important cause for free speech advocates. Lenny's papers had been donated by his daughter Kitty Bruce and underwritten with a grant from the Hugh M. Hefner Foundation. Speakers at the conference, including rant-comic Lewis Black, hailed Lenny Bruce for his groundbreaking observational humor style and lamented his tragic early death before he could be vindicated.

The punchline came a year later, when Brandeis canceled a play about Bruce. It was written by an alumnus, Michael Weller of the class of 1965, who also wrote the 1979 screenplay adaptation for the tribal love-rock musical *Hair*. Weller, who was receiving the Brandeis Creative Arts Award, used materials from the Bruce papers to craft a play-within-a-play about students and administrators taking offense at a play about Lenny Bruce. But art was imitating life a little too closely. When the script circulated, it met instant opposition from outraged progressive students and faculty. One critic called it "an overtly racist play" that would "be harmful to the student population if staged." A student said that Weller, an "older, straight gendered, able-bodied and white man," should not be "stirring the pot." Weller was forced to withdraw his work, which was tellingly titled *Buyer Beware*.[47]

The comic Penn Jillette, a proud graduate of the Ringling Brothers and Barnum & Bailey Clown College, said the fiasco underscored the uselessness of the modern university for anyone who wants real-world experiences. "If college is so comfortable and safe," he wrote, "I'm glad I'm not there." Lenny Bruce had inspired Jillette to go into comedy in part because his act was so shocking, but he also made people think. These days it is much more important for leftist students and faculty to have "safe spaces" in which they can nurture their radical worldviews free of intellectual challenges. This is one reason why other comics like Jerry Seinfeld have abandoned playing universities; it is simply not worth the ordeal of facing the humorless hair-triggered social justice robots. Or as Penn Jillette pithily concluded in his piece, "F 'em."[48] As for poor Lenny Bruce, he was too vulgar for the conservative power structure of his era, and too honest for the intolerant Left today.

Free speech is under broad attack. Theories of "subjective victimization" empower college cupcakes to brand any idea they don't like as "unsafe" or "threatening" or even "verbal violence," justifying censorship.[49] The *New York Times* ran a regrettable column that purported to demonstrate the scientific basis for restricting speech that causes anxiety, concluding, "It's reasonable, scientifically speaking, not to allow a provocateur and hatemonger like Milo Yiannopoulos to speak at your school."[50] One wonders how the *Times* would react to dressing up censorship as science if the censorship were aimed at it. Arguments like this only empower those most prone to be offended, who are the last people who should have a say over who gets to speak.

Taking matters a step further, the student paper at Hillary Clinton's alma mater, Wellesley College, editorialized that in dealing with those who are "given the resources to learn and either continue to speak hate speech or refuse to adapt their beliefs, then hostility may be warranted." The editorial, running under the Orwellian headline "Free Speech Is Not Violated at Wellesley," goes on to argue that when faced with those who support (in their view) "racist politicians" and ideas that "will lead to the harm of others," then "it is critical to take the appropriate measures to hold them accountable for their actions." And hostility is warranted because "shutting down rhetoric that undermines the existence and rights of others is not a violation of free speech."[51] Shut up, Wellesley explains.

This kind of thinking encourages groups like the thuggish Antifa to resort to violence, which they justify as self-defense against "verbal violence,"—a rhetorical word game meant to validate cracking heads. The advent of these "black bloc" gangs has spurred a reaction by radical right-wing groups who are also interested in "a bit of the old ultra-violence." And the possibility of such confrontations has handed school administrators a rationale to clamp down on speech in the name of "public safety," or to charge student groups who want to host controversial speakers exorbitant security or insurance fees, which has a substantial chilling effect.[52]

School administrators themselves can be targeted by the extremists they have helped create. University of Oregon President Michael H. Schill was shouted down and driven from the stage when he tried to present his state of the university speech. Radicals were upset with, among other things, Schill's support for free speech, which they said perpetuated "fascism and white supremacy." President Schill, whose extended family perished in the Holocaust, wrote a response in the *New York Times* that pointed out that the tactics the protesters were using were in fact those of fascism. But he said that "the accusation that American universities somehow shelter or promote fascism is odd and severely misguided."[53] He then outlined all the steps the university was taking to placate the progressives, perhaps hoping that the unbalanced protesters will be convinced by the calm logic of his argument. He could have written a shorter and more effective essay titled "You are all expelled."

TOO MUCH BOOK LEARNIN'

Many Americans are never exposed to this toxic university environment. While 90 percent of Americans have high school degrees or equivalent, only about 60 percent have had some college. Nearly 45 percent graduated with an associate's or bachelor's degree, and only around 10 percent have graduate or professional degrees. There are around 17.5 million full- and part-time students at the college level, and for most of them these issues are probably merely a bizarre sideshow.

But what is lost in the debate is education's traditional civic purpose. The drive to frame the latest victim class and to partition the country between the putatively privileged and oppressed is dangerous and divisive. It is not generating a healthy social or political environment. It is not, as Jefferson said, "necessary to good government and the happiness of mankind." If anything, it achieves the opposite. A study by the Bradley Foundation on America's national identity warned that "the next generation of Americans will know less than their parents about our history and founding ideals. And many Americans are more aware of what divides us than of what unites us."[54] It is the "house divided" that Lincoln warned us cannot stand.

Many have understandably grown dissatisfied with the primary education system, as the rise of home schooling suggests. Around 3 percent of students between the ages of five and seventeen are home schooled, and the number is rising. Opposition to the Common Core is another indicator. Supporters of stronger local control of schools were happy to hear Education Secretary Betsy DeVos say that in her department, Common Core was dead.[55]

Republicans have dramatically soured on higher education in recent years. In 2015, a Pew Research Center poll found that 37 percent of Republicans believe colleges and universities have a harmful influence on the country. By 2017 this number had soared to 58 percent, and according to Gallup, 67 percent of Republicans have only "some" to "very little" confidence in higher education.[56] Around a third of the dissatisfied Republicans say that schools are too liberal, while, not surprisingly, only 1 percent of Democrats agree.[57]

Other critiques of the education system focus on its increasing cost, declining quality, misdirected teaching, and poor leadership. The cost is especially concerning. Since 1996, college tuition has risen more than 200 percent, growing at double the rate of health care. Much of the increased cost is due to the inordinate growth of school bureaucracies, which has far outpaced faculty and enrollment growth.[58] And given the easy availability of student loans, schools have been able to run up their prices with relative impunity, saddling students with more than a trillion dollars of debt in the process.

At the same time, school endowments have grown immensely—for example, Harvard's was $37.1 billion in 2017. The outsized wealth of some of these nonprofit institutions is why President Trump's 2017 tax reform bill included a provision for a 1.4 percent tax on net investment income for schools with endowments in excess of five hundred thousand dollars per student. Even this relatively modest effort to have universities pay their fair share drove opponents to declare the tax a "serious threat to higher education institutions and their ability to provide need-based financial aid to their students."[59] The hyperbolic response to the measure from elite institutions, filled with left-wing professors who never met a tax they didn't like, speaks volumes about how out of touch with the country they are.

There is also a growing awareness that the value of a college education may have been oversold. The emphasis since the 1970s and '80s on sending high school graduates to colleges at the expense of vocational schools has left the country with a shortage of skilled laborers and a surplus of graduates, many of whom will never use their degrees. Over-credentialed job requirements have also forced people to get degrees for jobs that could as well be done without the sheepskin. Bryan Caplan argues in *The Case Against Education* that while a bachelor's degree tells an employer you are disciplined enough to achieve something, college imparts few useful skills, which could be learned less expensively.[60]

Professor David McGrath, an alumnus of the College of DuPage, argues that the unfair stigmatization of vocational education is driving large numbers of students into college when they should be doing something more productive. The "it's college or nothing" idea has steered "youngsters unwilling or unsuited for academic study into frustration, failure and depression." He believes that "a campaign of public relations, parental education and cash is needed to combat the stigma."[61] People in skilled trades are more likely to be employed and to stay employed, since there will always be a demand for their skills. This is not to argue that no one should go to college, but higher education is not a panacea for our national challenges.[62] State and federal governments should increase funding for vocational education by reducing excess support for colleges and universities. The United States can't get back to being a country that builds things if no one knows how.

Home Depot is donating fifty million dollars to train twenty thousand disadvantaged youth, high school students, and veterans over the next ten years to mitigate the skilled labor shortage.[63] Mike Rowe, the former host of television's *Dirty Jobs*, is a firm believer in closing the skills gap. He thinks it is "fundamentally corrupt" to tell kids that the best way to pursue a career is also the most expensive way, when there are millions of important jobs available that they can prepare for at substantially lower cost. Decades of institutional support for the college track and disparaging portrayals of blue-collar workers in entertainment and the media, he thinks, have caused "entire categories of education" to be ignored and have culturally "marginalized an entire chunk of the workforce."[64] To help correct this imbalance, he established the mikeroweWORKS Foundation, which gives scholarships to kids for trade school education. And his television program showed the country a variety of little-seen but necessary jobs that are open to anyone who isn't afraid of getting dirty.

Education must not be an incubator of hatred of our country or a workshop for constructing grievances. Manufactured grudges and entitled anger cannot replace the American spirit of optimism and opportunity. These are dangerous messages for a country that wants to survive. Yet ultimately it is up to American families to preserve the country's story and keep alive the spirit of freedom. Ronald Reagan said that "lesson number one" about this country is that "all great change in America begins at the dinner table." American families need to inculcate American values and pass along the legacy of the American epic. They should breathe life into American traditions. Parents need to discuss with their kids what they have learned about America in school and be equipped to contradict any disparaging progressive propaganda. And as the Gipper said, it is a two-way street. "Children," he said, "if your parents haven't been teaching you what it means to be an American, let them know and nail them on it. That would be a very American thing to do."[65]

NINE

ERASING THE BORDER

In 2003, the former Democratic governor of Colorado Richard D. Lamm gave a short satirical speech titled "I Have a Plan to Destroy America."[1] He said that history shows that the surest way for a great country to die is by suicide. For those who felt the United States was "too smug, too white bread, too self-satisfied, too rich," he offered a simple eight-step plan for the country to annihilate itself:

1. Become bilingual.
2. Invent and promote multiculturalism to sustain differences.
3. Celebrate diversity by reinforcing differences rather than finding harmony.
4. Make sure the unassimilated are also undereducated.
5. Invest in a grievance industry to encourage minority groups to blame the majority for their troubles.

6. Establish dual citizenship and promote divided loyalties—again, to "celebrate diversity."
7. Shut down criticism of all the above by labeling it "racist" and "xenophobic."
8. Make it impossible to enforce immigration laws.

Governor Lamm could not have predicted the future more accurately. These eight points precisely reflect current progressive immigration priorities, which seek to enhance left-wing political power and wipe out the traditional view of America as a melting pot.

THE MELTING POT AND ASSIMILATION

The American people are the product of centuries of immigration. Immigrants started coming to what is now the United States in the 1500s, with more permanent settlements following in the next century. Millions of Americans of European descent can trace their family histories in North America back three or four hundred years. These settlers came for many reasons, but all were seeking freedom—freedom from the circumstances of their place of origin and freedom to govern themselves in communities of their own making. There were also unwilling immigrants, slaves brought from Africa from the early 1600s until 1808, when the slave trade ended. These families can also trace a long American history. Yet most immigrants came here willingly, seeking freedom and opportunity and overcoming hardships great or small. Each wave of immigrants bolstered the idea that this was a country of, by, and for free people.

"We are a nation of immigrants," the *Richmond State Journal* wrote in 1874, in one of the earliest uses of that expression, "and immigrants' children." The paper, editorializing in favor of immigration to restore the fortunes of postwar Virginia, noted the spirit of enterprise of the person who strikes out to live in a new country. "It is the strong man who summons up resolution, packs up his goods and crosses the ocean in search for better things for himself and family. The weak one stays at home and suffers. Hence it is that we get a very desirable class of immigrants, full of determination and work."[2]

This spirit of initiative built the country, whether it was farmers, ranchers, and miners taming America's vast undeveloped lands or merchants and industrialists fueling the development of the cities. The immigrants who contributed to the growth of the United States brought their determination to make good in their new home. And they left the conflicts, feuds, and national animosities of the Old World behind them.

Assimilation has always been the national norm. People who came to the United States did so to be Americans, to adopt the values of their new country, to honor its history and institutions. They brought with them their native customs, tastes, languages, and fashions, but these did not impede immigrants from adopting an American way of life, nor was it argued that they should actively resist the Americanization process. The "hyphenated American" was still expected to be primarily an American, even while contributing the best of what his native culture had to offer to the country's multicultural mix.

The expression "melting pot" to describe this blending of many peoples into the American nation was popularized by an early twentieth-century play of the same name by Israel Zangwill, the British-born son of Jewish immigrants from Latvia and Poland. He wrote the play in the midst of the great surge of immigration, begun in the late nineteenth century, that brought him to this country. The character David Quixano, fleeing a pogrom that took the lives of his family, entreats immigrants at Ellis Island to forget their past conflicts and plunge into the new life awaiting them. "Germans and Frenchmen, Irishmen and Englishmen, Jews and Russians," he says, "into the crucible with you all! God is making the American."[3]

Today about 13 percent of those living in the United States are foreign-born, up from under 5 percent in 1970 yet slightly below the level it was when *The Melting Pot* premiered in New York in 1908.[4] Policymakers then faced the same challenges as today: integrating newcomers who spoke a variety of languages and had different customs, faiths, backgrounds, education levels, outlooks, and aspirations. But there's a crucial difference: a century ago, the idea of Americanization—the assimilation of immigrants into American society—was the norm, supported by American policymakers and immigrant groups alike. Today no small number of progressives and radical immigration activists oppose the idea of assimilation and instead promote ethnic division.

The ideal of Americanization is still important to the vast majority of Americans. For example, a 2015 poll found that 66 percent thought speaking English was a very important part of being truly American, and 23 percent thought it was somewhat important.[5] Resistance to learning English is part of the progressive program, but the melting pot continues to simmer. While the number of Hispanic Americans has increased, the proportion who speak Spanish in the home is decreasing.[6] And while 97 percent of foreign-born Americans with Hispanic ancestry self-identify as Hispanic, by the third generation this has dropped by a quarter, and by the fourth generation it is down by half.[7] Despite the Census Bureau's efforts to keep people in tightly defined ethnic boxes, increasing numbers of previously self-identified Hispanics are instead identifying themselves as white.[8]

A study by the Hudson Institute finds a "patriotic integration gap" between native-born Americans and immigrants, a problem that has been largely self-inflicted. Barriers to assimilation "have developed gradually through a combination of federal bureaucratic policies, congressional activities, executive orders and court decisions." The authors conclude that the challenge of assimilation is a moral issue, pitting the traditional American focus on individual rights against the progressive multicultural focus on group identity. They recommend "cutting off federal funding for any programs promoting multicultural education, bilingual education, diversity training, and any so-called multicultural or cultural competency training."[9]

THE AMERICANIZATION IDEAL

Immigration has become a critical fault line in American politics. Immigration policy was one of the most important factors in driving large numbers of white voters who supported Barack Obama in 2012 into the Trump column in 2016.[10] Polls show that Democratic voters back measures that will allow illegal aliens (or as they prefer, undocumented Americans) to transition quickly to citizenship. For Republicans, the top priority is to tighten border security and strengthen law enforcement. Democrats strongly oppose building a wall along our border with Mexico; Republicans strongly support it. Democrats by and large do not see illegals as more likely to commit serious crimes. Republicans definitely do.[11] The senseless death in 2015 of Kate Steinle, shot on a San Francisco pier by the previously deported illegal alien Jose Ines Garcia Zarate, became a rallying point for conservatives opposed to San Francisco's sanctuary city policy and the Obama administration's lax enforcement of immigration laws. Donald Trump frequently mentioned the case on the campaign trail, and in 2017, when Zarate was acquitted of murder and manslaughter charges, the president tweeted that the verdict was a "complete travesty of justice," adding "BUILD THE WALL!"[12]

President Trump's immigration reform measures—which included restricting family-based immigration, reducing refugee admissions, eliminating the visa lottery, ending the Obama administration's Deferred Action for Childhood Arrivals program, and other restrictions—are generally popular among Republicans and have been denounced by Democrats as heartless, racist, and un-American.

But the current debate clearly illustrates the Democrats' radical drift. Not long ago there was bipartisan agreement on many of the immigration basics. In his 1995 State of the Union address, President Bill Clinton said that all Americans "are rightly disturbed by the large numbers of illegal aliens entering our country," which is why his administration "moved aggressively to secure our borders," hired new border guards, increased deportations, cracked down on illegal hiring, and "barr[ed] welfare benefits to illegal aliens." Clinton said that "it is wrong and ultimately self-defeating for a nation of immigrants to permit the kind of abuse of our immigration laws we have seen in recent years, and we must do more to stop it."[13] If President Trump read Bill Clinton's 1995 speech verbatim today, Democrats would call it hateful, racist, and cruel.

President Clinton also touted a report by the U.S. Commission on Immigration Reform, chaired by the former congresswoman and African American civil rights leader Barbara Jordan. The commission recommended reducing immigration to 550,000 persons per year from 720,000 in 1995. (By 2016 the number had risen to 1.2 million.)[14] More importantly, Jordan promoted the "Americanization ideal," which meant helping immigrants become part of the broader nation. "Those who choose to come here," she wrote, "must embrace the common core of American civic culture. We must assist them in learning our common language: American English. We must renew civic education in the teaching of American history for all Americans. We must vigorously enforce the laws against hate crimes and discrimination. We must remind ourselves, as we illustrate for newcomers, what makes us America."[15]

Even then-Senator Barack Obama could say back in 2006, "Those who enter our country illegally, and those who employ them, disrespect the rule of law. And because we live in an age where terrorists are challenging our borders, we simply cannot allow people to pour into the United States undetected, undocumented, and unchecked." He recommended that "before any guestworker is hired, the job must be made available to Americans at a decent wage with benefits. Employers then need to show that there are no Americans to take these jobs."[16]

Obama's views obviously "evolved" after he took office. Democrats generally have moved far away from this bipartisan view of immigration and Americanization. The extent of the shift was evident when Senator Diane Feinstein of California lost the Democratic Party's endorsement for her 2018 reelection bid in part because of her former immigration stance. Supporters of her main challenger, the state senator Kevin de León, circulated a video of Senator Feinstein saying in 1994, "I think we should enforce our borders" and questioning the costs to California of babies born to illegal immigrants. She also noted that 17 percent of the prison population was "illegal immigrants who come here and commit felonies—that's not what this nation is all about." Feinstein said then that "the way you protect the front door of legal immigration is to close the back door of illegal immigrants, which you can't control and you can't well provide for." De León, who championed California's "sanctuary state" law, snarked, "she represents California, not Arkansas."[17]

The reason for the Democrats' lurch to the left is the surging influence of progressives in the party and the need to replace the moderate voters being alienated by their increasingly radical politics. A memo circulated by the Center for American Progress Action Fund during the 2018 immigration debate said that the "fight to protect Dreamers" is "a critical component of the Democratic Party's future electoral success," and that losing the fight "will jeopardize Democrats' electoral chances in 2018 and beyond."[18] The objective is to quickly transform illegal immigrants into voters, since foreign-born voters give 80 percent of their votes to Democrats. It's a reasonable strategy, and it works. In Virginia, once reliably conservative, one in nine voters is now foreign-born, and Republican influence is evaporating. The "Turn Texas Blue" movement is one of the more conspicuous Democratic drives to weaponize immigrant votes.

To this end Democratic politicians are doing everything in their power to protect undocumented aliens, from declaring sanctuary cities to impeding federal enforcement of immigration laws. California's "Immigration Worker Protection Act," for example, limits employers' cooperation with federal immigration enforcement agents. It also bears a striking resemblance to the logic of the nullification doctrine promoted by Senator John C. Calhoun of South Carolina in the 1830s to evade federal tariffs. This issue came to a head in early 2018 when Mayor Libby Schaaf of Oakland tweeted out a warning to illegals about a planned Immigration and Customs Enforcement raid in the Bay Area. She said that "law abiding immigrants" deserved "fair warning when that threat appears imminent."[19] Of course, ICE was only interested in the law-breaking immigrants, who were also warned of the sweep, and eight hundred managed to evade justice. The Justice Department initiated a review of the tweets as possible obstruction, and Attorney General Jeff Sessions brought suit against California over its sanctuary policies. In the escalating war of words, Governor Jerry Brown said that this was tantamount to a declaration of war. The Golden State may regret giving President Trump an opportunity to emulate his hero Andrew Jackson, who practiced his art of the deal during the Nullification Crisis by threatening to invade South Carolina unless the state backed down.[20]

Note that sanctuary policies are not widely popular. A Harvard-Harris national poll found that 80 percent believed illegal immigrants arrested for other crimes should be turned over to immigration authorities.[21] In California, opinion is about evenly divided on the issue.[22]

Progressives even question whether being a citizen is necessary to vote. Some cities have already authorized noncitizen suffrage. College Park, Maryland, allows undocumented immigrants, student visa holders, and residents with green cards to vote in local elections. Former mayor Andrew Fellows said the city "should experiment in inclusivity wherever we possibly can."[23] San Francisco and Chicago allow noncitizens to vote for school boards. Chicago also recently came under scrutiny for a new municipal ID called CityKey, which would be issued to undocumented immigrants and also be valid identification for registering to vote. The card was seen as a way for the unpopular mayor Rahm Emanuel to boost support from Hispanics in what is expected to be a difficult 2019 reelection bid, but was also criticized as facilitating voter fraud.[24] Estimates of voter fraud in the 2016 election ran from none into the millions, but an attempt by the Trump administration to investigate the issue was stymied by the same states most likely to have seen widespread fraud, such as California.

Citizenship and borders seem like old-fashioned notions to some globalists. They argue that increasing international economic integration, wealth imbalances, and transnational challenges like climate change require more multilateral governance and free movement of peoples. By this view, illegal immigration "might actually be considered a justifiable form of resistance and civil disobedience against the economic injustice of the global order."[25] Alex Tabarrok, an economics professor at George Mason University, argues that "all people should be free to move about the earth, uncaged by the arbitrary lines known as borders," elevating the aspirations of immigrants over those of people "lucky to have been born in the right place at the right time."[26] The Mexican-American artist Ana Teresa Fernandez sought to symbolically erase the border and "pull down the sky" by painting the international border fence at Sonora blue. She said that "for me, the border, the border wall, is like a tombstone."[27] Fernando Romero, an architect, has proposed a utopian binational city on the border near El Paso as a means of promoting trade and overcoming the "primitive" border limit.[28]

YOU DON'T HAVE TO LIVE LIKE A REFUGEE

The question of admitting refugees from conflict zones was another immigration-related issue that divided the political parties in the 2016 election. The Syrian civil war had generated a refugee crisis in Europe and the United States that showed no signs of abating.

With some exceptions—most notably turning away Jewish refugees from fascism in the 1930s—the United States has welcomed people fleeing oppression in their homelands. We gave safe haven to refugees fleeing the systematic massacres of Assyrian Christians in Syria, Iraq, and Iran during the First World War, around the same time as the more well-known Armenian genocide. In one case from 1915, several thousand Christians were under siege by jihadists in the village of Geogtapa, near

Urmia in northwest Persia. The American missionary Harry P. Packard negotiated a ceasefire with the leaders of the attacking force, then walked through the no-man's-land between the lines carrying an American flag, the sight of which then gave even the renegade Muslim fighters pause. Packard was able to escort the Christians to at least temporary safety, and many eventually came to the United States.[29]

The journalist James Morgan witnessed a group of such Christian refugees from Syria boarding a train to the port of Beirut, where they would board a ship bound for America. As the train departed "many of those left behind knelt by the track in prayer." And a crowd of young men, "in their eagerness to follow the fortunes of the emigrants to the promised land," clung to the side of train until it had to stop, and Ottoman soldiers removed them. As Morgan wrote, "a Mayflower sails every day."[30] Repudiating that tradition, the Obama administration barred Middle Eastern Christians facing new massacres. The State Department would not classify them as refugees since they were being wiped out by non-state actors like ISIS and not their home governments. And when twenty-seven Iraqi Christians managed to make their way to the United States, they were rounded up to be deported.[31] It was like the Mayflower in reverse.

One hundred years ago the American flag was respected abroad—enough to intimidate jihadists—and there was no question that the refugees of 1915 would arrive in their new home with a spirit of gratitude. It would have been incredible to suggest that they or their children would one day start killing Americans simply for being Americans.

Today, sadly, this is not the case. The American flag no longer commands the respect it once did. Refugees come for a variety of reasons, some with no sense of gratitude. And terrorists mingling with the refugees have infiltrated Western countries and establish underground networks to continue their jihad from within.

When the Obama administration began importing thousands of refugees from war-torn Syria, the American people were assured that this humanitarian gesture posed no risk to them. A thorough vetting process would weed out potential terrorists, said Press Secretary Josh Earnest: "Those individuals who seek to enter the United States through the refugee resettlement program do so only after undergoing the most intensive screening of anybody who attempts to enter the United States."[32]

But even Obama administration officials soon cast doubt on the effectiveness of the vetting process. FBI Director James Comey told Congress in October 2015 that he couldn't "sit here and offer anybody an absolute assurance that there's no risk associated with this." The Department of Homeland Security warned that the Islamic State was printing false documents to enable movement across international borders. CIA Director John Brennan testified in 2016 that ISIS "has a large cadre of Western fighters who could potentially serve as operatives for attacks" and that the group was "exploring a variety of means for infiltrating operatives into the West, including refugee flows, smuggling routes and legitimate methods of travel."

Obama's refugee program was not popular. A Chicago Council on Global Affairs poll in June 2016 showed that only 36 percent of Americans favored admitting Syrian refugees, with sharp differences between Republicans and Democrats.[33] And the threat was real: the perpetrators of the November 13, 2015, terror attacks in Paris infiltrated Western Europe posing as refugees and migrants. The FBI began re-investigating dozens of Syrian refugees who passed the vetting system despite red flags in their backgrounds. But because the Obama White House had set an arbitrary quota of ten thousand Syrian refugees by the end of the year, the already questionable vetting period was slashed to twelve weeks. And it was impossible for the public to evaluate whether this move could keep them safe because the administration kept the details classified.

This was the background to the Trump administration's attempt to make the refugee vetting system safe and effective— measures denounced by critics as a "Muslim ban." And incendiary criticism of the policy opened up further divisions in a relationship with Muslims complicated by the 9/11 attacks and their aftermath.

For progressives, efforts to ensure that we do not welcome terrorists into the United States as "refugees" is another front in the diversity struggle. President Obama routinely exaggerated Muslim influence in early American history, and for the first time ever it was debated whether the Constitution was "Shariah compliant." The progressive doctrine of "intersectionality" even prompted non-Muslim feminists to don the hijab during the protest march in Washington after President Trump's inauguration.[34] A popular poster promoted the traditional head covering as an all-American symbol of freedom.

Yet for women in the Muslim world who are forced to cover their heads, the hijab can be a tool of oppression. Traditional

Muslim countries regularly rank at the bottom of the global scale for women's rights. During the Iranian uprising in December 2017 a lone woman dressed in black waving a white hijab on a stick became an international icon of resistance. The "Girl of Enghelab Street" was later arrested and sentenced to twenty-four months in prison. Thirty-five-year-old Manijeh Tafaghod Rezaei, who illegally worked as a model in Iran, was interrogated after sharing videos of herself uncovered on social media. She kept protesting but fled the country after being threatened with "acid spraying, rape and abuse."[35]

The Iranian teenager Dorsa Derakhshani, the second-highest-ranked female chess player in Iranian history and the holder of the number-two ranking among the world's female youth chess champions, stopped wearing the hijab while competing in Spain, and Tehran banned her from future chess competitions. (Her brother was also banned for having played a game against an Israeli.) "Time and time again," Dorsa said, "those in charge of the Iranian national team showed that they cared more about the scarf covering my hair than the brain under it." She moved to the United States, where she is "surrounded by people who respect me as a player and don't care or notice what I look like." She said that "the choice to stop covering felt morally right," and she "never felt a shred of guilt" about her decision.[36] So while misguided American feminists don the headscarf for a "day of resistance," brave women elsewhere face severe penalties simply for taking it off.

Mattel jumped onto the identity bandwagon by introducing a devout Muslim version of the popular Barbie doll, inspired by American Olympic fencer Ibtihaj Muhammad. The doll has brown eyes and dark skin, dresses modestly, and has long dark hair in a bun that you can't see. Muslim modesty is in, both as a fashion and political statement. And this political angle is why we are unlikely to see other avatars of feminine modesty such as evangelical Barbie wearing a cross or *frum* Orthodox Jewish Barbie in her *sheitel*. How about Amish Barbie? Buggy sold separately.

One obvious market for hijab Barbie is the progressive, non-Muslim parent who wants to make a statement to the world about tolerance and intersectionality. This is the kind of person who dresses a baby boy in pink to trap the unwary passerby into an uncomfortable/sanctimonious discussion about gender roles. But kids love to experiment with juxtaposition, so what happens when their girls (or boys, whatever!) immediately put hijab Barbie into a skimpy bikini? Odds are they will get a stern lecture on cultural sensitivity. Because really, kids, this isn't about your having fun; it's about your parents sticking it to Trump.

Another potential market is in conservative Muslim parents who want a toy that expresses and helps transmit their values. There is certainly nothing wrong with that. It ties into the country's history as a haven for religious groups seeking to build communities that practice a way of life based on their beliefs. And a strong and vibrant nation is rooted in family values, an expression that conservatives use with affection and one that makes liberals wince.

So hijab Barbie may help preserve a form of cultural identification. But on the other hand, it would be a mistake to assume that all kids born into a given culture want to remain in it. This is one of the most important intellectual shortcomings of identity politics, the insistence that you are defined by a group affiliation over which you have no choice.

But part of living in a free country is the ability to adopt a way of life different from the one you grew up with or inherited from a country where such choices are non-existent. First-generation or newly arrived Muslim kids in traditional families may gravitate toward the more free and easy social conventions of their new home. This has always been the lure of American culture. It is the melting pot that softens or erases the hard edges of successive waves of immigrant cultures through the innumerable choices individuals make once they get here. Pray five times a day, or fewer, or none? Eat halal, or try the bacon? Wear the hijab, or don't? For Muslim immigrants and refugees from tradition-bound countries, these are the kinds of choices—and opportunities—they may be facing for the first time in their lives.

Mattel says hijab Barbie is about empowerment. And yes, in recent decades Barbie has been all about feeding aspirations. Small children have big dreams. The real life-changing moment of empowerment might come when Muslim American girls in traditional homes make the choice to take Barbie's hijab off—and leave it off.

COMING TO AMERICA

Immigration policy—which touches on states' rights, executive powers, national security, criminal justice, assimilation, voting rights, and citizenship—is becoming the subject of a national crisis. Polls show a majority of Americans back President Trump's proposals and agree with his assertion that "Americans are dreamers too." A Harvard-Harris poll found that 65 percent of Americans support a deal "that ends chain migration, eliminates the random visa lottery and secures the border with a wall," and 80 percent believe that "immigration should be based on merit and skills," and that it is preferable to have secure borders rather than open borders.[37]

But the larger issue is how the United States can return to the historical norm of promoting Americanization and assimilation. In part, this involves talking Democrats off the identity-politics ledge, which is only leading to sharper and more intractable national divisions. The planks of Governor Lamm's satirical but all-too-true eight-point plan for annihilating the country must be repudiated, and institutional support for programs that maintain divisions must come to an end. It's time to let the magic of freedom turn newcomers into Americans, as it has done throughout our history.

Ronald Reagan never lost his confidence that the United States is "a beacon, still a magnet for all who must have freedom, for all the pilgrims from all the lost places who are hurtling through the darkness, toward home."[38] America has always had a multicultural society, but it cannot be a multinational country. Many peoples live in the United States, and many cultures thrive, but there is and can be only one nation, which is American.

TEN

DIVIDING
AMERICA

*The enemy of the moment always represented absolute
evil, and it followed that any past or future agreement
with him was impossible.*
—George Orwell, *1984*

The conflicts discussed thus far—over history, heritage, the
Founders, the flag, religion, holidays, and immigration—are
all symptoms of the breakdown of a shared sense of nationality
and a growing division in American life. In an NBC News poll
on perceptions of national unity, 80 percent responded that the
United States is mainly (59 percent) or totally (21 percent)
divided. Only 1 percent believed the country was totally united.[1]
One aspect of the current hyperpolarization is the "big sort" of
the country into groups of people with almost mutually exclusive
worldviews. And a related, more serious problem is the growing
dislike and distrust between the two sides that reinforces the
breakdown of national unity.[2] A Pew study showed that between
1994 and 2017, the average political views of Republicans and
Democrats moved strongly toward their respective extremes,
decreasing the amount of overlap between the two parties.[3] At
the same time, America's institutions are growing weaker,

popular passions are more intense, and the national sense of purpose is vanishing.

The 2016 election laid bare the extent of the national division. Unlike previous Republican candidates who attempted to skirt the issue, Donald Trump made a point of highlighting the fracture zones and advocating a return to traditional American ideals. His blunt approach defied the conventional wisdom of pundits and professional electioneers, but it resonated with enough voters for Trump to defeat sixteen other Republican candidates, some of whom were pillars of the establishment. And he stuck to his message to defeat Hillary Clinton, who ran one of the most expensive campaigns in history and who had been plotting for the job since her childhood. Trump by contrast was a novice to electoral politics, and the presidency was his entry-level position. But he spoke to an important belief in America that was powerful enough to give him the win.

WHAT HAPPENED?

Hillary Clinton produced a long list of reasons why she lost the 2016 election. She blamed Russia, sexism, Bernie Sanders, Barack Obama, the Democratic National Committee, WikiLeaks, clueless journalists, low-information voters, James Comey, the "basket of deplorables," and even herself, in a self-pitying way. President Trump's win was so counter to the conventional wisdom, so stubbornly at odds with the pollsters, that vast numbers of progressives concluded that the election had been rigged. They latched onto the paranoid notion that "1,000 Russian agents" had overthrown American democracy using Facebook ads and

Twitter bots. This narrative became the rationale for a slow-motion coup attempt against the new president.

These conspiratorial notions can easily be refuted by looking at a map. The Democrats' problem was not just that the Clinton campaign failed to devote sufficient time and resources to key states they mistakenly assumed were behind their "blue wall." The Trump phenomenon was broad-based and national. Precinct-level voting maps compiled by Ryne Rohla reveal that the shift in Republican support from Romney in 2012 to Trump in 2016 was geographically widespread, with particularly strong shifts of +20 percent or more in a sweeping arc of the Northern heartland stretching from western New York through Pennsylvania and Ohio, and including the Great Lakes states, with important additional pockets of strength in Florida, North Carolina, Iowa, and Missouri.[4] County-level data showed the same pattern, including clusters of counties in Iowa, Wisconsin, and Michigan that had flipped from voting for Obama in 2012 to Trump four years later, helping hand those states to the GOP.[5]

Hillary Clinton should have remembered the slogan from her husband's winning 1992 race, "It's the economy, stupid." Democratic talking points notwithstanding, Barack Obama's eight years in office had produced anemic economic growth in which only upper-income groups and those with political connections were rewarded. The Democrats offered nothing to inspire the middle-class Americans being slowly squeezed out of prosperity. But Donald Trump spoke directly to their concerns: work, faith, family, pride, and culture.

Democrats might have recognized this if they had been paying attention. In December 2015, Nate Cohn, a poll analyst, noted that Donald Trump's core primary supporters were "self-identified Republicans who nonetheless are registered as Democrats…concentrated in the South, Appalachia and the industrial North." This was the very cohort that provided the margin of victory eleven months later.[6] A May 10, 2016, DNC internal email bore the uncharacteristic subject line, "Trump on to something." Attached were the results of a Quinnipiac University Swing State Poll of the battleground states Florida, Ohio, and Pennsylvania showing historic Democratic weakness among white men, who never had a compelling reason to vote for Hillary to begin with, and even among white women, who were mostly in the Trump camp.[7]

But the too-clever-by-half Democrats completely misread this signal. Early in the presidential campaign season they wanted Republicans like Donald Trump, Ted Cruz, and Ben Carson to do well in the GOP primaries because they saw the success of their message as an advantage for Hillary. An April 2015 DNC discussion memo called these candidates the "pied pipers" who would lead the GOP to the right and "undermine their credibility among our coalition (communities of color, millennials, women) and independent voters." The memo suggested "elevating" these candidates and encouraging the press to take them seriously.[8]

Democrats did not notice the perils of this strategy until it was too late. The "abandoned white working-class voter" suddenly vaulted to prominence after it became clear that ignoring over half the electorate was not a winning strategy. Robert Reich, Bill Clinton's secretary of labor, blamed the elite liberal power structure for deserting the traditional working-class Democratic base in favor of financiers, corporations, and upper-middle-class voters in swing suburbs.[9] The progressive super-PAC Priorities USA found that voters in key states who shifted from Obama to Trump were mostly from the white working class, and economic anxiety played the most important role in their switch (along with a highly unfavorable impression of Hillary Clinton).[10] And a study of white working-class voters funded by George Soros's Open Society Foundations, oddly titled "The Other America," found that white working-class voters, who saw Donald Trump as strong, hardworking, and honest, responded to Trump's slogan, "Make America Great Again," which evoked "a golden past" and aroused hope "for a better future."[11] So while Hillary Clinton was busy delivering the bad news that traditional America was never coming back, Donald Trump won its votes by responding, in effect, "Not so fast."

"DRAIN THE SWAMP"

Much of the country felt a strong sense of alienation from Washington, a town that was getting rich from government while middle-class incomes flattened or descended. The region surrounding the national capital is the richest part of the country for no other reason than federal patronage. This healthy skepticism about government is also one of the pillars of conservatism. Out-of-control federal spending was making the country poorer and running up ruinous debt. Increasing taxation and regulation stifled the spirit of innovation and entrepreneurship that had made the United States a world economic leader. And government's thirst for power and regulation of daily life increased markedly in the Obama years, a trend that Hillary Clinton was eager to continue.

While government was expanding, there was no sense it was becoming more effective. Americans' trust in their institutions was at historical lows, and there was a pervasive sense that the system was broken. The country lurched from crisis to crisis. Members of Congress couldn't work together or with the president, who believed executive leadership meant circumventing Congress instead of doing the hard work to find compromises. Hillary Clinton pledged to do the same thing. And liberal federal judges were increasingly brash in imposing their personal policy preferences under the pretense of interpreting the laws or the Constitution. The three branches of government, as well as the press, the education system, and other important traditional bulwarks of national unity, came to be seen as untrustworthy, incompetent, and unresponsive to public concerns. A poll taken weeks before the 2016 election showed only 52 percent had faith in democracy, while 40 percent said they had lost faith, and 6 percent said they never had it.[12]

Donald Trump's slogan "drain the swamp," which arose spontaneously at his rallies, summed up how the base viewed his basic mission. And they trusted him to get it done; Trump was the man who could not be bought, because he was already wealthy, and there was nothing Washington could offer that he could not have on his own.

But Democratic leaders were either unaware of this political dynamic or did not care. Their working model was the "coalition of the ascendant"—the growing numbers of youth, minorities, and unmarried women who supposedly represented the political future. They did not court traditional white middle-class voters because they felt they didn't have to. Barack Obama won in 2012 with only 39 percent of white voters, and all Hillary had to do to repeat the win was to motivate the progressive base.[13]

As far as the Democrats are concerned, demography is destiny, and the browning of America will lead naturally to a more progressive society. Nancy Pelosi revealed the absurd lengths to which they are willing to take this conviction when she proclaimed it "a proud day" when her grandson made a birthday wish that he "had brown skin and brown eyes" like his Guatemalan friend Antonio. "So beautiful," she gushed. "So beautiful. The beauty is in the mix. The face of the future for our country is all-American. And that has many versions." Except, apparently, her grandson's "Irish, English, whatever, whatever, and Italian-American" heritage.[14]

THE DEPLORABLES

Progressives' belief in the inevitability of their triumph, reinforcing their natural elitism, has bred a remarkable degree of condescension and smugness among the urban Left toward supposedly less sophisticated conservatives and the people of rural America. They simply didn't care if much of the country's traditional way of life was disrupted. If the yokels objected loudly enough, surely Washington bureaucrats could placate them with some kind of handout.

There is a sense among progressives that rural and working-class whites are simply too stupid to know how to vote. This is the thesis of Thomas Frank's 2004 book *What's the Matter with*

Kansas? in which he asserts that Republicans have exploited cultural conservatism to dupe rural blue-collar voters to support the supposed moneyed interests of the GOP instead of backing Democrats, who would reward them with government assistance (and of course all the control that goes with it). A lengthy pre-election article in *Vox* cautioned liberals that their belief in "the failure of half the country to know what's good for them" comes across as a "condescending, defensive sneer toward any person or movement outside of its consensus, dressed up as a monopoly on reason."[15] *The Atlantic* proved this point by running an article arguing that Trump supporters are racists but are too ignorant to know it.[16] House Minority Leader Nancy Pelosi piled on with her assertion that non-college educated white males are irrational bumpkins who vote "against their own economic interests because of guns, because of gays, and because of God, the three G's."[17]

Progressive contempt was why Hillary Clinton's "basket of deplorables" comment became a badge of honor for many Trump supporters. When the Democratic nominee spoke down (her accustomed rhetorical posture) to the "racist, sexist, homophobic, xenophobic, Islamophobic" core Trump supporters, she launched the "revolt of the politically incorrect."[18] It was reminiscent to the outset of World War I, when the imperious Kaiser Wilhelm II allegedly ordered his generals to "to exterminate first the treacherous English and walk over [British] General French's contemptible little army." British troops adopted the nickname the "Old Contemptibles" and proved in battle that walking over them was easier said than done. Likewise, Donald Trump immediately understood the power of the moment. At a rally in Miami days after Hillary Clinton's insult, he came on the stage to the anthem "Can You Hear the People Sing" from *Les Misérables*, in front of a Trumpified mockup of the show's poster reading "Les Deplorables." The crowd went wild when he opened his speech with, "Welcome to all of you deplorables."[19]

When the inconceivable happened and Donald Trump won, the left-wing cognoscenti simply could not process the news. A distraught Ana Kasparian, cohost of the progressive online news show *The Young Turks*, told Trump voters on election night, "You got fooled by a simpleton who uses simple sentences that appeal to you." She said they were "people who voted against their best interests." Another Young Turk countered that Trump voters were not fooled, that "tens of millions of Americans are totally fine with a man who is driven almost purely by racism and sexism and islamophobia, of hatred of everyone unlike him, and they want that."

Shell-shocked Hillary supporters filled the airwaves predicting an apocalypse. The economy was going to collapse, the stock market was going to tank, immigrants would be sent to prison camps, the United States would become embroiled in nuclear war, and minorities would be sent to the back of the bus.

Progressives doubled-down on their hostile critique of Trump's America. The Silicon Valley tech executive Melinda Byerley spoke for many of them when she offered the helpful advice to flyover country that "big corporations" ignore them because "no educated person wants to live in a shithole with stupid people." She said super-smart people like herself would "like to live a more rural lifestyle" but "won't sacrifice tolerance or diversity to do so." She would rather not dwell among "violent, racist, and/or misogynistic" people who "don't want brown people to thrive" in towns with "nothing going for them." She said if these places "clean up their act" maybe liberals will grace them with their presence, but the "best and brightest" young people "would rather scrape by in SF than live in a huge house somewhere if it meant dealing with bigots and backwards ideologies every day."[20] Meanwhile, in Silicon Valley the tech lords work in isolated utopian campuses and live in gated communities, while in downtown San Francisco interactive maps help pedestrians navigate around discarded hypodermic needles and piles of human excrement. Shithole indeed.

Some, however, sought to understand what happened. After the election a number of news outlets ran articles like one by ABC News, in which reporters spent a year talking to people in the "most pro-Trump town in America" because "ABC News wanted to learn and observe."[21] The stories read like accounts of anthropological expeditions to the Amazon jungle, in which reporters ventured out into the undeveloped hinterlands to experience Trump supporters in their natural habitat.

Sometimes human connections were possible across the great divide. Ruth Mayer of Charlotte, North Carolina, was furious about the "national nightmare" of Donald Trump's election and drank her morning coffee from a cup that read, "I hate to wake up when Donald Trump is President." She hated the people who were either too biased or too stupid to resist voting for him. But as she drove home through Virginia after the post-inaugural protest march, a large piece of plastic under the front bumper of her Prius came loose, and she had to pull off the highway. Almost immediately a local man and his teenaged son pulled over to help and managed to quickly make the car drivable again. "Just ask any redneck like me what you can do with zip ties," he said, "—well, zip ties and duct tape. You can solve almost any car problem. You'll get home safe." She later thought about the encounter with the Virginia good old boy and concluded that even though "Trump's cruelty and mendacity demand outrage and the most vigorous resistance a nation can muster," maybe "if we treat one another with kindness and gratitude" the nightmare could be "more bearable."[22] To the "redneck" who stopped to help her, kindness and gratitude probably come naturally.

Kindness is in short supply in American politics. Rhetoric has become harsher and more polarizing. There has always been tough language in American politics, but there is a new willingness to stake out extreme positions and to characterize opposing viewpoints in purely ideological terms. It is now commonplace to shove opponents into categories ending with –ist, which serve as instant and thoughtless character judgments, rather than addressing the substance of the debate. Everything comes down to good or evil. Politicians and pundits can't seem to do without clichés like "all in" or "full throated." Political oratory has been replaced by paranoid threatening language with the tone of a pressure-group fundraising letter.

In 2011, Senator Chuck Schumer, a New York Democrat, was overheard by the press on a conference call with his colleagues during budget debates saying, "I always use the word 'extreme,' that's what the caucus instructed me to do the other week."[23] Maybe it was a rhetorical flourish back then, but now extremism is the temper of the times on the Left. Senator Schumer got a sense of how far the radicalism on his side has gone shortly after the 2016 election. Schumer made the kind of statement you would want and expect from a Senate minority leader, namely that he would work with President Trump where their interests overlapped and oppose him where they had differences. This was a standard American statement of bipartisanship.

But progressives pounced on Schumer for compromising their program of massive resistance. "No Democrat should ever legitimize that corrupt xenophobic white supremacist Russian puppet," the blogger Markos Moulitsas declared.[24] Diane Feinstein was slammed when she rejected the idea of impeaching President Trump and instead counseled people to be patient. "We don't owe Trump patience," a prospective primary challenger, state senator Kevin de León, thundered, "We owe Californians resistance."[25] And Maine Republican Susan Collins was blasted by feminists for her work in crafting the 2017 tax bill. She had gotten every addition to the bill she wanted, and by traditional political standards she did an excellent job in forging compromises. But to progressives she was a traitor to women for collaborating on the bill whatsoever.[26]

A political system that was designed for compromise can't function with progressives hell-bent on mindless resistance with no sense of the national interest. A CBS News poll in June 2017 asked about the overall tone and civility in American politics. More than two-thirds of the respondents said the level of civility was getting worse, and only 7 percent thought things were getting better.[27] This view was consistent across all partisan lines. In the same poll, 73 percent believed that the "tone of America's politics and political debate is encouraging violence among some people." It hardly helps when you have Terry McAuliffe, the former governor of Virginia, suggesting he would punch President Trump if he got too close to him in a debate or former Vice President Joe Biden saying he would "beat the Hell out of him."[28] Of the latter threat, President Trump responded, "He doesn't know me, but he would go down fast and hard, crying all the way. Don't threaten people, Joe!"[29] We may be on the verge of bringing back the time-honored American custom of dueling, Alexander Hamilton's fate notwithstanding.

Old-school liberal and self-described "tone-deaf curmudgeon" Jon Tevlin, in a column lamenting Al Franken's being driven from the Senate over sexual harassment charges, said that "we're into a period of political and social nihilism and we no longer want to win, we want to destroy each other. There are no rules and no limits to the mean. Add to that the churlish, insatiable beast of social media and the toxicity is overwhelming."[30] The former Facebook vice president Chamath Palihapitiya says he feels "tremendous guilt" about the damage his company has done to the social landscape. "I think we have created tools that are ripping apart the social fabric of how society works," he said. With online interaction there is "no civil discourse, no cooperation; misinformation, mistruth." And he added that this is "not an American problem—this is not about Russians ads. This is a global problem."[31]

Sometimes people rise above the mean spirit of the times. In September 2017, pro-Trump demonstrators faced off with Black Lives Matter protestors in Washington, DC, in dueling rallies that some pundits expected (or hoped) would turn to violence. There was some trash-talking, but then the organizer of the pro-Trump rally invited Hawk Newsome of the BLM group up on his platform to speak, because "whether they disagree or agree with your message is irrelevant. It's the fact that you have the right to have the message." Mr. Newsome took up the offer and said, "I am an American, and the beauty of America is that when you see something broke in your country, you can mobilize to fix it." He added, "If we really want to make America great, we do it together." By the end of the event the two sides had not solved the nation's ills, but they were engaging each other in a productive spirit. Arthur C. Brooks, the president of the American Enterprise Institute, wrote that the two sides "saw each other as people" and escaped the toxic social media cages that reduce others to faceless slogans.[32] But just when it looks like we might be on the verge of a breakthrough in understanding, Howard University researchers inform us that this type of "whiteness-informed civility" erases "racial identity" and reinforces "white racial power."[33] Traditionalists might just call it good manners.

The fractured, balkanized media landscape contributes to the incivility. People become isolated in social media-powered information bubbles. The idea of objective journalism has broken down, and journalistic standards have eroded under the pressure to maximize online clicks. Some reporters and organizations have even embraced "resistance" as a norm. Public confidence in the media was low going into the 2016 election cycle, and the mistakes and distortions that crept into coverage allowed Donald Trump to make "fake news" a rallying cry.

Even with only 5 percent positive coverage Trump was able to set the press agenda by using Twitter to reach the American people directly without media filters. As the president said, he uses social media not because he likes to but "because it is the only way to fight a VERY dishonest and unfair 'press,' now often referred to as Fake News Media. Phony and non-existent 'sources' are being used more often than ever. Many stories & reports a pure fiction!"[34] A Harvard-Harris poll showed bipartisan agreement on this point, with 65 percent saying that there is a lot of false information in the mainstream media.[35]

The digital age has given humanity access to more information than ever before, but this access has provoked balkanization as people are drawn to sources that tend to confirm their pre-existing biases. Fake news and the influence of social media in spreading it exacerbate this problem. The country is increasingly divided into antagonistic camps armed with their own facts and opinions, which may or may not be based on reality, while Internet trolls and bot-armed activists stoke the fires of outrage simply for the sake of causing trouble.

The age of the Big Three networks, dominant national newspapers, and wire services was not perfect, but at least there were common terms for the debate. Extreme views were mostly limited to newsletters and small-circulation newspapers.[36] But the Internet broke this oligopoly. Information was no longer bound by printing presses and broadcast studios. News organizations foolishly started giving away their only product—information—for free, killing their business model in the process. And aggregators, such as the Drudge Report, achieved click dominance by providing fresh editorial discretion more suited to the temper of the times.

The old-school norm of press objectivity was a myth, but it was therapeutic. In the Trump era many journalists have cast off even a pretense of objectivity. But making news more overtly opinionated further compromises public trust and makes it easier for skeptical people to dismiss it. The *Washington Post*'s self-satisfied Trump-era slogan "Democracy dies in darkness" is singularly inapt in an age of information abundance. The real problem is the echo chamber where no alternative voices are heard. One might say, "Democracy suffocates in a vacuum." And technology has reduced what passes for political dialogue in America to bumper sticker arguments, splashy headlines, online memes, and incessant tweets.

The harsh political tone and media breakdown, reflecting a rejection of the concept of a national good and making unity impossible, have aided the rise of race-based identity politics. The lines in the culture war have also grown starker. America used to be a place where like-minded people could form communities to live the way they wanted, resulting in a patchwork of different community values and standards. Freedom of choice was the norm. If you didn't like one community, you could try to change it or move to another. If you didn't want to do business with one establishment, go next door. Now Americans are being forced to accept a one-size-fits-all radical worldview, and those who object face pressure groups eager to shame or sue them into submission.

Progressives reject traditional American values of marriage, faith, and hard work. Militant culture warriors, backed by activist courts, are attempting to force all Americans into not simply tolerating but affirming and celebrating ways of life that they find distasteful, sinful, or dangerous. Those who advocate traditional values are not simply to be disagreed with but destroyed, taken to court, boycotted, fired. And there are enough progressive judges, administrators, bureaucrats, and others who agree with these tactics to make it a national issue. This newly intensified culture war has for example made the expression "Christian baker" into an emblem of intolerance to the Left, in what conservatives see as a contrived civil rights struggle that is needlessly ruining lives. Whether a Muslim baker would be forced to make a Mohammed cartoon cake has yet to be adjudicated.

THE BIG SORT

The cultural divide has framed what the journalist Bill Bishop called the "big sort" of people grouping geographically based on their politics and way of life.[37] In the Trump era, it has gone as far as *Harper's Bazaar* urging persons to divorce a spouse who supports the president.[38] This is already happening. The former Miami Dolphins cheerleader Lynn Aronberg split with her husband, Dave, a Palm Beach prosecutor and a Democrat, in part because she, a Republican and supporter of President Trump, "felt increasingly isolated in the marriage."[39]

That is an extreme example of the political divide, but it is true that the political map has evolved into archipelagoes of urban liberal enclaves surrounded by more conservative rural areas. In general, the divergence of urban and rural interests is one of the oldest facts of political life in our republic, dating back to the days of the Federalists and the Jeffersonian Democrats, when 95 percent of Americans lived in rural areas. One hundred years ago, the rural-urban split was about even. Today 80 percent of Americans live in urban areas comprising only 3 percent of the nation's landmass.[40] But if we include suburban areas in the breakdown, the picture becomes more nuanced. Half of voters live in suburban areas, and only about a third in cities proper; the remaining 17 percent are in the countryside. Exit polls from 2016 showed urban voters going for the Democrats 59-35, rural voters going Republican 62-34, and the battleground suburbs picking Trump by 50-45.[41] Yet almost two-thirds of Americans lived in uncompetitive counties where the winning candidates racked up margins of 20 percent or higher, and for a fifth of the population the margin was 50 percent or more.[42]

Self-sorting is nothing new. This has always been a nation on the move. From the earliest days Americans have searched out the places that suited them, driven by work, weather, adventure, education, marriage, faith, or chance. Even before the Revolution, Virginia's royal governor Lord Dunmore observed that Americans "acquire no attachment to place: but wandering about seems engrafted in their nature."[43]

The wandering began on the East Coast, then moved into the mountains, the plains, and beyond. Americans have traditionally established communities that reflected their values and ideas of the good life. This has been true in cities, suburbs, and rural areas. If people tired of one place, didn't like how it was run, or lost economic opportunities, they moved and set up shop elsewhere. This resulted in a patchwork of communities and cultures based on historical circumstances, immigration patterns, and so forth, differing in some respects but united by the idea of America. And this commonality of difference, enshrined in the Tenth Amendment, gave rise to the idea of states as "laboratories of democracy" in which innumerable experiments could take place.

This dynamic worked best when all agreed to differ on what constituted the good life and leave each to his own way. It was a model of true diversity, unlike the sham diversity of progressives. But the withdrawal from this plural democracy and the slide toward uniformity, encouraged by judicial and executive fiat, is breaking the old system down. Centralization and cookie-cutter government and national-level restrictions and mandates have produced a winner-take-all mentality that is inimical to the spirit of compromise on which the Constitution is based. And it has led to movements by some to simply get out.

ELEVEN

A MORE PERFECT DISUNION

S ecession is an increasingly popular topic in politics, particularly in the context of California's resistance to federal enforcement of immigration laws. There are proposals to split off all or part of the state into a new liberal utopia, perhaps combining with other states or areas on the West Coast. There have also been active secession movements in other states. It is a dream born in frustration. Wouldn't it be great to not have to deal with the other side? Wouldn't it be so much better, so much easier, to call it quits? It's the question behind every divorce, every separation, when things have broken down to the point where it is just not worth the fight any more, where differences become irreconcilable and require a parting of the ways.

This was the logic spelled out in the Declaration of Independence, an insistence that sometimes "in the course of human events, it becomes necessary for one people to dissolve the political bands which have connected them with another." Some

Americans today feel that continued political association is intolerable. Jefferson's and Madison's Kentucky and Virginia Resolutions of 1798 (declaring the federal Alien and Sedition Acts unconstitutional) were an expression of this same spirit. The Yankee merchants of the Essex Junto at the 1814–1815 Hartford Convention discussed secession as a way to check federal power. Talk of disunion was rampant during the Nullification Crisis of 1832–1833, and in the decades leading up to the Civil War secession was touted by radicals on both sides of the Mason-Dixon Line.

When the Confederate States finally seceded, they argued that their separation was in the spirit of the Declaration of Independence and that theirs was the second American Revolution. As the slave states started peeling off from the Union, the response in some abolitionist circles was "good riddance." But most in the North were willing to fight to preserve the Union, and the Civil War settled the long-standing question whether unilateral secession was permissible under the Constitution. A series of subsequent Supreme Court decisions dressed up in legal language what force of arms had decided.

The history of the 1860s has left the notion of secession linked in the popular imagination to civil war, but one does not necessarily lead to the other. Peaceful partitions are possible, such as the 1993 "Velvet Divorce" of the Czech Republic and Slovakia. On a larger scale, the dissolution of the Soviet Union into its fifteen separate states was achieved for the most part without widespread violence. There is no reason to think that a breakup of the United States need be violent either. It is an article of faith among many conservatives and libertarians that liberals and collectivists are not necessary for a prosperous society. Likewise, liberals and progressives aren't much enamored of the conservatives in their midst, although the collectivist Left relishes the opportunity to force dissenters to submit. Perhaps mutual disdain would ensure a peaceful parting. The political arrangements that have grouped us together were not created by us—and they can be altered by us. History in this sense need not be destiny. If progressives hate America so much, why stay together? If the Constitution is fundamentally racist and flawed, why live under it? If American society is as bad as they say it is, why don't they take their toys and go home?

One challenge would be drawing the lines for the new countries. In the case of the Soviet Union, the splits were along the pre-existing republican borders, and fighting broke out where the borders divided national groups, or where smaller national movements sought independence, such as in Chechnya. This is also the source of the fighting in Ukraine. When Yugoslavia split up, Slovenia was able to separate with relative ease because it was territorially and nationally compact. But in ethnically mixed Bosnia a brutal conflict broke out between Serbs, Croats, and Bosniaks. So it is important to draw lines that won't themselves become a cause for war.

California is a prime example of this challenge. The state used to be competitive for Republicans. In fact, between 1952 and 1988 the state supported the Republican presidential candidate in nine out of ten races and gave the country two presidents, Richard Nixon and Ronald Reagan. But Republicans lost California in 1992 and have never won there since. And while in the last winning year of 1988 the Republican share of the vote in the

Golden State tracked only slightly below the GOP's national share, in the year 2000 California voted 6 percent less Republican than the nation as a whole, and in 2016 it was sixteen points down. Victor Davis Hanson, a fifth-generation Californian, chronicled the rapid change in the state in *Mexifornia*, noting that the combination of an influx of cheap labor and progressive identity politics have changed the composition of the state's population and prevented the newcomers from fully assimilating.

The idea of "Calexit" originated before the 2016 election but became much more popular after Donald Trump won. Proponents of the idea, such as the group Yes California, believe the forty million inhabitants of the state have become a nation apart. They note that independent California would be the sixth-largest economy in the world and would have everything necessary to sustain itself.[1] An attempt to place a secession measure on the 2018 ballot failed, but talk of independence intensified when the state began to resist the enforcement of the Trump administration's immigration policies. It is amusing to hear progressive Californian politicians making Confederate-style arguments for states' rights, though the fact that over 45 percent of California is owned by the United States government complicates the matter.

But even before Calexit there were proposals to split up the Golden State into two, three, four, or even six states, based on existing cultural, economic, and geographic divisions. For example, in January 2018 the New California movement issued a Declaration of Independence seeking to split the eastern part of the state off from the coastal counties because the state has become a "tyranny" that is basically "ungovernable."[2] These proposals illustrate how independence means different things in different parts of the state. Secession might also mean partition, for which there is a precedent: Virginia lost its western trans-Appalachian counties during the Civil War. The West Virginia border was largely determined by the results of Virginia's 1861 secession referendum. A similar referendum in California giving residents the option to vote on staying or leaving could also be the basis for determining a new and more stable border. And the "Cal-3" proposal to divide the state into three parts gained enough support to be placed on the November 2018 ballot.

A broader secession movement would face similar border challenges. Progressive bastions are geographically isolated throughout the United States, primarily along urban corridors on the coasts and sections near the Great Lakes. A more comprehensive move to divide the country along political lines would have to take that into account, perhaps with the East and West Coast groups forming their own independent countries. There might also be economic advantages to forming microstates on the American periphery that could sustain themselves through trade, banking, serving as data hubs, or other innovative economic models. Once the process was underway the possibilities would be endless.

But the breakup would be difficult. Secession would involve complex negotiations over shares of state and national debt, commitments like social security, pensions, and other contractual payments, ownership of federal lands and other assets, military bases and forces, exclusive economic zones at sea, space-based assets, riparian rights, citizenship, trade, currency and finance, and a host of other issues. The complex negotiations between Britain and the European Union over Brexit show how difficult separation can be.

And it would be wrong to believe that secession would be a political cure-all. Areas that split from the United States would find their politics redefined by new issues and internal divisions. Radicals would be fully aware of the revolutionary potential of the new situation. The shift might get messy and could even lead to internal violence as the balance of power is sorted out. This is the major risk for progressive separatists: war not with the United States or with conservatives who would be happy to see them go, but with their own factions and factions of socialists and anarchists for whom even the means justify the means. And in cities with huge numbers of dependent populations this could get ugly very fast.

CIVIL WAR 2.0

But suppose a war did break out? An essay published in the *Saint Louis Union* ten years before the Civil War predicted accurately what would happen when things fell apart in the United States. "Let once the dogs of war be let loose, and scenes of horror would ensue, to which history can present no parallel, and which not even the wildest imagination could picture," the columnist wrote. "Once lighted, the flames of civil discord would reach from one ocean to the other, excepting no region of our happy country. ... And all for what? The question is more easily asked than answered."[3] A former Army Special Forces officer recently summed up the similarity between those days and today: "It is like 1859, everyone is mad about something and everyone has a gun."[4]

Civil wars erupt when the agreed-upon means of distributing power in a political system break down. They happen when one or more sides see the system as fundamentally illegitimate, when the central institutions of government are weak, when compromise becomes impossible, when every issue becomes a case of winner-take-all. They happen when political leaders fail to inspire faith in themselves or the system they represent. And they happen when the people begin to reject the ideals of unity and teamwork, no longer envisioning a future in which the other side plays a constructive role.

Factions resort to force when there is no longer any other perceived legitimate means of resolving disputes or when one side sees it as opportune because of an apparent fatal weakness on the other side. And violence is encouraged by a sense of otherness, when the two sides, no longer recognizing the ties that bind, reject the commonalities that inhibit or deter the use of force. At such times it becomes harder to resist conflict than to go ahead with it.

"All dreaded [the impending Civil War], all sought to avert it," Abraham Lincoln said in his second inaugural address. "Both parties deprecated war, but one of them would *make* war rather than let the nation survive, and the other would *accept* war rather than let it perish, and the war came." Compromise collapsed, diplomacy failed, radicals on both sides stirred the pot, and armies began to march.

We see some of the same preconditions for civil conflict in the United States today. A small catalyst could lead to a rolling crisis in which the masks were dropped and violence was viewed as the only remaining solution to the country's differences. And though some might think such a conflict would be brief, painless, and definitive, internal wars in Europe, Africa, and the Middle East—not to mention our own Civil War—point to a long, harsh, and destructive conflict. People who say it can't happen here must reckon with the reality of what it would look like if it did.

Ultimately civil conflicts—and many wars in general—break out when compromise collapses. The White House chief of staff General John Kelly made this point when he said during an interview with Fox News's Laura Ingraham that "the lack of an ability to compromise led to the Civil War, and men and women of good faith on both sides made their stand where their conscience had made them stand."[5]

Pundits, professors, and politicians launched a massive attack on the general, calling his view "bizarre mythology," a "racialist misreading of history," and simply wrong on the facts.[6] But Kelly was right. The political compromises that preceded the American Civil War began with the Constitutional Convention and were embedded in the document itself. In the seven decades leading up to the war, the country faced several major sectional crises over slavery and other issues that were resolved through compromises, among them the Missouri Compromise in 1820, the Compromise of 1850, and the Kansas-Nebraska Act in 1854. And during the secession crisis of 1860–1861, there were several attempts to forestall a conflict, most notably the failed Crittenden Compromise.

Yes, there were some uncompromising voices, such as the Southern firebrands who preached secession and the abolitionist William Lloyd Garrison, who called the American Constitution "'a covenant with death and an agreement with Hell,' which ought to be annulled now and forever."[7] But the desperate search for a deal to avert war was the most prominent political issue from the time of South Carolina's secession in December 1860 to the firing on Fort Sumter in the following April. The discussion filled the newspapers of the day. We have the *New York Herald* reporting on the last-ditch attempts to stave off conflict "in the matter of a Union-saving compromise...or, failing in that, the maintenance of the Union by force of arms."[8] We have a headline in the *Richmond Telegraph*, "The Free States in Favor of Coercion and Against Compromise."[9] We have the *Washington Evening Star* editorializing against factions on both sides of the crisis who would "prefer a long and bloody civil war to any compromise."[10] It cannot be an exaggeration to say that every history book ever written on the outbreak of the American Civil War notes the failed attempts to find a compromise solution.

In Ken Burns's 1990 documentary *The Civil War*, the historian Shelby Foote said that "Americans like to think of themselves as uncompromising. Our true genius is for compromise. Our whole government's founded on it." But when the Civil War threatened, "it failed." The historian Stephanie McCurry, who charged that Kelly's remark "tracks all of the major talking points of this pro-Confederate view of the Civil War," made the same point herself in *Confederate Reckoning* (2010), observing that moderate pro-Union Southerners tried to "hold their states back from the precipice of secession" but had "no power to deliver the compromise necessary" to prevent it—and soon the "hopes for compromise and peace came crashing down."[11]

The faux outrage over Kelly's comment shows the impossibility of having a rational discussion about that era. The public debate becomes especially confused when fed by professors and pundits with an anti-Trump axe to grind. The White House press secretary, Sarah Huckabee Sanders, pushed back hard against journalists who insinuated that Kelly's remarks implied that President Trump was soft on slavery, calling the suggestion "disgusting and absurd." It is ridiculous to try to "re-litigate the Civil War," she said, and Kelly's point was that "because you don't like history doesn't mean that you can erase it and pretend that it didn't happen."[12]

The catalyst for a new civil war could be something large or small. It could arise from a poorly handled move toward secession, for example. Perhaps a pro-Union resistance struggle within a seceding state, supported by the federal government, escalates into general war. Or a seceding state's attempted seizure, Fort Sumter-style, of a federal military installation. Rolling violence could be sparked by a politically-charged event—a riot, a police shooting, an assassination, a separatist uprising, or a palace coup in the White House (as some progressives openly advocate). A *New York Times* column speculated that President Trump is already raising an army of "zombie zealots" to defend himself against removal from office by force.[13] The outbreaks of violence might be exploited by foreign powers or other groups seeking to benefit from the chaos, or be fanned by media with an interest in sensationalism, drama, and division.

Civil War 2.0 would undoubtedly be devastating. It is hard to estimate its destructive potential. The original Civil War was the deadliest conflict our country ever fought, and the greatest war of the nineteenth century, with the largest armies in history up to that time. In today's heavily-armed society the scale of conflict would also be immense.

At the onset of the Civil War, most Americans on both sides assumed that it would be a short conflict, probably determined by one or two battles, maybe stretching into the fall of 1861, definitely over by Christmas. This confidence was reflected in the initial three- and six-month terms of enlistment. Optimists foresaw a brief and glorious conflict followed by a return to some type of normality, a grand compromise that could be cobbled together once people came to their senses. A month before the war ended, President Lincoln noted that neither party expected "the magnitude or the duration" of the war, and "each looked for an easier triumph, and a result less fundamental and astounding." But some sensed that the coming war would be neither brief nor glorious but a hard and deadly slog of uncertain outcome. "It is useless to hope or to suppose that the coming struggle will be a bloodless one or one of short duration," Cadet George A. Custer wrote from West Point in May 1861, weeks before seeing action at Bull Run. "It is certain that much blood will be spilled and that thousands of lives lost, perhaps I might say hundreds of thousands."[14]

Likewise, a new civil war would be complex, ugly, and festering, a Syria writ large. Much would depend on what parts of the armed forces would join which side, and it is difficult to predict how the vast U.S. arsenal would divide itself. Servicemen would go where conscience or calculation led them. Army and Marine units might fracture and disperse, or stay together and take a side. State governors would mobilize their National Guard units, but not all of them would report to the same governor for duty.

Naval forces would face a more complex situation since they need friendly port facilities, and air units would require bases and their support systems. Strategic nuclear forces would, one hopes, be uninvolved, but controlling them would be a critical factor in negotiating—perhaps even deciding—the outcome.

There are also many trained and experienced veterans who could join the forces of the various sides or form their own independent militias. There would be no clean lines, and violent internal conflicts within the contending sides would be possible. Terrorism and unconventional warfare would be prevalent on the margins; in some cases they would be a central aspect of strategy. Cyberwarfare would target communications infrastructures, satellites, air traffic control networks, power grids, financial structures, and any other networked assets. Drone warfare would come into its own, and killer robots would crawl the streets. The ingenuity of American vs. American is horrifying to contemplate.

If the initial geographic breakdown followed partisan political lines, then one side would hold mostly urban ground, the other the suburbs and countryside. Cities have some advantages—complex urban terrain is particularly useful for the defense. Sun Tzu said that urban warfare was the "lowest form of war," meaning it was something only unskilled generals get sucked into. Frontal attacks on cities could lead to high-casualty fiascos like the Russian incursion into Grozny, Chechnya, in 1995.

Yet cities have important disadvantages as well. Complex terrain has complex needs. Population densities are high, and people need food, water, and power, much of which comes from outside. Placing cities under siege might work, depending on circumstances. Food supplies would quickly run low without access to outside sources. Water might also be cut off for cities relying on distant reservoirs. External power lines could be cut, and lack of power would render some modern high-rise buildings uninhabitable. Garbage and waste would accumulate, disease would spread, and medical supplies would run out. Coastal cities might be able to import supplies, depending on the control of the sea. Complications like extremes of weather would also make life under siege more difficult. In the end, weak urban civic cultures would contribute to eventual social meltdown and anarchy, making further defense of the city impossible.

The nature and conduct of the war would be determined by the restraints each side would impose on itself. The original Civil War, which in many respects was a total war, still had some limits. The contending sides shared many values and conducted themselves accordingly. But the divisions today are starker. A new American civil war would take on aspects of complex, fourth-dimensional warfare and ethnic war, which is always more devastating, with higher casualties among combatants and noncombatants alike.

Foreign powers would seek to exploit the conflict, directly or indirectly, pursuing their interests abroad while the United States was preoccupied. Adversary states might support one or both sides in the American war to keep the carnage mounting and further weakening the once-United States. Terror groups, international organized crime syndicates, and others would seek to exploit the situation in various ways. The nuclear dimension is especially troubling since U.S. nuclear weapons might be used by one side or the other or even by rogue actors. Yet foreign states would also have a legitimate concern that the U.S. nuclear arsenal might get into the wrong hands and be used against them. A disabling counterforce strike against the American nuclear arsenal might look like a good option, especially in a situation where U.S. nuclear command and control was disrupted and an effective counterstrike was unlikely. Yet any foreign state would also be coping with the economic turmoil that would be generated by an American civil conflict. The global economic ripple effect would be catastrophic. And the absence of the United States as a global stabilizing force would compound uncertainties and intensify the likely global economic collapse.

Would such a war end with the magnanimity of Appomattox? With show trials and retribution? With ethnic cleansing and genocide? War objectives would evolve and harden as the conflict continued and costs of war mounted. What would have passed for peace at the start of the war would be deemed unacceptable later on. There are multiple conflict termination scenarios: military victory, economic and political collapse, nuclear strike, foreign intervention, Sherman-style devastation, mass starvation and epidemic, perhaps even a peaceful negotiated settlement. The political system that emerged from that war might not look anything like the United States. And the idea of America, a nation of free people upholding the values expressed in the Declaration of Independence and embodied in the U.S. Constitution, might cease to exist.

TWELVE

THE MYSTIC CHORDS OF MEMORY

Everything faded into mist. The past was erased,
the erasure was forgotten, the lie became truth.
—George Orwell, *1984*

How did America get here, and what does the future hold? There are no easy answers, but we know times are changing. The economy is in flux. New technologies are disrupting communications, transportation, energy, food, and medicine, and altering forever much of daily life. Immigration is surging, and the influx of new peoples is affecting American culture. There are divisions between urban and rural populations, between rich and poor, men and women, young and old. It seems like everything is moving and no one knows where we are going.

Yet this is nothing new. Rapid change is natural to this country. The challenges just mentioned are the same that confronted the country at the dawn of the twentieth century. The historian John P. Roche (1923–1994), in his classic 1963 book on civil rights, *The Quest for the Dream*, noted the sense of optimism of his father's generation: "They were at home in their universe and they knew its rules," he wrote. "Above all, they knew that the Future was Progress." That generation of Americans and their children weathered the coming storms and coped with change while holding onto the country's heritage. They scraped through the Great Depression, fought two world wars, and made America the most powerful and influential nation in the world. In the conclusion of his book, Roche, with all the confidence of Kennedy-era New Frontier liberalism, said there was "more respect for freedom and dedication to equality in the United States than we have ever known before," and that in 1963 "every indicator points toward the future elaboration of these libertarian principles."[1]

Unfortunately, things did not work out as planned. The old-style rational liberalism that John Roche represented was overwhelmed by the progressive New Left. Vietnam, Watergate, student radicalism, and race riots spawned a new, angrier, and anti-American leftism. The student radicals of the 1960s became the professoriate that trained the progressives of today. And when old-school social democrat Professor Roche returned to Brandeis University in 1968 after serving as a presidential advisor, student radicals firebombed his office and threatened his life.

Measurements of trust in government reflect our political rollercoaster ride. In October 1964, according to a Pew survey, 77 percent of Americans said they could trust the government in Washington to do what is right "just about always" or "most of the time." By March 1980, this figure had fallen to 26 percent. Ronald Reagan helped partially rebuild trust, though in the 1990s the numbers slumped and fluctuated, sagging to the teens by the end of George W. Bush's administration, where they have mostly remained since.[2] Another troubling indicator is that only

23 percent of likely voters think that the federal government has the consent of the governed, the basic requirement of the social contract. It is a sad comment on the state of public confidence in the political system.[3]

The difference between the twentieth-century era of American greatness and the challenges we face today is the diminished sense of optimism and national purpose. Ronald Reagan said that when he grew up the love of country was in the air, and we could use a fresh breeze of that feeling today.

It seems strange to have to make the case for loving and respecting America. Such feelings should be automatic. It is good to be proud of this country because, despite the revisionists, there is a lot to be proud of. This country was not built by slavery; it overcame and abolished slavery. This is not a land of rampant discrimination but of a people in active pursuit of the more perfect union. This is not a country of grinding exploitation but of limitless opportunity. It is not an imperialist country but the greatest proponent of freedom in human history.

The United States is the realization of Jefferson's "Empire of Liberty," the country that took the lead in defeating fascism and communism and is still fighting radical threats to freedom. Our troops and veterans are not baby killers and torturers; they are pillars of their communities who have served the country nobly and with honor. The Founders were not fundamentally evil. Though flawed, they were great men who left a great legacy. We do not suffer the American nightmare; we live the American dream. For all its faults, for all its past mistakes, for all its present foibles, our country is still worth all the devotion we can muster.

One bit of good news is that patriotism endures. Gallup polling going back to the 1980s shows that 70 to 80 percent of respondents are very or extremely proud of being American. The figures for those who are only a little or not at all proud of the country are consistently in single digits.[4] And the American Dream is back in fashion. According to a more recent Pew Survey, 82 percent say that they either have achieved the dream or are on the way to achieving it.[5] The fact is that people want to be inspired and feel good about their country. They desire a national narrative that supports their dreams. They are proud to be part of a noble experiment in human freedom.

Skeptics who snort at feel-good narratives can hardly defend their feel-bad alternative. And it is no coincidence that those most driven to disparage their country's history are also those most hostile to liberty. Progressive thinking is reflexively autocratic, seeking to broaden and deepen government and bureaucratic control over daily life. That's why it is hostile to history, which undermines it. Every authoritarian system has to rewrite the past.

The globalists who think Americans should aspire to be better international citizens should also be aware that there is a lot going on in the world that Americans need no part of. Whatever the shortcomings of the United States, the rest of the world is no garden spot. Americans have a healthy appreciation for their country that should be maintained. In a survey of people around the world asking whether they prefer being a citizen of their country to being a citizen of any other, the United States ranked first with 74 percent strongly agreeing, followed by Japan (61 percent) and Canada (58 percent).[6] Maybe Americans don't need to be more international as much as the world needs to be more American.

Americans can also try to reach across the political divide and foster a renewed appreciation for each other. A CBS poll in the summer of 2017 showed that while two-thirds of Americans felt that civility in politics was getting worse, a slim majority (55 percent) was optimistic that "Americans of different political views can still come together and work out their differences."[7] This attitude cut across party lines. Even Bill Clinton recently lamented that "tribalism based on race, religion, sexual identity and place of birth has replaced inclusive nationalism, in which you can be proud of your tribe and still embrace the larger American community."[8]

One way to overcome this tribalism is by cultivating a can-do culture instead of a victim culture. This has historically been the American way, a code of competence and spirit of achievement. After "In God We Trust," the national motto could well be "Git 'er done." It is what built the country and made it a world leader in industry, finance, technology, information, and culture. Promoting the ideology of victimhood—especially when based on past events that contemporary people had no part of—engenders a helplessness and sense of entitlement that is antithetical to the American competitive spirit. And those who believe in hard work and other "bourgeois values" can legitimately shrug off progressive guilt-tripping and move on.

A fair appreciation of history informs that onward motion. The project to make America great again is forward-looking and aspirational and seeks above all to recapture the ambitious American spirit. The progressives, despite their label, are backward and beholden to discarded ideas of socialism and tribalism that have already failed. Reawakening the American spirit begins with rediscovering the greatness of the American story. This is not a country that succeeded in spite itself or by accident. Our country's wealth, influence, and freedom are a decisive counter-argument to those who see only the worst in our history.

Ronald Reagan spoke to the necessary connection between history and advancement when he said that progress "would not mean rejection of the past" but "must be rooted in traditional values—in the land, in culture, in family and community—and it must take its life from the eternal things, from the source of all life, which is faith." This leads to "new understandings, new opportunities, to a broader future in which the tradition is not supplanted but finds its full flowering."[9]

At its simplest, this is a choice that every generation faces: to be part of the solution or part of the problem. To nurture our union or to allow it to erode and collapse. We all play a role. "We the people" is truer today than it was in 1787—more citizens than ever before are positioned and empowered to take part in civic life. And our nation's history is being made by us, now.

Education in history and civics should be informed by the concept of public interest, not self-flagellating narratives that tear down the country. Schools across the country are starting to pay more attention to teaching the values enshrined in the founding documents. Kids can also get a practical education by travel within and outside of America, to see that never have so many had so much. They can also learn from immigrants who chose America for themselves and their families.

Justice Clarence Thomas stresses the need for students simply to be good citizens, to focus on improving their personal conduct rather than nursing grievances against others. He told graduates of Hillsdale College that he learned from his grandfather, who experienced the worst of segregation, to revere "duty, honor [and] country," and that even though "not nearly perfect, our constitutional ideals were perfectible if we worked to protect them rather than to undermine them." He urged students as they go through life to "try to be that person whose actions teach others how to be better people and better citizens." And he resisted the urge to exhort students to go out and change the world because their own challenges were hard enough, but through "discharging their daily duties in their daily obligations" they would be doing their part to preserve the nation.[10]

Private sector educational efforts also play a role. The American Security Council Foundation launched "Step Up America: The Call to Good Citizenship" to promote engagement through schools, civic and religious organizations, law enforcement and veterans' groups, scouting troops, and other civic institutions. The goal of the program is to introduce young people to American principles and institutions, increase engagement with community organizations, and foster a positive and informed outlook on civic life. In another effort, the actress Janine Turner is doing her part with her "Constituting America" foundation to educate students about the Constitution and the freedoms it guarantees. The foundation hosts lectures, essay- and song-writing contests, and conferences with the objective of honoring "our country, the founding documents and the future generation of Americans."[11] Efforts like these seek to reinforce respect for the autonomy of the individual—freedom coupled with opportunity.

In addition to educating future generations about American history and values, it is important to cultivate a sense of gratitude and responsibility. It requires imagination to lift our eyes to the horizon and ask what kind of country do we want to pass on to our children. Americans have inherited a magnificent, centuries-old legacy, but it is ours only temporarily. We are its custodians, and when we pass it on it should be in good condition. It is not a fortune to be squandered, not an estate to be reduced to a shell. We have an obligation to the future to hand over an inspiring past. It is a debt incurred from those who did the same for us, the keepers of the flame and watchers on the walls who added to the story and passed it along. We cannot be the generation to fail to defend this legacy, to bring about the extinction that Ronald Reagan warned about.

One of the most meaningful ways to transmit the American legacy to future generations is to tell family stories. Every family has its own American narrative, whether it reaches back one generation or many. Knowing the family story helps make the American sense of opportunity tangible for the next generation and those to come. More tools than ever are available for people to research, compile, preserve, and distribute their family tales. Studying them brings history to life, strengthens family bonds, and forges a personal connection to the story of America.

Renewed optimism, a spirit of solidarity, and love of country will secure both the country's history and its future. Our best leaders have called on us to be bigger than ourselves, to view the past with understanding, to view the present with gratitude, and to view the future with optimism. President Lincoln invoked the unifying power of the "mystic chords of memory, stretching from every battlefield and patriot grave to every living heart and hearthstone all over this broad land," when touched by "the better angels of our nature." So it is today. America cannot be erased so long as it lives in the hearts of its people.

NOTES

ONE: ERASING AMERICA

1. Peter Manso and Michael McClure, "Brautigan's Wake," *Vanity Fair*, May 1985. At the time, in the 1970s, Brautigan estimated America only had a hundred years left.
2. James S. Robbins, "One nation, divisible," *The Washington Times*, November 6, 2012.
3. "The People's State of the Union," Buzzfeed News, January 29, 2018.
4. Thomas Jefferson, *Notes on the State of Virginia* (Philadelphia: Prichard and Hall, 1788), 159.
5. Ronald Reagan: "Farewell Address to the Nation," January 11, 1989. Online by Gerhard Peters and John T. Woolley, *The American Presidency Project*, http://www.presidency.ucsb.edu/ws/?pid=29650.
6. Ayn Rand, "A Preview," *The Ayn Rand Letter*, I, 24, 5.
7. Ayn Rand, *Philosophy: Who Needs It* (New York: Signet, 1984), 10.

8.   Kimiko de Freytas-Tamura, "George Orwell's '1984' Is Suddenly a Best-Seller," *New York Times*, January 25, 2017.

9.   Ross Douthat, "Who Are We?" *New York Times*, February 4, 2017, https://www.nytimes.com/2017/02/04/opinion/who-are-we.html.

10. Joy Reid (@JoyAnnReid), Twitter, January 31, 2018.

11. David Smith, "I saw hate in a graveyard–Stephen Fry," *The Guardian*, June 5, 2005, https://www.theguardian.com/uk/2005/jun/05/religion.hayfestival2005.

12. James S. Robbins, "One nation, divisible," *The Washington Times*, November 6, 2012.

13. Saul Alinsky, *Rules for Radicals: A Pragmatic Primer for Realistic Radicals* (New York :Vintage Books, 1972). It wasn't an offhand nod to Satan. When asked in one of his final interviews about the afterlife, Alinsky said he would rather go to Hell because "they're my kind of people." See "Playboy Interview: Saul Alinsky," *Playboy Magazine* (March 1972). Alinsky became young Hillary Clinton's mentor and inspiration. He and his methods were the subject of Hillary's ninety-page senior thesis at Wellesley, "'There is only the fight…': An Analysis of the Alinsky Model." When *Rules for Radicals* was published, Hillary described it in a letter to Alinsky as "the fulfillment of Revelation."

14. "Quotes From Donald Trump's Convention," *New York Times*, July 23, 2016, https://www.nytimes.com/2016/07/24/opinion/campaign-stops/quotes-from-donald-trumps-convention.html.

15. Kelly J. Baker, "Make America White Again?" *The Atlantic*, March 12, 2016, https://www.theatlantic.com/politics/archive/2016/03/donald-trump-kkk/473190/.

16. Josh Delk, "Congressional Black Caucus chairman: Trump's slogan code for 'make America white again,'" *The Hill*, January 11, 2018, http://thehill.com/blogs/blog-briefing-room/368644-congressional-black-caucus-chairman-trump-slogan-code-for-make.

17. Lori Brandt Hale and Reggie L. Williams, "Is This a Bonhoeffer Moment?" *Sojourners*, February 2018.

18. No one objected when Bill Clinton used "make American great again" in his announcement that he was running for the presidency in October 1991.

19. Ronald Reagan, "Address to the annual meeting of the Phoenix Chamber of Commerce," March 30, 1961, https://archive.org/details/RonaldReagan-EncroachingControl.

TWO: DRIVING DOWN OLD DIXIE

1. C. J. Hopkins, "The Year of the Headless Liberal Chicken," *Counterpunch*, December 8, 2017. Hopkins observed that, "never before have so few fascists owed so much to the mainstream media, which showered them with overwrought coverage, triggering a national Nazi panic."

2. Adam K. Raymond, "A Running List of Confederate Monuments Removed Across the Country," *New York Magazine*, August 25, 2017, http://nymag.com/daily/intelligencer/2017/08/running-list-of-confederate-monuments-that-have-been-removed.html.

3. H.R. 3660, introduced August 18, 2017. No significant action was taken on the bill.

4. Thomas Kaplan, "Call to Remove Confederate Statues From Capitol Divides Democrats," *The New York Times*, August 17, 2017, https://www.nytimes.com/2017/08/17/us/politics/

pelosi-confederate-statues-capitol.html. Jefferson Davis and Robert E. Lee are among this group.

5.   "Birmingham mayor orders Confederate monument to be covered, exploring legal options for removal," WHNT News, August 15, 2017, http://whnt.com/2017/08/15/birmingham-mayor-orders-confederate-monument-to-be-covered-exploring-legal-options-for-removal/.

6.   Karma Allen, "Confederate statues removed from Memphis parks," ABC News, December 21, 2017, https://abcnews.go.com/US/confederate-statues-removed-memphis-park-city-council-vote/story?id=51924363. On the suspicious circumstances of the sale see Ed Hooper, "A Monumental Heist," HuffPost, December 28, 2017, https://www.huffingtonpost.com/entry/a-monumental-heist_us_5a45afefe4b06cd2bd03df1f.

7.   Alex Horton, "Protesters in North Carolina topple Confederate statue following Charlottesville violence," *The Washington Post*, August 14, 2017, https://www.washingtonpost.com/news/post-nation/wp/2017/08/14/protesters-in-north-carolina-topple-confederate-statue-following-charlottesville-violence/?noredirect=on&utm_term=.3cce1e1d6d0c.

8.   Scott Neuman, "Duke University Removes Robert E. Lee Statue From Chapel Entrance," NPR, August 19, 2017, https://www.npr.org/sections/thetwo-way/2017/08/19/544678037/duke-university-removes-robert-e-lee-statue-from-chapel-entrance.

9.   "Confederate statue in Georgia vandalized to the tune of $200G, officials say," Fox News, December 24, 2017, http://www.foxnews.com/us/2017/12/24/confederate-statue-in-georgia-vandalized-to-tune-200g-officials-say.html.

10. "Man charged in Frank Rizzo statue vandalism," Fox 29/ WTXF, August 17, 2017, and "Vietnam Veterans Memorial vandalized," Fox 5 DC, August 17, 2017.

11. Katie Hall, "Stevie Ray Vaughan statue vandalized by taggers," *Austin American-Statesman*, January 30, 2018, https://www.statesman.com/news/local/stevie-ray-vaughan-statue-vandalized-taggers/yX0ASMKvgDvBK69bpxaXwO/.

12. Karma Allen, "Confederate statues removed from Memphis parks," ABC News, December 21, 2017.

13. Mary Papenfuss, "'Saturday Night Live' Trolls The Stiff, Boring Democrats," HuffPost, November 12, 2017, https:// www.huffingtonpost.com/entry/snl-trolls-stiff-democrats_ us_5a07e987e4b0e37d2f37de4f.

14. "Penn: Shakespeare portrait is moving, not disappearing," *The Philadelphia Inquirer*, December 14, 2016. The student removal followed a faculty vote to "relocate" Shakespeare.

15. Kaplan, "Call to Remove Confederate Statues From Capitol Divides Democrats." *The New York Times*, August 17, 2017.

16. Donald J. Trump: "Remarks on Infrastructure and an Exchange With Reporters in New York City," August 15, 2017. Online by Gerhard Peters and John T. Woolley, *The American Presidency Project*.

17. James S. Robbins, "Trump is right — violent extremists on both sides are a threat," *USA Today*, August 17, 2017, http:// www.presidency.ucsb.edu/ws/index.php?pid=126765.

18. Peter W. Stevenson, "Rep. Keith Ellison blasts Trump, but says Democrats have a lot of work to do," *The Washington Post*, August 16, 2017, https://www.washingtonpost.com/news/the-fix/wp/2017/08/16/rep-keith-ellison-blasts-trump-but-says-democrats-have-a-lot-of-work-to-do/?utm_term=.81db37de0057.

19.   Amber Athey, "Keith Ellison Poses With Antifa Handbook,"
       The Daily Caller, January 3, 2018, http://dailycaller.
       com/2018/01/03/keith-ellison-poses-with-antifa-handbook/.

20.   John Blake, " 'White supremacists by default': How ordinary
       people made Charlottesville possible," CNN, August 24,
       2017, https://www.cnn.com/2017/08/18/us/ordinary-white-
       supremacists/index.html.

21.   Domenico Montanaro, "Poll: Majority Believes Trump's
       Response To Charlottesville Hasn't Been Strong Enough,"
       NPR, August 16, 2017, https://www.npr.
       org/2017/08/16/543957964/poll-majority-believe-trump-s-
       response-to-charlottesville-hasn-t-been-strong-eno. Notice
       how NPR's headline buried the lede on what was the most
       newsworthy aspect of the poll. A more attention-getting
       headline would have been, "Plurality of African Americans
       want rebel statues to stay up."

22.   Linette Lopez, "Every Confederate statue must come down—
       not because of what they are, because of why they are,"
       Business Insider, August 20, 2017, http://www.
       businessinsider.com/confederate-statues-after-charlottesville-
       rally-2017-8.

23.   *The Economist*/YouGov Poll, August 13–15, 2017.

24.   The Ordinances of Secession and declaration of causes of the
       various states are the best explanation of what motivated the
       secessionists. Northerners had a variety of reasons for
       fighting, and also differed on the causes and objectives of the
       war.

25.   Quoted in James Longstreet, *From Manassas to Appomattox*
       (Philadelphia: J.B. Lippincott Company, 1896), 624.

26.   Gregory P. Downs, "The Dangerous Myth of Appomattox,"
       New York Times, April 11, 2015, https://www.nytimes.

com/2015/04/12/opinion/sunday/the-dangerous-myth-of-appomattox.html. See also Elizabeth R. Varon, *Appomattox: Victory, Defeat, and Freedom at the End of the Civil War* (Oxford: Oxford University Press, 2013) which argues that Appomattox made things worse by fueling Southern defiance.

27. For a thorough description of the complexities of the time, see Jay Winik, *April 1865: The Month That Saved America* (New York: HarperCollins, 2001).

28. "Taft Chief Guest at Grant Dinner," *The Washington Herald*, April 28, 1909, 1. The speech was at the Union League Club in Philadelphia.

29. Quoted in Shelby Foote, *The Civil War: A Narrative, Red River to Appomattox* (New York: Random House, 1974), 951.

30. Morris Schaff, *The Spirit of Old West Point* (New York: Houghton, Mifflin and Company, 1907), 251–252.

31. Ibid. On Appomattox and the reunion, see James S. Robbins, *Last in Their Class: Custer, Pickett and the Goats of West Point* (New York: Encounter Books, 2006), 282–305.

32. These words are engraved on the north wall of the Lincoln Memorial.

33. Ulysses S. Grant, *Personal Memoirs of U.S. Grant* (New York: Charles L. Webster and Company, 1885).

34. Barack Obama, "Remarks at a Lincoln Bicentennial Celebration," February 12, 2009. Online by Gerhard Peters and John T. Woolley, The American Presidency Project, http://www.presidency.ucsb.edu/ws/index.php?pid=85760.

35. "General Sherman Won't Do," *The Evansville Journal*, November 20, 1867, 4. Sherman was speaking to veterans of the Army of the Tennessee. Sherman concluded that over

time the idea of the "Lost Cause" would "sink deeper and deeper into infamy."

36. In 1835 Andrew Jackson became the first and only president to preside over zeroing out the national debt. The debt ran back up because of the expenses of the Mexican-American War in the 1840s, and in 1860 the national debt was almost $65 million. By 1865, the debt stood at around $2.6 billion. The war cost the U.S. government $5.2 billion in direct expenditures and forced a complete overhaul of the federal financial system (U.S. Treasury data).

37. Jennifer Steinhauser, "Historical Symbols in Midst of a 'Purge Moment'," *New York Times*, September 1, 2015, https://www.nytimes.com/2015/09/02/us/historical-symbols-in-midst-of-a-purge-moment.html. The damaged desk is still in use, and is assigned to Mississippi senior Senator Thad Cochran.

38. Guy Gugliotta, "New Estimate Raises Civil War Death Toll," *New York Times*, April 2, 2012, https://www.nytimes.com/2012/04/03/science/civil-war-toll-up-by-20-percent-in-new-estimate.html?mtrref=www.google.com&gwh=532784 3276C101CD1C74AA06AF3BC299&gwt=pay.

39. In 1861 Greeley had run editorials headlined "No compromise!/No concession to traitors!"

40. Section 3 of the Fourteenth Amendment provides: "No person shall be a Senator or Representative in Congress, or elector of President and Vice President, or hold any office, civil or military, under the United States, or under any state, who, having previously taken an oath, as a member of Congress, or as an officer of the United States, or as a member of any state legislature, or as an executive or judicial officer of any state, to support the Constitution of the United States,

shall have engaged in insurrection or rebellion against the same, or given aid or comfort to the enemies thereof. But Congress may by a vote of two-thirds of each House, remove such disability."

41. Jimmy Carter: "Restoration of Citizenship Rights to Jefferson F. Davis Statement on Signing S. J. Res. 16 into Law," October 17, 1978. Online by Gerhard Peters and John T. Woolley, The American Presidency Project, http://www. presidency.ucsb.edu/ws/?pid=29993.

42. Robert Penn Warren, *Jefferson Davis Gets His Citizenship Back* (Lexington: The University of Kentucky Press, 1980).

43. "Amnesty: Speech of Hon. James G. Blaine in the House," *The Hillsdale Standard*, January 25, 1876, 1.

44. Ibid.

45. Jonathan Haidt and Marc J. Hetherington, "Look How Far We've Come Apart," *New York Times*, September 17, 2012, https://campaignstops.blogs.nytimes.com/2012/09/17/look-how-far-weve-come-apart/?mtrref=www.google.com&gwh =EDAD51D4110D90009EFFC7A1D3C03D5C&gwt=pay &assetType=opinion.

46. Barack Obama: "Proclamation 8654—Civil War Sesquicentennial," April 12, 2011. Online by Gerhard Peters and John T. Woolley, The American Presidency Project, http:// www.presidency.ucsb.edu/ws/index.php?pid=90254.

47. See Maya Kosoff, "Twitter Melts Down Over 'Treason' After Trump Praises Putin," *Vanity Fair*, December 30, 2016, https://www.vanityfair.com/news/2016/12/twitter-melts-down-after-donald-trump-praises-putin.

48. James C. Cobb, "How Did Robert E. Lee Become an American Icon?" *Humanities*, (July/August 2011).

49. *The Ingraham Angle*, FOX News, October 30, 2017.

50. Maggie Astor, "John Kelly draws ire for saying lack of compromise caused Civil War," *The Boston Globe*, October 31, 2017, https://www.bostonglobe.com/news/politics/2017/10/31/john-kelly-earns-ire-for-comments-praising-robert-lee/O5OXOKOxMU4fL2LHllP2yN/story.html.

51. Tina Nguyen, "John Kelly, in Spicer Moment, Calls Robert E. Lee 'An Honorable Man,'" *Vanity Fair*, October 30, 2017, https://www.vanityfair.com/news/2017/10/john-kelly-laura-ingraham-interview.

52. Lori Aratani, "Historic Alexandria church decides to remove plaques honoring Washington, Lee," *The Washington Post*, October 28, 2017, https://www.washingtonpost.com/local/social-issues/historic-alexandria-church-decides-to-remove-plaques-honoring-washington-lee/2017/10/28/97cb4cbc-bc1b-11e7-a908-a3470754bbb9_story.html?utm_term=.33712b851d55.

53. *The Ingraham Angle*, FOX News October 30, 2017.

54. Michelle Boorstein, "The Virginia church of Confederate Gen. Robert E. Lee has voted to drop his name," *The Washington Post*, September 20, 2017, https://www.washingtonpost.com/news/acts-of-faith/wp/2017/09/20/the-virginia-church-of-confederate-gen-robert-e-lee-has-voted-to-drop-his-name/?utm_term=.83d27c10576b.

55. Pasquale S. Toscano, "My University Is Named for Robert E. Lee. What Now?" *New York Times*, August 22, 2017, https://www.nytimes.com/2017/08/22/opinion/washington-lee-university-trump-nationalism.html.

56. Emily Cochrane, "National Cathedral to Remove Windows Honoring Confederate Generals," *New York Times*, September 6, 2017, https://www.nytimes.com/2017/09/06/

us/politics/washington-national-cathedral-stained-glass-confederate-lee.html.

57. "National Cathedral Should Not Be Stained With Confederate Flag, Dean Says," NPR, June 27, 2015, https://www.npr.org/2015/06/27/417981652/national-cathedral-should-not-be-stained-with-confederate-flag-dean-says.

58. "Cliff Seats, First Row," *The Winchester Star*, June 30, 2015, 4.

59. Nathan Fenno, "Traveler, USC's mascot, comes under scrutiny for having a name similar to Robert E. Lee's horse," *Los Angeles Times*, August 18, 2017, http://www.latimes.com/sports/la-sp-usc-traveler-20170818-story.html. Note also that the spelling of the name of Lee's horse varies by the source.

60. Brian Stelter, "Robert Lee: ESPN under fire for taking announcer off UVA game," CNNMoney, August 23, 2017, http://money.cnn.com/2017/08/23/media/espn-robert-lee-uva-game/index.html.

61. Austin Wright, "Lawmakers urge removal of Robert E. Lee statue at Antietam," *Politico*, August 19, 2017, https://www.politico.com/story/2017/08/19/lawmakers-urge-removal-robert-e-lee-antietam-241788.

62. Christopher Gwinn, "The Lee Controversy of 1903," From the Fields of Gettysburg: The Blog of Gettysburg National Military Park, December 19, 2013, https://npsgnmp.wordpress.com/2013/12/19/the-lee-controversy-of-1903/.

63. "The Gettysburg Gathering," *The Charleston Daily News*, August 26, 1869, 1.

64. Julie E. Greene, "Antietam's Confederate monuments to remain," *Hagerstown Herald Mail*, August 17, 2017.

65. Rex Curry, "Dallas removes Robert E. Lee's statue from city park," Reuters, September 14, 2017, https://www.reuters. com/article/us-dallas-statue/dallas-removes-robert-e-lees-statue-from-city-park-idUSKCN1BQ07Z.

66. Franklin D. Roosevelt: "Remarks at the Unveiling of the Robert E. Lee Memorial Statue, Dallas, Texas," June 12, 1936. Online by Gerhard Peters and John T. Woolley, The American Presidency Project, http://www.presidency.ucsb.edu/ws/?pid=15303.

67. Dwight D. Eisenhower: "Remarks at the Annual Convention of the United Daughters of the Confederacy," November 10, 1953. Online by Gerhard Peters and John T. Woolley, The American Presidency Project, http://www.presidency.ucsb. edu/ws/index.php?pid=9757.

68. Lyndon B. Johnson: "Remarks at a Fundraising Dinner in New Orleans," October 9, 1964. Online by Gerhard Peters and John T. Woolley, The American Presidency Project, http://www.presidency.ucsb.edu/ws/index.php?pid=26585. Johnson was quoting Lee's famous advice to a Confederate widow angry at the United States after the war. See Edward Lee Childe, *The Life and Campaigns of General Lee* (London: Chatto and Windus,1875), 331.

69. "Granting Lee Citizenship Gets Approval," AP, *Charleston Gazette,* July 23, 1975, 3B.

70. "General Robert E. Lee's Parole and Citizenship," *Prologue Magazine* 37 no. 1 (Spring 2005).

71. Quoted in Henry Alexander White, *Robert E. Lee and the Southern Confederacy* (New York: Putnam, 1897), 32.

72. Letter, Col. J. M. Moore to Maj. Gen. D. H. Rucker, Dec. 11, 1865. National Archives, RG 92: Records of the Office of the Quartermaster General, Records relating to functions:

cemeterial, 1829-1929. General correspondence and reports relating to national and post cemeteries ("Cemetery file"), 1865-c. 1914. Arlington, VA, Box 7, NM-81, Entry 576.

73. Quoted in Rosemary Rumbley, "Seeing FDR at Lee Park makes indelible print on memory," *Duncanville Today*, January 27, 1994, 4A.

74. Mrs. Kennedy chose that site from a group proposed by the cemetery director.

75. Michael Kammen, *Digging Up the Dead: A History of Notable American Reburials* (Chicago: University of Chicago Press, 2010), 105.

76. Sue Eisenfeld, "Should We Remove Confederate Monuments—Even If They're Artistically Valuable?" *Forward*, December 1, 2017, https://forward.com/culture/388595/should-we-remove-confederate-monuments-even-if-theyre-artistically-valuable/.

77. Dan K. Thomasson, "Is there room in Arlington—and in our memories—for Confederate soldiers?" *The Chicago Tribune*, June 26, 2017, http://www.chicagotribune.com/news/opinion/commentary/ct-confederate-soldiers-arlington-cemetery-20170626-story.html.

78. An address delivered for Memorial Day, May 30, 1884, at Keene, N.H., before John Sedgwick Post No. 4, Grand Army of the Republic.

79. Ambrose Bierce, "A Bivouac of the Dead," in *The Collected Works of Ambrose Bierce*, Volume XI, (New York: Neale Publishing Company, 1912), 395.

80. "America May Accept Inspiration from Civil War Veterans' Meeting at Gettysburg," *Oakland Tribune*, July 2, 1938, 40.

81. Franklin D. Roosevelt, "Address at the Dedication of the Memorial on the Gettysburg Battlefield, Gettysburg,

Pennsylvania," July 3, 1938. Online by Gerhard Peters and John T. Woolley, The American Presidency Project, http://www.presidency.ucsb.edu/ws/?pid=15669.

82. Barack Obama, "The President's Weekly Address," May 29, 2010. Online by Gerhard Peters and John T. Woolley, The American Presidency Project, http://www.presidency.ucsb.edu/ws/index.php?pid=87955&st=The+President%5C%27s+Weekly+Address&st1=.

83. Morris Schaff, *The Sunset of the Confederacy* (Boston: John W. Luce and Company, 1912), 288.

84. An address delivered for Memorial Day, May 30, 1884, at Keene, NH, before John Sedgwick Post No. 4, Grand Army of the Republic.

85. An address delivered for Memorial Day, May 30, 1884, at Keene, NH, before John Sedgwick Post No. 4, Grand Army of the Republic.

86. Eileen Jones, "The Cinematic Lost Cause," *Jacobin*, August 21, 2015, https://www.jacobinmag.com/2015/08/civil-war-cinema-confederacy-keaton-lost-cause.

87. "Deep South," *TV Tropes*, http://tvtropes.org/pmwiki/pmwiki.php/Main/DeepSouth.

88. Jones, "The Cinematic Lost Cause."

89. Gabriel Bell, "'Gone With the Wind' dropped from Memphis theater over racial concerns," *Salon*, August 28, 2017, https://www.salon.com/2017/08/28/gone-with-the-wind-dropped-from-memphis-theater-over-racial-concerns/.

90. Victor Davis Hanson, "The Strange Case of Confederate Cool" *National Review Online*, September 19, 2017, https://www.nationalreview.com/2017/09/confederate-chic-when-leftists-love-johnny-reb/.

91. Alessandra Stanley, "It's Mud and Blood, All the Livelong Day," *New York Times*, November 3, 2011, https://www. nytimes.com/2011/11/04/arts/television/hell-on-wheels-on-amc-review.html?mtrref=www.google.com&gwh=BD477D 87D7164781E938C83C4DB36F59&gwt=pay.

92. Note that the most often used "Confederate flag" is adapted from the battle flag of the Army of Northern Virginia and was not the official CSA flag. It is most similar to the Confederate Navy Jack of 1863–1865.

93. Bernie Cook ed., *Thelma & Louise Live!: The Cultural Afterlife of an American Film* (Austin: University of Texas Press, 2007), 28–29.

94. Rich McCormick, "Warner Bros. scraps Dukes of Hazzard car toys over Confederate flag controversy," *The Verge*, June 23, 2015, https://www.theverge.com/2015/6/23/8836571/ dukes-of-hazzard-car-toys-confederate-flag.

95. Jennifer Agiesta, "Poll: Majority sees Confederate flag as Southern pride symbol, not racist," CNN, July 2, 2015, https://www.cnn.com/2015/07/02/politics/confederate-flag-poll-racism-southern-pride/index.html. In the South, 75 percent of whites saw it as a pride symbol, and 75 percent of blacks as a sign of racism.

96. John C. Moritz, "Six Flags Over Texas will only fly American flags," *USA Today*, August 19, 2017, https://www.usatoday. com/story/news/nation-now/2017/08/19/six-flags-over-texas-only-fly-american-flags/582935001/.

97. Sid Miller, Facebook post, August 21, 2017.

98. "Statement from NASCAR Industry Members on Confederate Flag," Official NASCAR release, July 2, 2015, https://www.nascar.com/content/nascar/en_us/news-media/

articles/2015/7/2/statement-nascar-tracks-confederate-flag.
uploadImage.html.

99.   "Fans defend right to fly Confederate flag in Daytona infield,"
        Fox Sports, July 5, 2015, https://www.foxsports.com/nascar/
        story/confederate-flag-daytona-international-speedway-fans-
        defend-right-to-fly-070515.

100.   Ibid.

101.   Jessica Kwon, "Oops! Ivanka Trump Vacation Photo has
        Confederate Flag on Boat Behind Jared Kushner," *Newsweek*,
        December 27, 2017.

102.   @MichaelEMann, Twitter, December 26, 2017. On
        Climategate, see Neela Banerjee, "The most hated climate
        scientist in the US fights back," *Yale Alumni Magazine*,
        March/April 2013, https://yalealumnimagazine.com/
        articles/3648-the-most-hated-climate-scientist-in-the-us-
        fights-back.

103.   @KellerG2, Twitter, December 26, 2017.

104.   Debbie Truong, "Fairfax County school district votes to
        rename J.E.B. Stuart High," *Washington Post*, October 27,
        2017, https://www.washingtonpost.com/news/education/
        wp/2017/10/27/fairfax-county-school-district-votes-to-
        rename-j-e-b-stuart-high/?utm_term=.114a58e41b5c.

105.   Vernon Freeman, Jr., "Kings Dominion changes name of
        historic 'Rebel Yell' to 'Racer 75'," WTVR, February 3, 2018,
        http://wtvr.com/2018/02/02/kings-dominion-changes-name-
        of-historic-rebel-yell-to-racer-75/.

106.   Wade Sheridan, "Dolly Parton drops 'Dixie' from Dixie
        Stampede dinner attraction," UPI, January 10, 2018, https://
        www.upi.com/Dolly-Parton-drops-Dixie-from-Dixie-
        Stampede-dinner-attraction/9771515604060/.

107. Aisha Harris, "Springtime for the Confederacy," *Slate*, August 24, 2017, http://www.slate.com/articles/arts/culturebox/2017/08/visiting_dolly_parton_s_dinner_show_dixie_stampede.html.

108. Adam Ganucheau, "For Ole Miss sports, 'Dixie' is dead," *Mississippi Today*, August 19, 2016, https://mississippitoday.org/2016/08/19/for-ole-miss-sports-dixie-is-dead/.

109. Chris Campion, "Liner Notes," *Mickey Newbury – An American Trilogy*, Drag City Records, 2011.

110. Hillel Italie, "Helm, of The Band, dies at 71," AP, April 20, 2012.

THREE: KILLING THE DEAD WHITE MEN

1. Donald J. Trump: "Remarks on Infrastructure and an Exchange With Reporters in New York City," August 15, 2017. Online by Gerhard Peters and John T. Woolley, *The American Presidency Project*.

2. "Historians say Trump went afoul in lumping Robert E. Lee with founding fathers," PBS Newshour, August 16, 2017, https://www.pbs.org/newshour/politics/historians-say-trump-went-afoul-lumping-robert-e-lee-founding-fathers.

3. Johnita P. Due, "Governor's painful gaffe on Charlottesville," CNN, August 15, 2017, https://www.cnn.com/2017/08/15/opinions/jefferson-charlottesville-rally-opinion-due/index.html. See also Kerry Picket, "CNN Attorney: Founding Fathers Paved Way For White Supremacy In U.S.," *The Daily Caller*, August 16, 2017, http://dailycaller.com/2017/08/16/cnn-attorney-founding-fathers-paved-way-for-white-supremacy-in-u-s/; and James. S. Robbins, "Trump is winning the statue war," *USA Today*, August 25, 2017,

https://www.usatoday.com/story/opinion/2017/08/25/trump-winning-statue-war-ames-robbins-column/595178001/.

4. Jeffrey Blount, "Dear Gov. McAuliffe: Racism and Bigotry Are Indeed Virginia Natives," *The Huffington Post*, August 15, 2017, https://www.huffingtonpost.com/entry/dear-gov-mcauliffe-racism-and-bigotry-are-indeed_us_5992508be4b0caa1687a631e.

5. "CNN's Angela Rye Calls for Washington, Jefferson Monuments to Come Down," Fox News Insider, August 17, 2017.

6. Charlie Rose, August 14, 2017.

7. Katie Brooke & Catherine Doss, "Thomas Jefferson statue uncovered after Black Lives Matter protest," WSET News, September 13, 2017. On the gaps in the Jefferson/Hemings theory, see Robert F. Turner, "The Myth of Thomas Jefferson and Sally Hemings," *The Wall Street Journal*, July 11, 2012.

8. "Chicago bishop wants George Washington's name taken off park in black neighborhood," Fox News, August 17, 2017.

9. *The Ingraham Angle*, FOX News, October 30, 2017.

10. Ben Kamisar, "Va. gov: Leave Confederate statues alone," *The Hill*, June 24, 2015.

11. "Virginia Gov. Terry McAuliffe calls for Confederate monuments to be removed in the state," *The Washington Examiner*, August 17, 2017.

12. John F. Kennedy: "Speech of Senator John F. Kennedy, Raleigh, N.C., Coliseum," September 17, 1960. Online by Gerhard Peters and John T. Woolley, *The American Presidency Project*. Kennedy beat Nixon in North Carolina by 4 points.

13. J. Franklin Jameson and J. W. Buel, *Dictionary of American History* (New York: I. W. Wagner Publisher, 1901), 350–351.

14. See John P. Roche, "The Founding Fathers: A Reform Caucus in Action," *American Political Science Review* 55, no. 4 (December 1961): 799–816. This was the most reprinted article in the history of the APSR.

15. Mya Berry, "Changing the name of James Madison Memorial High School," Change.org, May 2017.

16. Tabitha Sawyer, "Poll shows overwhelming support for NOT renaming James Madison University, despite our founder's slave-owning past," *The Tab*, June 16, 2017.

17. Kenzie O'Keefe, "Patrick Henry's problematic legacy," *North News*, November 25, 2016, 7.

18. John Fabian Witt et al., "Report of the Committee to Establish Principles on Renaming," President's Office, Yale University, November 21, 2016.

19. Ibid.

20. Roger Kimball, "The College Formerly Known as Yale," *Wall Street Journal*, August 8, 2016.

21. Rama Lakshmi, "What did Mahatma Gandhi think of black people?" *Washington Post*, September 3, 2015.

22. David J. Garrow, "The FBI and Martin Luther King," *The Atlantic*, July–August 2002.

23. Courtland Milloy, "Marion Barry's statue captures the essence of the man—his strengths and his vulnerabilities," *Washington Post*, March 4, 2018.

24. Matthew Yglesias, "The huge problem with Trump comparing Robert E. Lee to George Washington," *Vox*, August 17, 2017.

25. "CNN's Angela Rye Calls for Washington, Jefferson Monuments to Come Down," Fox News Insider, August 17, 2017.

26. Caleb Ecarma, "MSNBC Guest Claims America Based on 'Backbone of Racism,'" *Mediaite*, November 18, 2017.

27. Edward Baptist, "America's Economy Was Built on Slavery, Not White Ingenuity—Historians Should Tell It Like It Is," *Alternet*, November 1, 2016.

28. Donie O'Sullivan and Dylan Byers, "Exclusive: Fake black activist accounts linked to Russian government," CNN, September 28, 2017.

29. "A Declaration of the Immediate Causes which Induce and Justify the Secession of the State of Mississippi from the Federal Union," The Avalon Project, Lillian Goldman Law Library, Yale University, New Haven, Conn.

30. For a comprehensive compilation of polling data see Karlyn Bowman and Eleanor O'Neil, "Polls on Patriotism," AEI Public Opinion Series, July 2017.

31. Neetzan Zimmerman, "Connecticut Dems remove Thomas Jefferson from dinner name over slavery," *The Hill*, July 23, 2015.

32. "Name Our Annual Dinner," Colorado Democratic Party, Google Docs.

33. Ernest Luning, "Public TV pundits ponder new name for Colorado Democrats' annual fundraising dinner," *Colorado Politics*, December 11, 2017, https://coloradopolitics.com/public-tv-pundits-ponder-new-name-colorado-democrats-annual-fundraising-dinner/.

34. Grace Guarnieri, "Obama Family Replaces Slaveholders Jefferson and Jackson as Name of Colorado Democrats' Fundraising Dinner," *Newsweek*, December 19, 2017.

35. Jackie Calmes, "Harriet Tubman Ousts Andrew Jackson in Change for a $20," *New York Times*, April 20, 2016.

36. Jarvis DeBerry, "Take 'em Down NOLA says Andrew Jackson's statue must go," *New Orleans Times-Picayune*, September 17, 2016.

37. Doug MacCash, "Joan of Arc statue in French Quarter tagged with 'Tear It Down' graffiti," *New Orleans Times-Picayune,* May 4, 2017.

38. Statement of Senator John F. Kennedy, Chairman, Special Committee on the Senate Reception Room, to be Delivered on the Senate Floor, May 1, 1957, https://www.jfklibrary.org/Asset-Viewer/7nx00fI0lEWTNCfSX7KM5A.aspx.

39. "Statue to Foster," *Waterbury Evening Democrat*, October 11, 1900, 6.

40. Dan Majors, "City's art commission unanimous: Statue of Stephen Foster needs to go," *Pittsburgh Post-Gazette*, October 25, 2017.

41. Adam Brinklow, "San Franciscans demand removal of anti-native monument," *Curbed San Francisco*, August 22, 2017.

42. Ruben Vives, "St. Junipero Serra statue vandalized in Mission Hills," *Los Angeles Times*, August 20, 2017.

43. Ibid.

44. Brad Williams, "'Native American' statues in La Crosse not so native?" WIZM, December 7, 2017.

45. Brad Crawford, "ESPN's Max Kellerman says Notre Dame's nickname is offensive," *247 Sports*, January 31, 2018.

46. Clay Travis, "MSESPN Host: Notre Dame Fighting Irish & Leprechaun Is Offensive, Should Be Banned," *Outkick the Coverage*, January 30, 2018, and @LrElias3, Twitter, January 30, 2018.

47. Glenn Effler, "Reimagine the Alamo?...OK, but this master plan doesn't," *San Antonio Express-News*, April 29, 2017.

48. Allen R. Myerson, "For Alamo's Defenders, New Assault to Repel," *New York Times*, March 29, 1994. The quotation is from Travis's February 25 letter from the besieged Alamo.

49. James S. Robbins, "Master Thespians," *National Review Online*, March 15, 2007.

50. See Debbie Nathan, "Forget the Alamo," *Texas Monthly*, April, 1998.

51. "How I Learned to Stop Worrying and Love the Alamo," *King of the Hill*, first aired April 18, 2004.

52. Effler, "Reimagine the Alamo?...OK, but this master plan doesn't."

53. Jonathan Tilove, "Texas GOP Raises Questions about George P. Bush's Alamo Stewardship," *Austin American-Statesman*, September 24, 2017.

54. Justin Wm. Moyer, "Lincoln Memorial vandalized with red spray paint," *Washington Post*, August 15, 2017; Wilbert L. Cooper, "Donald Trump says removing confederate statues is a slippery slope that could get out of control. Maybe he's right—would that be such a bad thing?" *Vice*, August 17, 2017.

55. Fran Spielman and Mitch Dudek, "Alderman says Lincoln bust in West Englewood burned," *Chicago Sun-Times*, August 17, 2017.

56. Abraham Lincoln, *Political Debates between Lincoln and Douglas* (Cleveland: Burrows Bros. Co., 1897), 137.

57. Jack E. White, "Was Lincoln a Racist?" *Time*, May 7, 2000.

58. "Lincoln Called Racist," UPI, January 24, 1968.

59. For a good discussion of the complex politics of the Emancipation Proclamation, see "What The Emancipation Proclamation Didn't Do," NPR, January 9, 2013.

60. Martin Luther King Jr. on the Emancipation Proclamation, New York Civil War Centennial Commission's Emancipation Proclamation Observance, New York City, September 12, 1962, https://www.nps.gov/anti/learn/historyculture/mlk-ep.htm.

61. Jenny Price, "Abraham Lincoln Statue," *On Wisconsin*, Spring, 2010.

62. Megan Provost, "Wunk Sheek, supporters promote Indigenous People's Day with 'die-in' on Bascom," *UW Daily Cardinal*, October 10, 2016.

63. Riley Vetterkind, "Movement for racial justice at UW keeps momentum," *UW Badger-Herald*, January 26, 2015.

64. Zach Swaim, "'Systematic oppression' of Abraham Lincoln up for debate again at UW-Madison," *The College Fix*, October 6, 2017.

65. "New York City 'Symbols of Hate' Purge Could Target Columbus Statue, Grant's Tomb," CBS New York, August 22, 2017.

66. Yoav Gonen and Kirstan Conley, "De Blasio opens historical can of worms, faces barrage of monument questions," *New York Post*, August 22, 2017.

67. "General Grant in Love and War," Smithsonian.com, February 14, 2012, https://www.smithsonianmag.com/history/general-grant-in-love-and-war-94609512/.

68. John Russell Young, *Around the World with General Grant*, Part Seven (New York: The American News Company, 1879).

69. Jamelle Bouie, "The Unlikely Paths of Grant and Lee," *Slate*, April 9, 2015.

70. Jonathan Sarna, "Why the Rush to Tear Down Grant's Tomb Is Ignorant," *Forward*, August 24, 2017.

71.   Ibid.

72.   Ibid.

73.   Colin Moynihan, "Protesters Deface Roosevelt Statue Outside Natural History Museum," *New York Times*, October 26, 2017. James Earle Fraser's works are ubiquitous in Washington, D.C., one prominent example being the Hamilton statue at the U.S. Treasury building; he also sculpted the George Patton statue at West Point, designed the Navy Cross, and the Buffalo nickel.

74.   Gloria Pazmino, "Councilman calls for removal of Civil War–era portrait from City Hall," *Politico*, August 22, 2017.

75.   William Neuman, "No Traveling for New York's Columbus Statue, Mayor Decides," *New York Times*, January 12, 2018.

76.   Basil Davidson, *The African Slave Trade* (Boston: Little, Brown and Company, 1980), 110.

77.   Neuman, "No Traveling for New York's Columbus Statue, Mayor Decides."

78.   "Legendary Playwright, Historian Howard Zinn Dead at 87," NPR, January 28, 2010.

79.   Danielle Abreu, "Christopher Columbus Statue Vandalized with Red Paint, 'Black Lives Matter'," *New England Cable News*, July 1, 2015.

80.   "Christopher Columbus statue vandalized in Houston's Bell Park," KHOU, August 18, 2017.

81.   Abby Phillip, "Someone took an ax to the Christopher Columbus statue in Detroit," *Washington Post*, October 12, 2015.

82.   Luke Broadwater, "Baltimore official says damaged Columbus monument will be repaired, rededicated," *Baltimore Sun*, October 9, 2017.

83. "San Jose City Council Votes to Remove Columbus Statue," KPIX News, January 31, 2018.

84. Edward Murphy, "Gregori, World-Famous Painter Who Spent a Life Time Under Hoosier Skies at the University of Notre Dame Has Left There the Indelible Mark of His Genius," *South Bend News-Times*, November 7, 1920, 1.

85. John P. Slattery et al., "It's Time for the Murals to Go," *The Notre Dame and Saint Mary's Observer*, November 28, 2017.

86. ABC News Poll. August 16–22, 1999.

87. Marist Poll, September 2017.

88. "Christopher Columbus Statue In Little Italy Defaced Again On Columbus Day," CBS2 Chicago, October 9, 2017.

89. "Legendary Playwright, Historian Howard Zinn Dead At 87."

90. "October 12: Day of Indigenous Resistance," teleSUR, October 11, 2015.

91. This section is adapted from James S. Robbins, "Give Seattle Back to the Indians," *Rockit News*, October 13, 2014.

92. Daniel Beekman, "Seattle council faces backlash from Italian-American group," *Seattle Times*, October 9, 2014.

93. Daniel Beekman, "Native Americans cheer city's new Indigenous Peoples' Day," *Seattle Times*, October 6, 2014.

94. Ibid.

95. Albert Bates, "The Gospel of Chief Seattle: Written For Television," *Medium*, July 30, 2017.

96. Cooper, "Donald Trump says removing Confederate statues is a slippery slope that could get out of control. Maybe he's right—would that be such a bad thing?"

97.   Manuel Bojorquez, "Confederate removal fight extends to KKK birthplace Stone Mountain," CBS News, August 17, 2017.

98.   Somak Ghoshal, "Who Owns the Sublime?" *The Telegraph* (India), January 24, 2008.

FOUR: TAKING A KNEE

1.   James S. Robbins, "The NFL is Kneecapping Itself," *Political Vanguard*, September 26, 2017.

2.   Steve Wyche, "Colin Kaepernick explains why he sat during national anthem," NFL.com, August 27, 2016.

3.   Alysha Tsuji, "President Trump says NFL players who protest anthem should be fired," *USA Today*, September 22, 2017, https://ftw.usatoday.com/2017/09/donald-trump-nfl-anthem-protest-alabama-rally-video-quotes-kneeling-fired-soft-concussion.

4.   "Kneeling for Justice," *Sports Pundit*, February 2, 2018.

5.   Mike Florio, "Goodell calls Trump comments divisive, disrespectful," NBC Sports, September 23, 2017, https://profootballtalk.nbcsports.com/2017/09/23/goodell-calls-trump-comments-divisive-disrespectful/,

6.   "Colin Kaepernick Is GQ's 2017 Citizen of the Year," *GQ*, November 13, 2017, https://www.gq.com/story/colin-kaepernick-cover-men-of-the-year.

7.   James S. Robbins, "NFL commits suicide by Trump with politically correct protests," *USA Today*, September 26, 2017, https://www.usatoday.com/story/opinion/2017/09/26/fl-stop-self-destructive-grandstanding-and-just-play-football-james-robbins-column/701472001/.

8. Reprinted in Dave Anderson, "Star-Spangled Habit Plays On," *Lincoln Sunday Journal and Star*, January 21, 1973, 35.

9. Michael MacCambridge, *America's Game: The Epic Story of How Pro Football Captured a Nation* (New York: Anchor, 2005), 231.

10. Dick West, "The 200 Year Old Football Draft Choice," UPI, October 7, 1975.

11. Alex Fitzpatrick et al., "The 25 Most Influential Super Bowl Ads of All Time," *Time*, January 31, 2017, http://time.com/4653281/super-bowl-ads-commercials-most-influential-time/.

12. "NFL Draft shows shift of America's Game," WDAY News, April 25, 2013.

13. "The Fans Who Say They're Walking Away from the NFL," *Sports Illustrated*, September 27, 2017.

14. Will Leitch, "Is This the End of the NLF?" *New York*, November 25, 2017.

15. Philip A. Garubo Jr., "The Last Legal Monopoly: The NFL and its Television Contracts," *University of Miami Entertainment & Sports Law Review* 4 (October 1, 1987): 358.

16. Leitch, "Is This the End of the NFL?" and Kimberly Schimmel, "Not an 'Extraordinary Event:' NFL Games and Militarized Civic Ritual 1," *Sociology of Sport Journal*. 34 (March 2017): 79-89.

17. Jenny Vrentas, "The NFL Moves On From Pink October," *Sports Illustrated*, December 13, 2016.

18. Drew Harwell, "Women are pro football's most important demographic. Will they forgive the NFL?" *The Washington Post*, September 12, 2014.

19. "NFL hires domestic violence advisers," ESPN, September 15, 2014.

20. Will Brinson, "NFL won't let Cowboys wear decals supporting Dallas police in regular season," CBS Sports, August 11, 2016.

21. Mike Triplett, "Saints RB Alvin Kamara fined $6K for wearing Christmas-themed cleats," ESPN, December 29, 2017.

22. Brinson, "NFL won't let Cowboys wear decals supporting Dallas police in regular season."

23. Saj Chowdhury, "London 2012: George Foreman's Olympic salvation," *BBC Sport*, May 17, 2012.

24. John L. Paustian, "Notes and Notions," *Appleton Post-Crescent*, May 9, 1976, E-2.

25. Maury White, "Wottle Sorry He Forgot Cap," *The Des Moines Register*, September 3, 1972.

26. Anderson, "Star-Spangled Habit Plays On."

27. Dan Steinberg, "A Redskins running back once squabbled with Bills fans after allegedly snubbing the anthem," *Washington Post*, August 31, 2016; "Buffalo fans want Rozelle to fine Thomas," UPI, August 22, 1973.

28. Matthew Van Tryon, "Here's why more than 20,000 say they will boycott NFL games for Veterans Day," *Indianapolis Star*, November 10, 2017.

29. Robbins, "NFL commits suicide by Trump with politically correct protests."

30. "Marshawn Lynch only stands for Mexican national anthem," *New York Post*, November 19, 2017.

31. Dakin Andone, "The first controversy of the Winter Olympics—and it's over the flag," CNN, February 9, 2018.

32. "Americans Agree With Trump on National Anthem," Remington Research Group, September 25, 2017.

33. Quinnipiac University Poll. Oct. 5-10, 2017. N=1,482 registered voters nationwide. Margin of error ± 3.

34. Kathryn Casteel, "How Do Americans Feel About The NFL Protests? It Depends On How You Ask," *FiveThirtyEight*, October 9, 2017.

35. John Bowden, "Poll: NFL drops as favorite US sport," *The Hill*, October 7, 2017.

36. A. J. Perez, "NFL TV viewership takes heavy hit again in 2017," *USA Today*, January 3, 2018.

37. Nielsen Media Research; 2016-17 NFL regular seasons; Live+Same Day, nationally-televised broadcasts only (CBS, FOX, NBC, ESPN – Excluding NFL Network) compiled by Jason Clinkscales in "The NFL's 2017 ratings slide was mainly fueled by white viewers and younger viewers," *Awful Announcing*, January 8, 2018.

38. Jimmy Traina, "All Four NFL Playoff Games See Double-Digit Ratings Decrease," *Sports Illustrated*, January 8, 2018.

39. Dominic Patten, "Eagles' 1st Super Bowl Win Draws 103.4M Viewers, Smallest Audience In Nine Years," *Deadline*, February 5, 2018.

40. Eben Novy-Williams, "NBA's TV Ratings Are Up, and NFL's Are Down, Even on Christmas Day," *Bloomberg*, December 26, 2017.

41. Jeff Barker, "Ravens, NFL scramble as fans stay home," *The Baltimore Sun*, December 2, 2017.

42. Chad Calder, "Saints season-ticket holder sues for refund over player protests: 'One way or another they'll pay,'" *New Orleans Advocate*, December 12, 2017.

43. Robbins, "NFL commits suicide by Trump with politically correct protests."

44. Jerry Brewer, "I have loved football for years, but this NFL season is making me queasy," *Washington Post*, September 8, 2017.

45. "The Fans Who Say They're Walking Away from the NFL," *Sports Illustrated*, September 27, 2017.

46. Ibid.

47. Ibid.

48. Ibid.

49. Ibid.

50. Juliette Akinyi Ochieng, "How My Dad Stopped Me from Becoming One of Those Women," DaTechGuyBlog, December 23, 2017.

51. Kathy Barnette, "To NFL millionaires on Thanksgiving, be thankful and get off your knees already," Fox News, November 23, 2017.

52. Mark W. Sanchez, "Cops are launching their own national anthem counter-protest," *New York Post*, September 3, 2017.

53. Karen Roberts, "'I Am So Sick of White Guys' coloring book hits a nerve," *Journal News*, December 22, 2017.

54. Data from the online Washington Post Police Shootings Database, www.washingtonpost.com/graphics/national/police-shootings-2017/ .

55. Kathleen Joyce, "Florida man dragged, kicked and punched deputy before he was shot by police, video shows," Fox News, December 12, 2017.

56. Valerie Richardson, "FBI report finds officers 'de-policing' as anti-cop hostility becomes 'new norm,'" *Washington Times*, May 4, 2017.

57. "2017 sees highest murder rate ever in shrinking Baltimore," CBS News, January 2, 2018.

58. Lauren Frayer, "Baltimore Residents Blame Record-High Murder Rate on Lower Police Presence," NPR, December 31, 2017.

59. Heather Mac Donald, "As Chicago backs off policing, its murder rate skyrockets ever higher," *New York Post*, December 27, 2016.

60. Ibid.

61. "The 2017 Imagination Report: What Kids Want to Be When They Grow Up," *Fatherly*, December 22, 2017. The scientific survey of 1,000 children was sponsored by insurer New York Life.

62. Mark W. Sanchez, "Steelers confused about teammate's public anthem salute," *New York Post*, September 25, 2017.

63. Bryan DeArdo, "Ben Roethlisberger issues statement on National Anthem decision," *247 Sports*, September 25, 2017.

64. "Salute to Service," NFL website, http://www.nfl.com/salute.

65. Ibid.

66. Matthew Van Tryon, "Here's why more than 20,000 say they will boycott NFL games for Veterans Day," *Indianapolis Star*, November 10, 2017.

67. Lindsey Young, "Flag Carried During Vikings Intros was Flown by U.S. Army Sgt. In Afghanistan," Vikings.com, November 19, 2017.

68. Sara Boboltz, "NFL Pledges Donations to Military Nonprofits in Hashtag Campaign," *Huffington Post*, November 5, 2017.

69. Helena Andrews-Dyer, "Colin Kaepernick tours African American Civil War Museum in Washington on Veterans Day," *Washington Post*, November 13, 2017.

70. *Tackling Paid Patriotism: A Joint Oversight Report* by U.S. Sens. John McCain and Jeff Flake, November 2015, https://

www.mccain.senate.gov/public/_cache/files/12de6dcb-d8d8-4a58-8795-562297f948c1/tackling-paid-patriotism-oversight-report.pdf.

71. Darren Rovell, "NFL returning $723K for sponsored military tributes," ESPN, May 19, 2016.

72. Melanie Schmitz, "How the NFL sold patriotism to the U.S. military for millions," *ThinkProgress*, September 25, 2017, https://thinkprogress.org/nfl-dod-national-anthem-6f682cebc7cd/.

73. Cavan Sieczkowski, "Jesse Williams: NFL National Anthem Is 'A Scam' to Boost Military Recruitment," *Huffington Post*, September 25, 2017.

74. Anderson, "Star-Spangled Habit Plays On."

75. "Kneeling for Justice," *Sports Pundit*, February 2, 2018.

76. Mark Viviano, "Ravens Letter to Fans: We Need Your Support," CBS Sports, December 22, 2017.

77. Christian Red, "Dolphins owner Stephen Ross on national anthem protests: 'All our players will be standing,'" *New York Daily News*, March 5, 2018.

78. John Aidan Byrne, "Ex-NFL star takes stand against national anthem protests," *New York Post*, November 19, 2017.

79. Burgess Owens, "Ex-NFL star Burgess Owens: The flag and why I stand," Fox News, August 31, 2017.

80. Shelby Steele, "Black Protest Has Lost Its Power," *Wall Street Journal*, January 12, 2018.

81. Amber Randall, "Black Conservatives List the Issues Football Players Should Actually Be Protesting Against," *Daily Caller*, October 1, 2017.

82. Jim Hodges, "NBA Sits Abdul-Rauf for Stance on Anthem," *Los Angeles Times*, March 13, 1996.

83. Scott Rafferty, "Eric Reid Calls NFL's 'Social Justice' Donation a 'Charade,'" *Rolling Stone*, December 1, 2017.

84. Robbins, "NFL commits suicide by Trump with politically correct protests."

85. "NFL Partners with Morehouse College and RISE to Host Advocacy in Sport Workshop," NFL Press Release, December 5, 2017, https://nflcommunications.com/Pages/NFL-PARTNERS-WITH-MOREHOUSE-COLLEGE-AND-RISE-TO-HOST-ADVOCACY-IN-SPORT-WORKSHOP.aspx.

86. Thomas Barrabi, "NFL's Patriots fly Parkland students on team plane for DC gun control rally," Fox Business, March 23, 2018.

87. Norman Spinrad, "The National Pastime," in *Nova 3*, Harry Harrison ed. (Toronto: Fitzhenry & Whiteside, 1973). This story has been anthologized many times.

88. Norman Spinrad, personal correspondence with the author, January 18, 2018.

89. James S. Robbins, "If NFL players keep kneeling, they may soon find themselves in 'Combat Football,'" *USA Today*, February 2, 2018.

FIVE: LAND OF THE FREE AND THE HOME OF THE SLAVE

1. "Abolition Pioneers," *Washington Daily Union*, July 29, 1856, 3. Garrison further said, "To-day I renew my accusation against the American constitution, that it is 'a covenant with death and an agreement with Hell,' which ought to be annulled now and forever. To-day I pronounce the American Union a league of despotism, to perpetuate which is a crime against our common humanity, and a sin against God."

2.   John Sexton, "ACLU: That Photo Of A Flag-Waving 3-Year-Old We Just Posted Shows 'White Supremacy Is Everywhere'," *Hot Air*, August 23, 2017.

3.   Henry Ward Beecher, "The American Flag," in Frances P. Hoyle, *The Complete Speaker and Reciter for Home, School, Church and Platform* (Evanston: Cumnock School of Oratory, Northwestern University, 1905).

4.   James A. Moss, *Our Flag and Its Message* (Philadelphia: J. B. Lippincott Co., 1917). Moss was the Goat of the West Point Class of 1894, father of American military cycling, white officer with the Twenty-Fifth Infantry "Buffalo Soldiers" regiment, awarded the Silver Star for combat actions in Cuba, and tireless promoter of American patriotism.

5.   Quoted in Sally Jenkins, "How the Flag Came to be Called Old Glory," *Smithsonian*, October 2013.

6.   "A Flag Story," *Daily Green Mountain Freeman*, March 12, 1862, 2.

7.   Carroll Doherty, "Who Flies the Flag? Not Always Who You Might Think," Pew Research Center, June 27, 2007, http://www.pewresearch.org/2007/06/27/who-flies-the-flag-not-always-who-you-might-think/.

8.   Public Religion Research Institute/Religion News Service. June 10–14, 2015. N=1,007 adults nationwide. Margin of error ± 3.6.

9.   Frances Hooper, "Can You Find Your Star on the American Flag?" *The Warren Sheaf*, June 13, 1917, 2.

10.   Milton Richman, "Rick Monday: His Quick Action May Signal a Change," UPI, May 6, 1976.

11.   Ibid.

12.   Milton Richman, "Rick Monday, Flag Saver," UPI, September 28, 1976.

13. David Davis, "When Rick Monday Saved the American Flag From Being Burned at Dodger Stadium," *Vice*, April 25, 2016.

14. Danika Worthington, "A history of racism, the KKK, and crimes against American Indians: Colorado's struggle with divisive monuments started long ago," *Denver Post*, August 18, 2017.

15. Disarm NYPD event posted on Facebook for July 1, 2015. See Mike Pearl, "Activists Are Planning to Burn American Flags in Brooklyn on Wednesday," *Vice*, June 29, 2015, https://www.vice.com/en_us/article/qbxvjm/activists-are-planning-to-burn-american-flags-in-brooklyn-on-wednesday-382.

16. "Protesters Burn American Flag in Fort Greene Park; Opponents Rush In," CBS New York, July 1, 2015.

17. Chauncey Alcorn, "Calls to remove Confederate battle flag highlight racial tensions over the American flag," *New York Daily News*, July 3, 2015.

18. B. Drummond Ayres Jr., "Art or Trash? Arizona Exhibit on American Flag Unleashes a Controversy," *New York Times*, June 18, 1996.

19. Steve Johnson, "Dread Scott, artist who invited Chicagoans to walk on the flag, is back," *Chicago Tribune*, February 12, 2016.

20. Doug Bolton, "'Eric Sheppard Challenge' flag desecration divides Americans online," *The Independent*, May 10, 2015.

21. Adam Floyd, "Flag Fracas at Valdosta State," *Valdosta Daily Times*, April 17, 2015.

22. "Stepping on the American Flag at UCLA," YouTube, posted by Grace Lee, May 14, 2015, https://www.youtube.com/watch?v=qxVf0YsGFZ8.

23. Video posted to LiveLeak, April 25, 2015.

24. "Veterans respond to last week's flag protest at WSU," WHIO, April 24, 2015.

25. Susan Svrluga and Alejandra Matos, "Student protesters burn American flags at confrontation over Trump victory," *Washington Post*, November 9, 2016.

26. Jessica Lee, Dahlia Bazzaz, and Christine Willmsen, "5 arrested as Trump supporters, counterprotesters rally in Seattle," *Seattle Times*, February 10, 2018.

27. Hannah Scherlacher, "Mysterious man trashes American flags from 9/11 memorial," *Campus Reform*, September 11, 2017.

28. Autumn Price, "9/11 memorial TRASHED at Occidental," *Campus Reform*, September 11, 2016.

29. Peter Van Voorhis, "Gender studies prof rips down 9/11 memorial posters," *Campus Reform*, September 9, 2016; Matt Coker, "Lovett or Leave It," *OC Weekly*, September 27, 2001; "In the days after 9.11.2001 … ," *Revolutionary Worker* #1119, September 23, 2001.

30. Lemor Abrams, "UC Davis Student Senate Votes to Make American Flag Optional at Meetings," CBS Sacramento, April 14, 2017.

31. Todd Starnes, "Professors: U.S. flag symbolizes racism, should not be displayed on campus," Fox News, March 11, 2015.

32. Todd Starnes, "Teacher Deems American Flag 'Offensive,'" Fox News Radio, May 9, 2010.

33. James S. Robbins, "Stinko de Mayo," editorial, *Washington Times*, May 7, 2010.

34. Eugene Volokh, "Tinker plaintiffs' brief supporting right to display American flag at school," *Washington Post*, January 28, 2015.

35. "School reverses flag ban after protest," KARE, September 6, 2017.

36. "High School Reverses Flag Ban after Student Protest," Fox News, September 7, 2017.

37. Colin Campbell and Sean Welsh, "Baltimore to keep, clean defaced Francis Scott Key statue," *Baltimore Sun*, September 13, 2017.

38. Kimberly Eiten, "Baltimore's Star-Spangled Banner Centennial Monument Defaced," CBS Baltimore, January 15, 2018.

39. Carl Wilson, "Proudly Hailed," *Slate*, July 3, 2014.

40. Henry Allen, "Oh Say, Can You Seek a New Anthem? *Washington Post*, April 23, 1987.

41. Gersh Kuntzman, "Major League Baseball must permanently retire 'God Bless America,' a song that offends everyone," *New York Daily News*, June 30, 2016.

42. Westbrook Pegler, "Seconding Motion for New, Singable National Anthem," *El Paso Herald-Post*, March 2, 1943, 4.

43. "Our National Anthem," *The Alpine Avalanche*, April 9, 1943, 4.

44. See for example Harvey Wasserman, "We Need a New National Anthem," *The Progressive*, September 25, 2017.

45. "New York Debates National Anthem," *San Antonio Express*, October 21, 1935, 4. In the same debate New York City Community Church pastor John Haynes Holmes sniffed that the anthem "is abominable poetry, and as literature it is cheap and vulgar."

46. Wasserman, "We Need a New National Anthem."

47. This served a propaganda purpose as well as a military one, with its explicit appeal to the ideal of freedom, though slavery was legal in the British Empire until 1833.

48. *Annapolis Republican,* July 8, 1812, 3.

49. *London Morning Post*, December 18, 1804.

50. *Annual Register, or, A View of the History, Politics, and Literature for the Year 1800* (London: W. Otridge and Son, 1810), 34.

51. Reprinted in the Philadelphia *Gazette of the United States and Daily Evening Advertiser*, May 28, 1795, 2.

52. See, for example, William Finnigan, "Pass, American!" *New York Times*, September 27, 1988. Isaac Asimov used this scenario in the plot of his short story "No Refuge Could Save," the second of his Union Club mysteries.

53. Brent Staples, "Colin Kaepernick and the Legacy of the Negro National Anthem," *New York Times*, November 21, 2017.

54. Jesse J. Holland, "Some NBA teams played 'negro national anthem' at games," Fox 5 New York, February 28, 2018.

55. Samantha Grossman, "T. I. and Skylar Grey Lament America's Culture of Violence on Powerful 'New National Anthem,'" *Time*, August 21, 2014.

56. "Present Flag to Phillis Wheatley," *Detroit Tribune* (an African American paper), October 4, 1941, 1.

SIX: NO NATION UNDER GOD

1. Mark Landler, "Pushed by Obama, Democrats Alter Platform over Jerusalem," *New York Times*, September 5, 2012; Seema Mehta, "Villaraigosa defends vote revising DNC platform on Jerusalem, God," *Los Angeles Times*, September 8, 2012.

2. See for example, "Democrats Boo God, Jerusalem," Fox News, September 5, 2012.

3. Democratic Party Platforms: "2008 Democratic Party Platform," August 25, 2008. Online by Gerhard Peters and John T. Woolley, The American Presidency Project, http://www.presidency.ucsb.edu/ws/index.php?pid=78283; Democratic Party Platforms: "2016 Democratic Party

Platform," July 21, 2016. Online by Gerhard Peters and John T. Woolley, The American Presidency Project, http://www.presidency.ucsb.edu/papers_pdf/117717.pdf.

4. Democratic Party Platforms: "2004 Democratic Party Platform," July 27, 2004. Online by Gerhard Peters and John T. Woolley, The American Presidency Project, http://www.presidency.ucsb.edu/ws/index.php?pid=29613.

5. Democratic Party Platforms: "1996 Democratic Party Platform," August 26, 1996. Online by Gerhard Peters and John T. Woolley, The American Presidency Project, http://www.presidency.ucsb.edu/ws/index.php?pid=29611.

6. Quoted in Lily Rothman, "Is God Dead? At 50," *Time*, April 7, 2016.

7. Public Religion Research Institute/Religion News Service. June 10–14, 2015. N=1,007 adults nationwide. Margin of error ± 3.6.

8. Gregory A. Smith and Jessica Martinez, "How the faithful voted: A preliminary 2016 analysis," Pew Research Center, November 9, 2016, http://www.pewresearch.org/fact-tank/2016/11/09/how-the-faithful-voted-a-preliminary-2016-analysis/. Note that the Mormon vote, which typically goes 80 percent Republican, was depressed in 2016 by the independent candidacy of Mormon Congressional staffer Evan McMullin.

9. Kevin Quealy, "Your Rabbi? Probably a Democrat. Your Baptist Pastor? Probably a Republican. Your Priest? Who Knows," *New York Times*, June 12, 2017.

10. Frank Newport, "Religion Remains a Strong Marker of Political Identity in U.S." *Gallup News*, July 28, 2014.

11. Smith and Martinez, "How the faithful voted: A preliminary 2016 analysis."

12. Michael Lipka, "U.S. religious groups and their political leanings," Pew Research Center, February 23, 2016, http://www.pewresearch.org/fact-tank/2016/02/23/u-s-religious-groups-and-their-political-leanings/.

13. Ron Kampeas, "Poll shows Hillary Clinton trouncing Donald Trump among Jewish voters," Jewish Telegraphic Agency, September 13, 2016.

14. Tanveer Ali, "How Every New York Neighborhood Voted in the 2016 Presidential Election," *DNAinfo*, November 9, 2016.

15. Josh Nathan-Kazis. "MAP: How Donald Trump Swept Orthodox Brooklyn—and Blocked a Jewish Landslide for Democrats," *The Forward*, November 10, 2016.

16. Penny Young Nance, "Sorry, Joy Behar, prayer and belief are not mental illnesses," *The Washington Examiner*, February 22, 2018.

17. Rabbi Daniel Lapin, "A Rabbi's Warning to U.S. Christians," *Toward Tradition*, January 2007.

18. Letter to the Jews of Newport, August 18, 1790, Washington Papers, 6:284–285, quoting Micah 4:4. The role of America in preserving the lives of millions of people from European Jewish communities who immigrated in the fifty years before the Holocaust is nothing short of providential.

19. Joseph Story, *Commentaries on the Constitution of the United States* (Cambridge: Brown, Shattuck and Company, 1833), § 1873.

20. James Wilson and Bird Wilson, *The Works of the Honourable James Wilson, L.L.D.*, Vol I (Clark, N.J.: The Lawbook Exchange, Ltd., 2005), 106.

21. Benjamin Franklin, *The Select Works of Benjamin Franklin* (Boston: Phillips, Sampson and Company, 1855), 101.

22. Lydia Saad, "Record Few Americans Believe Bible Is Literal Word of God," *Gallup News*, May 15, 2017, http://news. gallup.com/poll/210704/record-few-americans-believe-bible-literal-word-god.aspx. Note that in 1976 38 percent believed the Bible was the literal word of God, so that number has declined.

23. The case arose over whether an 1880 law that forbade importation of foreign labor applied to a church hiring a pastor from abroad. The Court ruled that the law did not apply.

24. Lawrence Hurley, "U.S. Supreme Court backs Christian baker who rebuffed gay couple," *Reuters*, June 4, 2018.

25. Rebecca Riffkin, "In U.S., Support for Daily Prayer in Schools Dips Slightly," *Gallup News*, September 25, 2014. In this poll support for daily prayer in school stood at 61 percent vs. 37 percent against. Seventy-seven percent favored making public school facilities available to religious groups after hours.

26. *Madalyn Murray O'Hair et al. v. Thomas O. Paine et al.*, 432 F.2d 66 (5th Cir. 1970), September 22, 1970.

27. Martine Powers, "Federal appeals court upholds Metro's ban on Christmas-themed ad, at least for now," *Washington Post*, December 20, 2017.

28. Ann E. Marimow, "Towering cross-shaped monument on public land is unconstitutional, court rules," *Washington Post*, October 18, 2017.

29. *Salazar v. Buono*, 130 S. Ct. 1803 (2010).

30. *Van Orden v. Perry*, 545 U.S. 677 (2005).

31. "Atheist group wants to stop World Trade Center cross," CNN, July 26, 2011.

32. *American Atheists, Inc., et al. v. Port Authority of New York and New Jersey et al.*, United States Court of Appeals for the Second Circuit, Decided: July 28, 2014.

33. Harry S. Truman, "Address Before the Attorney General's Conference on Law Enforcement Problems," February 15, 1950. Online by Gerhard Peters and John T. Woolley, The American Presidency Project, http://www.presidency.ucsb.edu/ws/?pid=13707.

34. Cleve R. Wootson Jr., "Why one man keeps ramming his car into Ten Commandments statues on government property," *Washington Post*, June 28, 2017.

35. "Eagles Plan Great Bend Dedication," *Hutchinson News*, May 23, 1958.

36. "Set in stone by DeMille," *Variety*, March 6, 2005.

37. Justin Schneider, "Commanding," *Anderson Herald Bulletin*, September 16, 2006, 1.

38. Judi Currie, "Atheist flag to fly in Somersworth," *Fosters*, November 27, 2017.

39. "Satanic Temple looking for new home for Baphomet statue after Oklahoma Court's ruling," KFOR-TV, July 2, 2015. The case in which the Court ruled against cities being forced to display donated monuments was *Pleasant Grove City v. Summum*, 555 U.S. 460 (2009).

40. "Satanists unveil sculpture in Detroit after rejection at Oklahoma capitol," *The Guardian*, July 25, 2016.

41. Margaret T. Peters, *Virginia's Historic Courthouses* (Charlottesville: University Press of Virginia, 1995), 38.

42. Emily Brown, "A different kind of courthouse battle brewing in Nelson County," *Lynchburg News and Advance*, May 6, 2017.

43. Amanda Gerry, "Bible verse causes courthouse controversy in Henderson County," WBBJ TV, July 20, 2017.

44. Jessi Turnure, "'In God We Trust' Monument Adorns Malvern Courthouse Lawn," KARZ/*Arkansas Matters*, March 29, 2018.

45. John Boyle, "Is 'In God We Trust' divisive?" *Asheville Citizen-Times*, November 7, 2015.

46. Bill Vidonic, "Butler County OKs public 'In God We Trust' display," *Pittsburgh Tribune-Review*, April 26, 2014.

47. Kristina Davis, "Judge invalidates killer's death sentence based on Bible-quoting prosecutor," *Los Angeles Times*, December 9, 2015.

48. Dave Collins, "Court tosses appeal that cited witness's help from God," AP, December 26, 2017.

49. Emily Brown, "Nelson supervisors vote to temporarily cover historic lettering in courtroom," *Nelson County Times*, August 8, 2017.

50. Tamara Jones, "Supreme Court Won't Alter Frieze Depicting Muhammad," *Washington Post*, March 13, 1997.

51. "Catholic University's Muslim Students Should Have Prayer Rooms without Crucifix, Complaint States," *Huffington Post*, October 28, 2011.

52. Sajedah Al-khzaleh, "Religious Holidays Aren't Represented Equally on Campus," *Loyola Phoenix*, December 6, 2017.

53. Katherine Timpf, "'God Bless You' Listed among Anti-Muslim 'Microaggressions,'" *National Review Online*, March 14, 2018. The Arabic equivalent response after sneezing, *yarhamkum Allah*, is almost identical.

54. "The Last of the Tomahawks," *The Tomahawk*, January 7, 1955, 2.

55. "Hopes for College Weekly Realized as the Tomahawk Now Appears," *The Tomahawk*, February 17, 1925, 1, 3. The name was taken from an earlier fundraising letter for the school called Packachoag Tomahawk.

56. James Gallagher, "Last of the Crusader," and Jack Godar, "Up Next: The Spire," *The Crusader*, February 2, 2018.

57. Grant Welker, "Holy Cross to keep 'Crusaders' name," *Worcester Business Journal*, February 3, 2018. Holy Cross also reviewed Mulledy Hall, named for its founding president, Thomas Mulledy, who sold 272 slaves when he was at Georgetown University in the 1830s. It was renamed Brooks-Mulledy Hall for John Brooks, Holy Cross president (1970–1994), who helped racially diversify the student population. Fenwick Hall is named for the college's founder, Benedict Joseph Fenwick, S.J., bishop of Boston, who was born into a slave-owning family in Maryland.

58. James Gallagher, "Last of the Crusader," and Jack Godar, "Up Next: The Spire," *The Crusader*, February 2, 2018.

59. Jack Fowler, Facebook, February 2, 2018.

60. Bill Shaner, "Holy Cross looks to move on from Crusader controversy," *Worcester Magazine*, February 8, 2018.

61. Caleb Parke, "Jesus was 'drag king' with 'queer desires,' claims theology professor," Fox News, March 29, 2018.

62. Richard Halstead, "San Anselmo's San Domenico School creates stir by removing Catholic statues," *Marin Independent Journal*, August 24, 2017.

63. "America's Two Catholic Churches," Father Dwight Longenecker, personal website, November 21, 2017, https://dwightlongenecker.com/americas-two-catholic-churches/.

64. Ronald Reagan: "Remarks at an Ecumenical Prayer Breakfast in Dallas, Texas," August 23, 1984. Online by Gerhard Peters and John T. Woolley, The American Presidency Project, http://www.presidency.ucsb.edu/ws/?pid=40282.

SEVEN: UNHAPPY HOLIDAYS

1. Ben Kamisar, "Trump: 'We're saying merry Christmas again,'" *The Hill*, October 13, 2017.

2. Emily Tillett, "In call to troops, Trump says America is saying Merry Christmas 'very proudly'," CBS News, December 24, 2017.

3. Liam Stack, "How the 'War on Christmas' Controversy Was Created," *New York Times*, December 19, 2016.

4. Michelle Boorstein and Sarah Pulliam Bailey, "Hate saying 'Merry Christmas' now? Everyone has Trump on the brain," *Washington Post*, December 22, 2017.

5. James Hamblin, "What Is This 'Christmas' You Speak Of?" *The Atlantic*, December 6, 2017.

6. Ian Schwartz, "Don Lemon: Is Trump's Use of 'Merry Christmas' A Dog Whistle?" RealClearPolitics, December 21, 2017.

7. Cristina Maza, "How Trump and the Nazis Stole Christmas to Promote White Nationalism," *Newsweek*, December 24, 2017.

8. Yasmin Alibhai-Brown, "Why do Muslims get picked on at Christmas?" *International Business Times*, December 22, 2017, and John Shammas, "Chilling ISIS terror poster threatens Christmas ramming attack on Pope Francis and the Vatican," *The Sun*, November 17, 2017.

9. Edgar Sandoval, et al., "Terror suspect was wearing homemade bomb as he rode the subway from Brooklyn to Port Authority Bus Terminal," *New York Daily News*, December 11, 2017.

10. Jennifer McGraw, "Bell Ringer Beaten after Wishing Man 'Merry Christmas'," CBS Sacramento, December 20, 2017.

11. "Poll: Most Americans say 'Merry Christmas' during holiday season," CBS News, December 18, 2017. The familiar lyrics

to "The Christmas Song" ("Chestnuts Roasting on an Open Fire") were written by Bob Wells and Mel Tormé in 1945. Nat King Cole recorded the song the next year and it went immediately to number three on the pop and R&B charts.

12. Joseph Carroll, "Focus on Christmas," Gallup News, December 21, 2004.

13. Public Religion Research Institute, Dec. 7-11, 2016. N=1,004 adults nationwide. Margin of error ± 3.6.

14. Lydia Saad, "'Happy Holidays' Rings Hollow for Most Americans," Gallup News, December 15, 2005.

15. Stack, "How the 'War on Christmas' Controversy Was Created."

16. "Americans Say Religious Aspects of Christmas Are Declining in Public Life," Pew Research Center, December 12, 2017.

17. Harriet Beecher Stowe, "Christmas; or, The Good Fairy," *Washington National Era*, December 26, 1850. Note that the story was published a day late! See also Alison Hudson, "When Did Christmas Become So Commercial?" *Skeptoid*, December 19, 2013.

18. Michael Feldberg, "How Christmas Transformed Hanukkah in America," in American Jewish Historical Society, *Blessings of Freedom: Chapters in American Jewish History* (Hoboken: KTAV Publishing House, 2002).

19. "Americans Say Religious Aspects of Christmas Are Declining in Public Life."

20. *Lynch v. Donnelly*, 465 U.S. 668 (1984).

21. Jennifer Brooks, "Hundreds of nativity scenes spring up in Wadena after legal challenge," *Minneapolis Star Tribune*, December 11, 2015.

22. All quotations from Kyna Hamill, "'The story I must tell': 'Jingle Bells' in the Minstrel Repertoire," *Theatre Survey*, vol. 58, no. 3 (September 2017): 375–403.

23. "Politically correct students sign fake petition to ban the song White Christmas after being duped into thinking it is RACIST," *Daily Mail*, December 23, 2015.

24. Camilla Turner, "University College London apologises after 'dreaming of a white campus' tweet was deemed racist," *The Telegraph*, December 13, 2017.

25. Bev Betkowski, "4 Christmas songs that hit sour notes," *Folio*, December16, 2016.

26. Katherine Timpf, "Six Christmas Lyrics You Didn't Realize Were Offensive," *National Review Online*, December 15, 2015.

27. "Qutb in America," *The Atlantic*, January 23, 2007.

28. Carol Costello, "Is 'It's a Wonderful Life' sexist?" CNN, December 20, 2017.

29. Zachary Jason, "White! Christmas!" *Slate*, December 12, 2017.

30. Lisa de Moraes, "Basic Cable Network 2017 Ratings Rankings: Who's Up, Who's Down," *Deadline Hollywood*, January 5, 2018; Jana Kasperkevic, "Let's do the numbers on Hallmark's Christmas movie empire," *Marketplace*, December 27, 2017; Michael Schneider, "Hallmark's Cheesy Christmas Movies Are Already Dominating Cable This Holiday Season," *IndieWire*, December 1, 2017.

31. "Poll: Most Americans say 'Merry Christmas' during holiday season," CBS News, December 18, 2017.

32. AP, "Red-Nosed Rudolph Has Made History," *Delaware County Daily Times*, December 8, 1964, 14.

33. James Harwood Barnett, *The American Christmas: A Study in National Culture* (New York: Macmillan, 1954).

34. Kay Wilson, "Rudolph Rides Again!" *Bluefield Daily Telegraph*, December 6, 1964, 9.

35.   Ed Mazza, "Why Is Santa Such A Total Jerk In 'Rudolph The Red-Nosed Reindeer'?" *The Huffington Post*, November 29, 2017.

36.   Patrick Ryan, "'A Charlie Brown Christmas' almost never happened," *USA Today*, November 29, 2015.

37.   Ibid.

38.   The Peanuts music was played at Vince Guaraldi's funeral after his sudden death in 1976 at age 47. Lee Mendelson and Bill Melendez, *A Charlie Brown Christmas: The Making of a Tradition* (New York: HarperCollins, 2000), 91.

39.   Michael Cavna, "12 DAYS OF GRATITUDE: #10. Why the appeal of tonight's (uncut) 'A Charlie Brown Christmas' endures…" *Washington Post*, December 16, 2014.

40.   Bruce Schreiner, "Linus Could Still Talk About Christmas Under Kentucky Bill," *Aiken Standard*, February 12, 2017, 15C.

41.   Jon Herskovitz, "Texas judge allows 'Charlie Brown Christmas' poster to go back up," Reuters, December 15, 2016.

42.   Brady Hammond, "Greenface: Exploring green skin in contemporary Hollywood cinema," NECSUS, June 3, 2013.

43.   See Elizabeth Young, *Black Frankenstein: The Making of an American Metaphor* (New York: New York University Press, 2008).

44.   Robby Soave, "Librarian Rejects Melania Trump's Dr. Seuss Books as 'Racist Propaganda,'" *Reason*, September 29 2017.

45.   "First Lady Promotes Eating Right, Fitness at Book Reading," BET, January 21, 2015.

46.   Phil Demers, "Massachusetts librarian who compared Dr. Seuss books to 'blackface minstrelsy' once dressed as Cat in the Hat," *MassLive*, September 29, 2017.

47. @iowahawkblog, Twitter, September 29, 2017. "Unperson" is the term Orwell used in *1984* for those who were wiped from history and human memory.

48. UC Irvine, Office of Equal Opportunity and Diversity, "Celebrations." See also Katherine Timpf, "UC-Irvine: Have 'Fall, Winter, or Spring' Parties Instead of Christmas Parties to Be 'Inclusive,'" *National Review Online*, December 7, 2017.

49. Scott Jaschik, "War on Christmas? On Inclusivity?" *Inside Higher Ed*, December 7, 2015.

50. Alex McDaniel, "Ole Miss renames Christmas event to be more inclusive," AL.com, December 9, 2015.

51. Anthony Gockowski, "'Bows' and 'wrapped gifts' now offensive on campus," Campus Reform, December 15, 2017.

52. Kaitlyn Schallhorn, "UMaine Bans Christmas Decorations in the Name of Diversity," Fox News, December 11, 2014.

53. Missouri State University, Policy Library, Chapter Eleven: Campus Planning, Building and Grounds Policies, Holiday Decorations Guidelines.

54. Alisha Roemeling, "Bethel School District parents had little love for Valentine's Day celebration change," *Eugene Register Guard*, February 16, 2018.

55. Jim Stinson, "City renames 2 holidays deemed culturally insensitive," Fox News, November 20, 2016.

56. Katie Zavadski, "School District Renames Christmas Break 'Winter Break' Instead of Accommodating Muslim Holidays," *New York Magazine*, November 12, 2014.

57. "NJ Councilwoman Rescinds Resignation Over 'Christmas' Tree Lighting Ceremony," CBS New York, December 5, 2015.

58. Chad Felix Greene, "I Turned My Coworker into HR When She Gave Me a Christmas Card, And She Changed My Heart," *The Federalist*, December 18, 2017.

EIGHT: DON'T KNOW MUCH ABOUT HISTORY

1. Ronald Reagan: "Farewell Address to the Nation," January 11, 1989. Online by Gerhard Peters and John T. Woolley, The American Presidency Project, http://www.presidency.ucsb.edu/ws/?pid=29650.

2. Jeffrey M. Jones, "Americans Grade Math as the Most Valuable School Subject," Gallup News, September 4, 2013.

3. *The American Revolution and the Founding Era: What Americans Know or Want to Know* (Philadelphia: The American Revolution Center, 2009).

4. Thomas Jefferson, *Notes on the State of Virginia* (Boston: Lilly and Wait, 1832), 159.

5. 2014 U.S. History Assessment Report, National Assessment of Educational Progress (NAEP), U.S. Department of Education, Washington, DC.

6. Angie Mason, "Should high school students take the citizenship test?" *York Daily Record*, October 7, 2016.

7. "Poll: Americans' Knowledge of Government, History in 'Crisis,'" VOA News, January 19, 2016.

8. Sheldon Stern, *Effective State Standards for U.S. History: A 2003 Report Card* (Washington, DC: Thomas B. Fordham Institute, 2003), 23.

9. Quoted in J. Martin Rochester, "The Training of Idiots," in James Leming, Lucien Ellington, and Kathleen Porter, eds., *Where Did Social Studies Go Wrong?* (Washington, DC: Thomas B. Fordham Foundation, 2003), 24.

10. Quoted in Tom Gjelten, "Should Immigration Require Assimilation?" *The Atlantic*, October 3, 2015.

11. Chester E. Finn Jr., foreword to *Where Did Social Studies Go Wrong*, op. cit., iii. See also the debate in *History, Democracy, and Citizenship: The Debate over History's Role in Teaching Citizenship and Patriotism*, Organization of American

Historians, May 14, 2004, http://www.oah.org/about/
reports/reports-statements/history-democracy-and-
citizenship-the-debate-over-history-s-role-in-teaching-
citizenship-and-patriotism/.

12. "NEA 9/11 Lesson Plan Draws Critics," Fox News, August
20, 2002.

13. All quotations from Mary Grabar, "Transcending the Idea
of American History and Forgetting D-Day," Selous
Foundation for Public Policy Research, June 9, 2014.

14. Thomas Bender, *The La Pietra Report: A Report to the
Profession*, New York, September 2000. An OAH/NYU
project report on the internationalizing the Study of American
History, Organization of American Historians.

15. Laura Loomer, "Common Core Exec Reveals Anti-American
Agenda: Guns, STDs & Islam," Project Veritas, January 21,
2016.

16. All quotations from Grabar, "Transcending the Idea of
American History and Forgetting D-Day."

17. Reagan: "Farewell Address to the Nation," January 11, 1989.

18. Joe Kovacs, "'Burn in Hell!' for Singing 'God Bless the
USA,'" WND, June 19, 2012.

19. Democratic Party Platforms: 1992 Democratic Party
Platform," July 13, 1992. Online by Gerhard Peters and John
T. Woolley, The American Presidency Project, http://www.
presidency.ucsb.edu/ws/index.php?pid=29610.

20. Amy Wax and Larry Alexander, "Paying the price for
breakdown of the country's bourgeois culture," *Philadelphia
Inquirer*, August 9, 2017.

21. Heather Mac Donald, "Scandal Erupts over the Promotion
of 'Bourgeois' Behavior," *National Review Online*, August
29, 2017.

22. IDEAL Council, "An Open Letter to the University of Pennsylvania Regarding Hate Speech in Our Community," *Medium*, August 17, 2017.

23. Mac Donald, "Scandal Erupts over the Promotion of 'Bourgeois' Behavior."

24. George Yancy and John D. Caputo, "Looking 'White' in the Face," *New York Times*, July 2, 2015.

25. Dan Williams, "Williams: What is privilege and what do we do with it?" *Daily Iowan*, July 25, 2017.

26. Laurie H. Rubel, "Equity-Directed Instructional Practices: Beyond the Dominant Perspective," *Journal of Urban Mathematics Education*, vol. 10, no. 2 (2017).

27. "Mathematics Education Through the Lens of Social Justice: Acknowledgment, Actions, and Accountability." A joint position statement from the National Council of Supervisors of Mathematics and TODOS: Mathematics for ALL, 2016.

28. "Rigor mortis," *New Criterion*, vol. 36 no. 5, 3.

29. Owen Rickert's senior presentation "Division" is posted in Jon Miltimore, "Student: How Identity Politics Ruined My High School," *Intellectual Takeout*, December 1, 2017.

30. Robert Samuels, "The show was supposed to bring black and white students together. It almost tore them apart," *Washington Post*, December 30, 2017.

31. Robyn Pennacchia, "America's wholesome square dancing tradition is a tool of white supremacy," *Quartz*, December 12, 2017.

32. "Welcome (Back) to POC Talk," *The Cooper Point Journal*, September 26, 2017.

33. Matthew Stein, "Stanford University course to study 'abolishing whiteness,'" *The College Fix*, August 11, 2017.

34. Jodi L. Linley, "Teaching to deconstruct whiteness in higher education," *Taylor Francis Online*, August 7, 2017.

35. Nathan Rubbelke, "Conference teaches K–12 educators how to combat 'whiteness in schools,'" *The Campus Fix*, July 28, 2017.

36. Abraham H. Miller, "The Campus and the Tyranny of Diversity," *Daily Wire*, November 15, 2017.

37. Robert Sellers, "DEI work is critical at the University," *The Michigan Daily*, April 9, 2017.

38. Miller, "The Campus and the Tyranny of Diversity."

39. Paul Bond, "Alan Dershowitz to Appear in Adam Carolla's 'No Safe Spaces' Film," *Hollywood Reporter*, February 12, 2018.

40. Erika Christakis, "My Halloween email led to a campus firestorm—and a troubling lesson about self-censorship," *Washington Post*, October 28, 2016.

41. In fact the fictional town of Hooterville featured in *Petticoat Junction* and *Green Acres* was based on Eldon, Missouri.

42. Ashley Jost, "Mizzou likely to cut hundreds of positions amid expected 7 percent enrollment drop," *Saint Louis Post-Dispatch*, May 16, 2017.

43. Kimberly Hefling and Caitlin Emma, "Obama-era school sexual assault policy rescinded," *Politico*, September 22, 2017.

44. Laura Kipnis, "Eyewitness to a Title IX Witch Trial," *Chronicle of Higher Education*, April 2, 2017.

45. Michael Barone, "Justice Ginsburg and Secretary DeVos agree," *Washington Examiner*, February 19, 2018.

46. "Free Expression on Campus: What College Students Think about First Amendment Issues," Knight Foundation, March 12, 2018.

47. Rick Cogan, "Lenny Bruce is back, but Brandeis University doesn't want him," *Chicago Tribune*, November 17, 2017.

48. Penn Jillette, "If Brandeis wants to censor Lenny Bruce, I don't need college," *USA Today*, November 21, 2017.

49. Wendy Kaminer, "The progressive ideas behind the lack of free speech on campus," *Washington Post*, February 20, 2015.

50. Lisa Feldan Barrett, "When Is Speech Violence?" *New York Times*, July 14, 2017.

51. Staff editorial, "Free Speech Is Not Violated at Wellesley," *Wellesley News*, April 12, 2017.

52. Catherine Rampell, "The newest excuse for shutting down campus speech: 'Security,'" *Washington Post*, September 19, 2016.

53. Michael H. Schill, "The Misguided Student Crusade against 'Fascism,'" *New York Times*, October 23, 2017.

54. *E Pluribus Unum: The Bradley Report on America's Identity Crisis*, The Bradley Project, June 2008, http://c8.nrostatic.com/sites/default/files/EPUReportFinal.pdf.

55. Maureen Downey, "Betsy DeVos: Common Core is dead at U.S. Department of Education," *Atlanta Journal-Constitution*, January 17, 2018.

56. Brandon Busteed, "The Political Divide over Higher Education in America," Gallup Blog, December 12, 2017.

57. Frank Newport and Brandon Busteed, "Why Are Republicans Down on Higher Ed?" Gallup News, August 16, 2017.

58. Benjamin Ginsberg, "Administrators Ate My Tuition," *Washington Monthly*, September–October 2011.

59. Jonathan Marks, "Memo to Harvard: Shut Up," *Commentary*, December 22, 2017.

60. Steven Pearlstein, "This Professor Says College Isn't Worth It. He's a Little Bit Right," *Washington Post*, March 12, 2018.

61. David McGrath, "Let's quit brainwashing kids that it's a college degree or nothing," *Chicago Sun-Times*, March 11, 2018.

62. For a more detailed discussion see Bryan Caplan, "The World Might Be Better off Without College for Everyone," *The Atlantic*, January–February 2018.

63. Paul Davidson, "Exclusive: Home Depot to donate $50M to train construction workers, address severe shortage," *USA Today*, March 8, 2018.

64. "Rebuilding America's pool of construction workers," CBS Sunday Morning, October 1, 2017.

65. Reagan, "Farewell Address to the Nation," January 11, 1989.

NINE: ERASING THE BORDER

1. Governor Lamm's remarks were given October 18, 2003, and an audio recording was later posted by radio host Mark Levin. See "Former Dem Gov. Dick Lamm on How to Destroy America," The Mark Levin Show, posted January 30, 2017, http://www.marklevinshow.com/2017/01/30/former-dem-gov-dick-lamm-on-how-to-destroy-america-2/.

2. "Immigration," *Richmond Daily State Journal*, March 21, 1874, 2.

3. Israel Zangwill, *The Melting Pot: A Drama* (New York: Macmillan, 1909).

4. Fred Dews, "What Percentage of U.S. Population Is Foreign Born?" *Brookings Now*, October 3, 2013.

5. Public Religion Research Institute/Religion News Service. June 10–14, 2015. N=1,007 adults nationwide. Margin of error ± 3.6.

6. Jens Manuel Krogstad and Hugo Lopez, "Use of Spanish declines among Latinos in major U.S. metros," Pew Research Center, October 31, 2017.

7. Mark Hugo Lopez et al., "Hispanic Identity Fades Across Generations as Immigrant Connections Fall Away," Pew Research Center, December 20, 2017.

8. Nate Cohn, "More Hispanics Declaring Themselves White," *New York Times*, May 21, 2014.

9. John Fonte and Althea Nagai, "America's Patriotic Assimilation System Is Broken," The Hudson Institute, April 2013.

10. Steven Shepard, "Study: Views on immigration, Muslims drove white voters to Trump," *Politico*, June 13, 2017.

11. "On Immigration Policy, Partisan Differences but Also Some Common Ground," Pew Research Center, August 25, 2016.

12. Matt Stevens et al., "Trump Tweets 'Build the Wall' After Immigrant Is Acquitted in Kathryn Steinle Case," *New York Times*, November 30, 2017.

13. William J. Clinton: "Address Before a Joint Session of the Congress on the State of the Union," January 24, 1995. Online by Gerhard Peters and John T. Woolley, The American Presidency Project, http://www.presidency.ucsb.edu/ws/index.php?pid=51634.

14. *Yearbook of Immigration Statistics 2016*, Table 1. "Persons Obtaining Lawful Permanent Resident Status: Fiscal Years 1820 to 2016," Department of Homeland Security, Washington, DC.

15. Barbara Jordan, "The Americanization Ideal," *New York Times*, September 11, 1995.

16. Senator Barack Obama, Floor Statement on Immigration Reform, April 3, 2006, http://obamaspeeches.com/061-Immigration-Reform-Obama-Speech.htm.

17. Angela Hart, "'She represents California, not Arkansas.' Feinstein's rival presses her on immigration," *Sacramento Bee*, January 17, 2018.

18. "Defending Dreamers is a Moral Imperative and a Defining Political Moment for Democrats," Center for American Progress Action Fund, January 8, 2018.

19. Emily Jashinsky, "ICE says Oakland mayor's warning to illegal immigrants protected convicted criminals," *Washington Examiner*, March 7, 2018.

20. See James S. Robbins, "James Buchanan Was No Andrew Jackson," *Wall Street Journal*, May 2, 2017.

21. Jonathan Easley, "Poll: Americans overwhelmingly oppose sanctuary cities," *The Hill*, February 21, 2017.

22. Mark DiCamillo, "Californians hold divided and partisan views about sanctuary cities," Berkeley IGS Poll, March 29, 2017.

23. Rachel Chason, "Non-citizens can now vote in College Park, Md.," *Washington Post*, September 13, 2017.

24. John Byrne, "Chicago ID card would be valid voter identification," *Chicago Tribune*, February 16, 2018.

25. Guy Aitchison, "Should we be allowed to move across borders freely?" *World Economic Forum*, December 21, 2016.

26. Alex Tabarrok, "The Case for Getting Rid of Borders—Completely," *The Atlantic*, October 10, 2015.

27. "Artist tries to render U.S.-Mexico border fence 'invisible,'" CBS News, October 13, 2015.

28. Jessica Mairs, "Borders are 'primitive' limits says designer of U.S.-Mexico binational city," *DeZeen*, September 9, 2016.

29. See his personal account in Harry P. Packard, "Hallelujah! The Hakim Sahib Has Come!" in Delavan L. Pierson, ed., *Missionary Review of the World*, vol. 34 (1921), 644–646.

30. James Morgan, "America, the Great Immigrant Nation," *Washington Herald*, August 22, 1915, Feature Section, 3.

31. Hollie McKay, "While DC debates religion, refugees, Iraqi Christians feel Uncle Sam's boot," Fox News, November 21, 2015.

32. This section adapted from the author's "Trump's refugee order delivers on Obama's broken promise," *USA Today*, January 30, 2017.

33. "Poll: Most Americans Oppose Admitting Syrian Refugees, Favor Limited Military Involvement to Combat ISIS in Syria," Chicago Council on Global Affairs, August 15, 2016.

34. Be sure to note that these were people who made hotel reservations and travel plans for the expected Hillary gala and turned it into a protest instead.

35. Hannah Ritchie, "Threatened with 'acid, rape, abuse': Protesting Iran's compulsory hijab law," CNN, March 6, 2018.

36. Dorsa Derakhshani, "Why I Left Iran to Play Chess in America," *New York Times*, December 29, 2017.

37. Jen Kerns, "New polling proves President Trump is right— 'Americans are #Dreamers, too,'" *The Hill*, February 3, 2018.

38. Reagan, "Farewell Address to the Nation," January 11, 1989.

TEN: DIVIDING AMERICA

1. NBC News–Wall Street Journal Poll conducted by Hart Research Associates (D) and Public Opinion Strategies (R). August 5–9, 2017. N=1,200 adults nationwide. Margin of error ± 2.8.

2. See Alexander George Theodoridis, "The Hyper-Polarization of America," *Scientific American*, November 7, 2016.

3. "The Partisan Divide on Political Values Grows Even Wider," Pew Research Center, October 2017.

4. Sam Petulla, "See How Your Neighborhood Voted in 2016," NBC News, April 3, 2017.

5.   Mark Fahey and Nicholas Wells, "The places that flipped and gave the country to Trump," CNBC, November 9, 2016.

6.   Nate Cohn, "Donald Trump's Strongest Supporters: A Certain Kind of Democrat," *New York Times*, December 31, 2015.

7.   See James S. Robbins, "Democrats Admit Trump Is 'On to Something,'" *Daily Caller*, August 1, 2016.

8.   "2016 GOP presidential candidates," DNC discussion memo, April 7, 2015, https://www.politico.com/magazine/story/2016/11/hillary-clinton-2016-donald-trump-214428.

9.   Robert Reich, "Democrats once represented the working class. Not any more," *The Guardian*, November 10, 2016.

10. Greg Sargent, "Why did Trump win? New research by Democrats offers a worrisome answer," *Washington Post*, May 1, 2017.

11. H. Beider, S. Harwood, and K. Chahal, "The Other America: White working-class views on belonging, change, identity, and immigration," Centre for Trust, Peace and Social Relations, Coventry University, UK, 2017.

12. Nathaniel Persily and Jon Cohen, "Americans are losing faith in democracy—and in each other," *Washington Post*, October 14, 2016.

13. See Celinda Lake, Joshua E. Ulibarri, and Caroline Bye, "A Demographic Profile of the Rising American Electorate in 2016," Voter Participation Center, September 2017.

14. "Pelosi: My Grandson's Birthday Wish Was to Have Brown Skin, Brown Eyes; 'Face of the Future of Our Country,'" *RealClear Politics*, February 7, 2018.

15. Emmett Rensin, "The smug style in American liberalism," *Vox*, April 21, 2016.

16. Adam Serwer, "The Nationalist's Delusion," *The Atlantic*, November 20, 2017.

17. Mile Lillis, "Pelosi: Clinton struggling with white men because of 'guns,' 'gays' and 'God,'" *The Hill*, July 27, 2016.

18. Daniel Henninger, "Les Déplorables," *Wall Street Journal*, September 14, 2016.

19. Eli Stokols and Louis Nelson, "Trump channels 'Les Déplorables,' says Hillary Clinton's Secret Service detail should disarm," *Politico*, September 16, 2016.

20. Robert Donachie, "Tech Founder: Middle America Is Too 'Violent, Stupid and Racist' For New Jobs," *Daily Caller*, January 8, 2017.

21. Meghan Keneally et al., "Roberts County: A year in the most pro-Trump town in America," ABC News, January 17, 2018.

22. Ruth Mayer, "I detest Trump, but a 'redneck' fixed my Prius with zip ties," *Charlotte Observer*, February 2, 2018.

23. "As Congress Negotiates, Federal Shutdown Looms," NPR, March 30, 2011.

24. Markos Moulitsas, "Begin the resistance," *The Hill*, November 29, 2016.

25. Seema Mehta, "Sen. Feinstein called for 'patience' with Trump. Now she faces a liberal backlash as she ponders reelection," *Los Angeles Times*, September 1, 2017.

26. Adam Cancryn, "Collins decries coverage of her tax bill support as 'unbelievably sexist,'" *Politico*, December 19, 2017.

27. CBS News Poll. June 15-18, 2017. N=1,117 adults nationwide. Margin of error ± 4.

28. Fenit Nirappil, "Terry McAuliffe suggests he'd clock Trump if he hovered over him in a debate," *Washington Post*, January 11, 2018.

29. @realDonaldTrump, Twitter, March 22, 2018.

30. Jon Tevlin, "Sexual harassment purge turns 'Giant of Senate' Al Franken into a ghost," *Minneapolis Star Tribune*, December 9, 2017.

31. James Vincent, "Former Facebook exec says social media is ripping apart society," *The Verge*, December 11, 2017.

32. Arthur C. Brooks, "Empathize with Your Political Foe," *New York Times*, January 21, 2018.

33. Steve Salerno, "'White-Informed Civility' Is the Latest Target in the Campus Wars," *Wall Street Journal*, January 2, 2018.

34. @realDonaldTrump, Twitter, December 30, 2017.

35. Jonathan Easley, "Poll: Majority says mainstream media publishes fake news," *The Hill*, May 24, 2017.

36. Note also radio back in the day, an important source of alternative information for conservatives especially, a formula liberals tried but failed to duplicate.

37. Bill Bishop, *The Big Sort: Why the Clustering of Like-Minded America Is Tearing Us Apart* (New York: Houghton Mifflin Harcourt, 2009).

38. Jennifer Wright, "If You Are Married to a Trump Supporter, Divorce Them," *Harper's Bazaar*, August 11, 2017.

39. Avi Selk, "Why a woman blames Trump selfies for her divorce," *Washington Post*, July 30, 2017.

40. "New Census Data Show Differences between Urban and Rural Populations," United States Census Bureau, December 08, 2016.

41. "Election 2016: Exit Polls," *New York Times*, November 8, 2016.

42. David Wasserman, "Purple America Has All But Disappeared," *FiveThirtyEight*, March 8, 2017.

43. Lord Dunmore, to the Earl of Dartmouth, secretary of state for colonies. December 24, 1774, in R. G. Thwaites and L.

P. Kellogg, eds., *Documentary History of Dunmore's War* (Madison: Wisconsin Historical Society ,1905), 371–372.

ELEVEN: A MORE PERFECT DISUNION

1.   Katie Zezima, "'California is a nation, not a state': A fringe movement wants a break from the U.S.," *Washington Post*, February 18, 2017.

2.   Josh Hafner, "New California declares 'independence' from California in bid to become 51st state," *USA Today*, January16, 2018

3.   "What would follow from dissolution?" reprinted in the *Plymouth Pilot*, July 23, 1851, 1.

4.   Keith Mines, "Will we have a civil war? A SF officer turned diplomat estimates chances at 60 percent," *Foreign Policy*, March 10, 2017.

5.   *The Ingraham Angle*, Fox News, October 30, 2017.

6.   Juana Summers, "John Kelly gets Civil War history wrong," CNN, October 31, 2017; Jelani Cobb, "John Kelly's Bizarre Mythology of the Civil War," *The New Yorker*, November 1, 2017.

7.   "Abolition Pioneers," *Washington Daily Union*, July 29, 1856, 3. Garrison further said, "Today I renew my accusation against the American constitution, that it is 'a covenant with death and an agreement with Hell,' which ought to be annulled now and forever. Today I pronounce the American Union a league of despotism, to perpetuate which is a crime against our common humanity, and a sin against God."

8.   "Mr. Seward, Mr. Charles F. Adams, and Mr. Senator Mason on the Crisis—Is It Peace or War?" *New York Herald*, February 02, 1861, 6.

9.   *Richmond Enquirer*, February 15, 1861, 3.

10. "A Settlement Not Impossible," *Washington Evening Star*, January 2, 1861, 2.

11. Stephanie McCurry, *Confederate Reckoning: Power and Politics in the Civil War South* (Cambridge: Harvard University Press, 2010), 68.

12. Sarah Huckabee Sanders: "Press Briefing by Press Secretary Sarah Sanders," November 1, 2017. Online by Gerhard Peters and John T. Woolley, The American Presidency Project, http://www.presidency.ucsb.edu/ws/index.php?pid=129162.

13. Charles M. Blow, "Trump Raises an Army," *New York Times*, August 31, 2017.

14. Custer letter, May 31, 1861. Custer continued, "If it is to be my lot to fall in the service of my country and in defense of my country's rights I have or will have no regrets."

TWELVE: THE MYSTIC CHORDS OF MEMORY

1. John P. Roche, *The Quest for the Dream* (New York: Macmillan, 1963), 2, 267.

2. "Public Trust in Government: 1958–2017," Pew Research Center, May 3, 2017.

3. "Few Think Government Has Consent of the Governed," *Rasmussen Reports*, July 19, 2017.

4. Karlyn Bowman and Eleanor O'Neil, "Polls on Patriotism," AEI Public Opinion Series, July 2017.

5. Paul Bedard, "American Dream is back: 82 percent have 'achieved' or are 'on way to achieving,'" *Washington Examiner*, November 2, 2017.

6. Karlyn Bowman and Eleanor O'Neil, "Polls on Patriotism," AEI Public Opinion Series, July 2017.

7.   CBS News Poll. June 15–18, 2017. N=1,117 adults nationwide. Margin of error ± 4.

8.   Bill Clinton, "Americans Must Decide Who We Really Are," *New York Times*, December 4, 2017.

9.   Ronald Reagan: "Remarks and a Question-and-Answer Session with the Students and Faculty at Moscow State University," May 31, 1988. Online by Gerhard Peters and John T. Woolley, The American Presidency Project, http://www.presidency.ucsb.edu/ws/index.php?pid=35897.

10.   Joel Gehrke, "Clarence Thomas tells graduates to simply be good citizens," *The Examiner*, May 14, 2016.

11.   Sandra Engelland, "Actress inspires students to value the Constitution," *Fort Worth Star-Telegram*, December 14, 2017.

INDEX